Singles Ask

Singles Ask

Answers to Questions about Relationships and Sexuality

New Revised Edition

Harold Ivan Smith

Augsburg

MINNEAPOLIS

Friends

Every writer needs friends
who understand the writing process;
who understand what "thin ice" feels like;
who appreciate the outrageously extravagant grace
offered by a Galilean single adult;
who understand single life.

I have been blessed with three incredible friends
Charlie Shedd
Jerry Jones
Alice Peppler

Who have been "cheerleaders"
Who have listened to my ideas
offered suggestions
offered encouragement
and have said, at times,
"This isn't your best, yet."

So, with this dedication
I attempt to acknowledge
their contribution to my writing
and to my journey.

SINGLES ASK
Answers to Questions about Relationships and Sexuality
New Revised Edition

Interior design: Teresa Marrone

ISBN 0-8066-3646-7

The paper used in this publication meets the minimum requirements of American National Standard for Information Sciences—Permanence of Paper for Printed Library Materials, ANSI Z329.48-1984. ∞

Manufactured in the U.S.A.   AF 9-3646

04   03   02   5   6   7   8

CONTENTS

Introduction

I had spent the day enjoying Disney World and wanted a souvenir to capture the experience. Since I write for and work with single adults, I decided upon the ceramic figures of Prince Charming and the Princess Perfect. The clerk carefully wrapped them for the flight home, but, alas, by the time we got to Kansas City, the Princess had lost her head. So, I glued it back on with super glue. Good as new.

During one of my infrequent dusting episodes, I bumped the Princess the wrong way and she again lost her head. How true to life! Some single adults, male and female, always seem to be losing their heads romantically. I know I have.

These days a cloud of romantic grief hangs over Singleland and its 73,000,000 U.S. inhabitants. Out of the grief come questions and questioning. Lots of single adults grapple with serious questions that do not always have simple answers. Some questions begin with, "I don't know how to ask this . . ." Most questions focus on sexuality and on the emotional bruises of relationships, particularly, romantic wounds that won't heal or relationships that didn't make it to "the finish line" of marriage. Many single adults carefully camouflage their wounds and hide their pain. A few invest in well-rehearsed cynicism about the possibilities of healthy relationships. Eavesdrop on television talk shows or conversations over cappuccino in a cafe, and your enthusiasm for romance is well-dampened—if not doused!

Some who read *Singles Ask* when it was first published in 1988 are, like me, *still single!* Some of us still phrase the same questions deep in our hearts. Some of us are still trying to compose our questions, or trying to find someone who will take our questions seriously. Some of us are newly singled.

Some of us dread or even avoid family gatherings, because at some point, The Question is going to come up: "Why isn't a nice person like you married by now?" Those awkward moments, when we simply cannot come up with good answers (or answers we dare voice) can bruise the soul. Long after the dishes have been washed and the leftovers wrapped, even after the "Thank you" notes have been mailed, The Question—and its companion questions—roll like aftershocks through the long corridors of our souls. Let's see, why *am* I single?

Massive cultural change—from which no single adult is immune—has stimulated new questions. AIDS, cybersex, outercourse, bisexuality, sexual harassment, stalking, sexual compulsion, sexual addiction, family values, Internet romance, gay rights—such issues have stimulated serious reflection and acrimonious debate in families, single adult groups, churches, and legislatures. Old, ugly attitudes and new intolerance have turned discussions into scorching verbal battles devoid of civility.

Sadly, many single adults dare not ask their questions. Others cannot find the vocabulary with which to voice their questions. Many cannot find resource people patient enough to hear the circumstances that prompt their questions. Newly-singled adults, who thought they had the "All-American" marriage, find themselves trying to make sense of life in Singleland. And those who have been around recognize their questions: "Been there/asked that!"

Simplistic answers don't do it for most single adults. I believe a deep hunger for authentic, intimate, meaningful relationships is reaching critical mass. Wise single adults are now looking inside rather than outside for answers to the question, "What is it that I really want?" Increasingly, single adults find their romantic and sexual needs, interests, and longings linked to a hunger for spirituality. Many are willing to consider answers that go beyond the old, all-purpose advice: "Avoid sin." Writer Kathleen Norris insists that sin is not just specific acts or naughty misbehaviors—especially sexual ones—but rather something more troublesome. Sin is "any impulse that leads us away from paying full attention to who we are and what we are doing; any thought or act that interferes with our ability to love God and neighbor." [1]

Our lives as single adults become complicated when we do not pay full attention to our sexuality and our spirituality. When I do not pay attention to the enormous reality that the single adult I am dating, have dated, will date is my neighbor. This reality makes "casual dating" a polite oxymoron.

You are about to embark on an interesting journey of reading and reflection. Over the last decade, *Singles Ask* has prompted lots of reflection, discussion, even debate, among singles all over the country—from the energetic group of single adults who read the book aloud for nine hours, packed in a church van like sardines on the trek home from a single adults conference, to the single adult in the stunning condo overlooking Chicago's skyline, to the single parent in a mobile home on a farm in northern Arkansas. In question-and-answer segments of seminars and in one-on-one chats after a presentation, I have listened to the wonderings, puzzlements, doubts, frustrations, confusion, and predicaments of single adults. I have also listened to the pauses in their questions. Out of those moments new questions have found their way into this revised edition.

The openness and the vulnerability of the questioners has impressed me. Not all had well-phrased, well-rehearsed questions. Some questions emerged out of a verbal fog—others were ensconced in a thick shame. I remember that single adult who was struggling with sexual orientation, trying to reconcile his reality with his deep commitment to faith, who was stunned that I listened to him, that I did not condemn him, or whack him over the head with scriptural proof texts. I remember that mother of two who was involved with yet another married man, hoping that, this time, the promises would be "good." That senior adult widower who was ashamed that he masturbates—befuddled by my initial response, "So?" That gorgeous woman who had been abused, not just by her husband, but by church folk who told her that she *had* to go back and submit to his abuse in order "to be a witness." That incredible woman who stood and cried, amazed that I believed her when she disclosed sexual misconduct by her minister. The woman who had discovered that her ex-husband had led a secret sexual life and had AIDS, but was too frightened to be tested herself.

I didn't always have answers when I talked with these individuals. I don't have airtight answers in *Singles Ask*. I've learned that, while questions are plentiful, answers are rare. I do have responses—and some strong opinions—because I have been around the track a few times and because I hate "easy answers" that are loaded down with shame and bruise or indict the questioner.

I hope some of these questions and many of my answers will move you into serious reflection. I hope that reading *Singles Ask* will cause you to repeat the ancient declaration of the Psalmist, "I *am* splendidly made" (Psalm 139:13, translation mine). Certainly, *Singles Ask* is not the final word and is not designed to "fix" you, because singleness is not a problem to be fixed but an opportunity to be lived! Now!

I hope this new edition will be a friendly resource that will help you wrestle with the realities of life as a single adult, find insight into the struggle of a friend or colleague or someone you are dating. It may prepare you for those romantic "surprises" or relational "ambushes" that appear when we least expect them.

Not all of the questions will interest you; not all of the answers will please you. Bumper-sticker mentality and religious clichés are great for T-shirts but they don't do it for truck drivers like Al, computer programmers like Cynthia, or travel agents like Marge. Every question must be considered in light of the outrageously extravagant grace of God—a God, I would insist, who is "crazy" about you. The God who invites you—regardless of your sexual past or present—to sample and bask in "abundant living" (John 10:10). That's what Jesus, a single adult, said day after day to the outcasts and excluded and sexually tarnished, as well as the Pharisees, who thought they had all the answers.

In my religious tradition, a great prayer comforts me:

"Almighty God, unto whom all hearts are open and all desires known, and from whom no thoughts are hidden . . ."

In other words, "God, who knows my questions before I ask them," but also God, who encourages my questioning and pondering. God, who never chides his children for having questions, especially sexual questions.

Whatever your sexual realities, what's to keep you from now paying "full attention" to who you are: an adult, who happens to be unmarried, who has been endowed with the most incredible gift—sexuality. What does God expect out of you? To be a good steward of that gift. Remember, you are the only one who can be you and get it right!

Five fundamental principles undergird this book:

1. Single adults have a right to learn the extent of their ignorance and misinformation.

2. Single adults have a right to expect the Christian community to replace misinformation with facts—not with more misinformation.

3. Single adults with tough, seemingly unanswerable questions have a right to ask them and a right to expect respectful answers and/or responses.

4. Single adults, when enlightened, will make better decisions about the use of their God-given and God-applauded sexual capacities.

5. Single adults need what in Hebrew is called a *mehom hanekhama*, or safe place, to voice their questions, to admit their struggles, to ask someone to come alongside them when the world has disappointed them, or their hormones have gotten the better of them, again, or when they scream, "I'm *never* going to trust again!"

You can begin reading at any point in the book. You can read it straight through or skip around. Whatever the order, I do hope that you will read and perhaps reread each question and answer, and then put the book down and reflect: What does this response say to me?

CHAPTER 1

Single and Sane and Special

1. What's so great about being a single adult?

Beauty is in the eye of the beholder, even the beauty of singleness. Both singleness and marriage have benefits as well as liabilities. The old saying, "The grass is greener on the other side of the (relational) fence" really should be "the grass is greener where it is watered." I was surprised by a report that 17 percent of adults, almost one in five, were not planning to give their spouse or significant other anything on Valentine's Day—not even a card![1] Clearly, the grass is not always greener in the land of marriage or romance.

Lots of things are worse than being single, like being married to the wrong person, or being married to an abusive person. My friend Alice suggests a little exercise. On a legal pad draw a vertical line down the center. At the top of the pad on the left write: *What's Good About Being Married?* On the right side write: *What's Good About Being Single?* Put your feet up and begin jotting down responses. Ask both single adults and married adults for responses; record their answers, then ponder their words, some of which might surprise you. Remember, each status has both advantages and disadvantages. As Alice says, "There is no perfect life we can lead. Each status has pros and cons. So enjoy the life in which God has placed you, and if it changes, enjoy that life. God's blessings spill out over all life's styles."[2]

Whether married or single, I solidly concur with the sign I discovered in The Best Cheeseburger in Paradise, Lahana: *Live Your Life Now!!*

2. What am I supposed to say to people who tease or joke about my singleness?

Some single adults would say that you had better develop tough skin. Others would insist, "Dish it right back!" Sometimes people joke or tease to hide their discomfort with singleness in general or your singleness specifically. When I was first single—and very sensitive about it—one married friend used to joke crassly about my celibacy. Finally, I angrily confronted him: "How would you feel if your wife had left you? If I were teasing you?" The teasing stopped. By not taking the teasing, I opened the door to some significant conversations between us.

Historically, single adults, especially females, were teasingly labeled *old maids, unclaimed blessings,* and *spinsters.* There were no such derogatory terms for bachelors, but any male who was not married by age thirty was thought to be practicing vile habits unmentionable in polite society. Throughout American history, unmarried politicians and clergy have been targets of verbal potshots. Sam Jones, the Billy Graham of the late 1880s and 90s, thundered, "Whenever I see an old maid, I think some man hasn't done his duty. Whenever I see an old bachelor, I just think of an old hog."[1] Imagine what single adults felt when Theodore Roosevelt, President of the United States, gave his "family values" spiel: "The greatest privilege and greatest duty of a man is to be happily married, and no other form of success or service, for either man or woman, can be wisely accepted as a substitute or alternative."[2]

3. How can I handle times when I feel lonely?

I have been single, married, and single again, and I have been lonely in all three states. Loneliness is part of being human.

Even though we all feel lonely at times, we *choose* whether or not we stay lonely. There are a million and one things we can do to jump-start ourselves out of the doldrums. Some choices are, of course, more helpful than others. Two bags of Doritos or a huge bowl of Ben & Jerry's, while tasting good, might not be the best choice. Yet some single adults eat when they are lonely; others shop; some masturbate. Too many stand in front of a mirror and deliver a "Do you know what your problem is?" tirade. It's tempting to whine, "If only Mr. (Or Miss or Ms.) Right were here, I wouldn't be lonely." Or "I wish he would hurry up." One single friend adds, "And he'd better have a good excuse for where he's been all these years. . . ."

Here are some healthy alternatives to playing the "Poor Me Symphony in C Minor":

- Become more active in your church or a civic group.
- Become a secret Robin Hood and anonymously help someone.
- Go back to school and take a course that really interests you.
- Learn a new skill, perhaps cake decorating or karate.
- Volunteer for a political campaign.
- Take a gourmet cooking class—you'll get to eat your homework!
- Run for political office.
- Sell a product like Tupperware or Avon (useful products for single adults) that helps you meet new people.
- Volunteer in a hospital, senior adult facility, or an after-school tutoring program.
- Keep a "hit list" of household chores to be done.
- Read. Better still, hang out at the public library.
- Travel to some exotic place.
- Send lots of greeting cards: for birthdays, anniversaries, or simply encouragement.
- Give to and get involved in good causes.
- Exercise. It's almost impossible to be lonely and depressed while exercising, because those hyperactive little endorphins get loose in your body, dancing and screaming, "It's party time!"

In other words, do something *with* or *about* your loneliness. Take charge. Channel it into something productive. Make the most of this season! (Browse my book, *51 Good Things to Do While Waiting for the Right One to Come Along* (Broadman, 1996) for more practical suggestions.)

4.   I often feel that my standards are in conflict with today's attitudes. Am I that far out of touch?

Maturity requires that we come to terms with our bodies and sexuality. Many single adults have allowed talk show hosts, advice columnists, magazine pollsters, celebrities, and pop psychologists to determine or undermine their values. Work colleagues and dates can add to the pressures. Many single adults have reluctantly participated in the "fast lane scene" because they don't want to be labeled out-of-date, old-fashioned, or prudish.

Be glad you have problems accepting today's standards. Sure, occasionally you may feel you have missed out on something, and you have: feelings of guilt; the pain of ending a relationship with (or being "dumped" by) someone with whom you have been physically and emotionally vulnerable; the realization that someone may have been using you (or vice versa); the possibility of pregnancy or paternity; and possible exposure to a sexually transmitted disease.

Ironically, some single adults assume the Bible has a legalistic point of view about sex just because it insists that sexual acts have consequences for people and for their relationship with God. The apostle Paul, a single adult, insists that freedom in Christ does away with legalistic rules and regulations, even in physical matters (1 Corinthians 6; Romans 4–6, Galatians 3–54). But he contends that by their very nature, sexual relationships involve the whole person and not just the genitals.

Despite this culture's insistence on no-strings "recreational sex"—a separation of what our bodies do from who we are and what we believe—it just doesn't work. Most of us have our fair share of relational scars and wounds. We know from experience that our sexual behavior has a profound effect on our emotions, our self-image, and our relationship with our neighbors and with God.

In his book on dating, counselor Norman Wright identifies five benefits of resisting the "if it feels good, do it" mind-set:

1. No guilt for having disobeyed God;

2. No fears of conceiving a child and having to decide what to do next;

3. No temptation to compare a future spouse's sexual performance with that of past lovers ("Oh, you are in the upper twenty-fifth percentile!");

4. The self-control learned by waiting for marriage will be valuable for those inevitable periods of abstinence due to illness or work;

5. The pleasure of sexual satisfaction shared only with each other will bring excitement into your life and marriage.[1]

It's never too late to change your direction, to turn over a new leaf and reject current sexual standards. Remember, being out-of-step with our culture's values can be downright healthy—mentally, spiritually, and physically.

5.   How old is "too old" for romance?

As long as you are breathing, there is still hope for romance. One gentleman in a retirement home got married for the first time at age ninety-two, explaining to reporters, "Just wanted to see what all the fuss was about!" However, our culture can be uncomfortable with large age differences, particularly if the female is older than the male. Society is more willing to overlook age differences when the male is older (especially if he has money), although old enough to be your great-grandfather is pushing the envelope. Texans gasped (or grinned) in 1994, when twenty-something actress, model, and former waitress from Mexia, Texas, Anna Nicole Smith, married Houston oil tycoon, J. Howard Marshall II, age eighty-nine. All legal "hell" broke loose a year later when J. Howard "passed on to his eternal reward," leaving $500 million to be fought over.[1]

Given the increase in the number of unmarried senior single adults, romance among seniors is going to be a big item. It can be controversial. Children from a first marriage often oppose the new marriage because it muddies the children's rights to inherit. But many people have found great romance in the golden years of their lives. If comedian George Burns, always surrounded by beautiful women, ever battled loneliness as a single adult, he never admitted it.

6.   What about when I get older? Or old? Who will be there for me then? Who will take care of me?

My mother used to ask, "Well, singleness may be OK for right now but what about *later?*" I have also been blessed with friends who remind, "You know, you're not getting any younger!" Perhaps you've also been asked, "When are you going to settle down and get married?"

I am concerned with the last part of your question: "*take care of me.*" It suggests a rather limiting understanding of marriage. Today's reality is that you have to take care of yourself. If you did marry, your spouse could die first or leave you. Adult children may live halfway across the country or, as many senior adults have lamented, they may "have enough problems of their own without worrying about me."

Single adults need to assume that singleness will be lifelong; women need to assume that, married or single, they will live longer than men. You need to be saving not only for the proverbial rainy day, but also for your senior years, especially if you want them to be "golden." As one single adult wisely decided, "If I don't marry, it will not be a big disappointment. If I do marry, it will be a pleasant surprise. Either way, I am going to be one happy individual."

7.   I do not necessarily want a spouse, but I do want a child. Your advice?

Many single adults reach a point when they want a child. You may tire of waiting for "the right one" to come along and opt for single parenthood. Your two choices are: (1) artificial insemination, either with a known donor or with an anonymous donor, or (2) adoption.

Artificial insemination, with either an anonymous or known donor, is the choice many women have made. While this offers the opportunity to be a birth mother and to breast-feed, the donor's involvement needs to be carefully planned; you may not want him knocking at your doorstep, saying, "Remember me? I'm back."

Other single adults choose to adopt, although this can be an expensive and emotionally draining proposition. Whatever the method, not everyone will encourage you to single parent. Dream-dousers will share heart-wrenching adoption-gone-bad stories. If you resolve to go "full speed ahead," I suggest the following preparation:

• Talk to several single parents about their daily experiences.

• Talk to single adults who have gone through the adoption or artificial insemination process.

• Begin building a support network.

• Adoption and the transition to single parenthood will require lots of ca$h. Begin enhancing your financial profile. Pay off your credit cards. Build up a ne$t egg.

• Check out the policies and attitudes of your employer (formal and informal). Is your employer pro–single parent? Does your employer offer personal leave for adoption? How long will it be before the child is fully covered by your insurance?

• Tell your extended family and friends. Some may need time to get used to the idea.

• Unfortunately, it is extremely difficult for a single adult male to adopt. Be prepared to have every facet of your life put under intense scrutiny by an adoption agency. Consider adopting a "special needs" child. With some agencies, this may increase your chances of success.

My personal experience with adoption has been wonderful. A single woman friend wanted to adopt a baby from China. The best "cheer-leading" I've ever done was in helping her dream become a reality. What a special child; that single parent and her baby have certainly blessed my life and the lives of many others!

8.   Is there something wrong with me that I have never had a romantic relationship?

No. Just as physical maturation has a different timetable, so does romantic maturation. Many people would have been better off if they had slowed down the romantic process. Some people just haven't gotten around to it yet. My friend, Liz Curtis Higgs, did not marry until "later." She kept her wits about her through humor. "I never intentionally skipped marriage, it just happened that way. I woke up on my thirtieth birthday and said, 'Oh, my word, I forgot to get married!'"[1] Some of us have concentrated on our professions; some of us have cared for an elderly parent(s). Some of us have been "just friends."

CHAPTER 2

Single and "The Family"

9. Why is singleness such a issue for my parents? They drive me up the wall at times.

This is a generational issue many single adults are wrestling with. No doubt your parents love you and are genuinely concerned for your well-being. Parents want their children to be happy, but few can imagine a happy unmarried adult. Your parents grew up in a culture in which marriage of adult children demonstrated that the parents had done a good job. Your parents may also want grandchildren; so if your brothers or sisters are younger or have not had children, the heat gets turned up under you. In some families, the issue is continuing the family name, especially if an additional roman numeral is expected, say, III or IV.

Sometimes the simplest question from a parent, like, "Are you *seeing* anyone, dear?" sounds more menacing to you than they mean it to be. They may simply want you to know they are interested. Parents may also have questions that they are not sure how to ask. For example, they may wonder about your sexual orientation, but hesitate to bring it up.

This kind of miscommunication can often be cleared up with honest discussion. Appendix 2 offers some guidelines for "The Conversation," which is any kind of serious (and perhaps difficult) discussion about your singleness. Schedule The Conversation with your parents to help them understand how you hear their questions and concerns. If you think it will be hard to talk honestly with them, you might try holding The Conversation with a brother or sister first, as a kind of dress rehearsal for The Conversation with your parents.

10. My family thinks that I ought to spend all my holidays with them. I'd like to spend Christmas with friends or do something really unusual, especially on the four-day weekends. But my parents are elderly and won't be around much longer. I just cannot hurt their feelings.

But obviously you can hurt your own feelings. Everyone needs to audit their attitudes about holidays. One approach that I used was to reduce the time I spent with my family, particularly at Christmas, from a week down to four days. Eventually came the year when I didn't sing, "I'll Be Home for Christmas . . . " You have to prepare for all reactions—from anger to smoldering resentment to accusations like, "I hope you're happy. You just ruined Mom and Dad's Christmas!" or a guilt-engendering, "That's OK. We understand. It just . . . (some will use dramatic pauses) won't seem like Christmas if you're not here."

For some single adults, the holidays can be lonely times whether with family or alone. However, I can be lonely in the midst of the three-ring Norman Rockwell family Christmas, too. The Christmas "blues" are experienced not only by single adults sitting alone in a condo. Especially if sleeping arrangements at home are chaotic. Or if you are paying a lot of money to go home. Or if you have a highly dysfunctional family.

The issue becomes complicated in families that expect you to be home for *every* holiday (even for some that are not marked in red on the calendars). You're a big boy or girl. As a single adult (and the key word is *adult!*) it's time for you to start your own traditions. Turn off the radio when you hear, "I'll be home for Christmas . . . you can count on me." My home is not my childhood home—it's where I get my mail and answer my phone. So, I am *always* home for the holidays.

Practice your no's before you disclose the decision. Send an early letter or fax or e-mail, around Labor Day, to give your family time to get used to the idea of a holiday without you there. This is especially true if you come from a dysfunctional family that does not respect your singleness or your wishes. Don't give your family review or veto power over your holiday decisions. Too many single adults spend January trying to "get over" holiday time with the family. So, if you have a hankering for a ski Christmas or a Hawaii Christmas, go for it! Live your life *now!*

11. My mother has Alzheimer's disease and is still living at home. My brothers and sisters expect me to take care of her, since in one brother's words, "You don't have a family *of your own.*" I have a great job and need to support myself. But I never have any time for me, let alone for romance.

Many families cling to the notion that the unmarried son or daughter has an obligation to care for aging parent(s). Sadly, many middle-aged and senior single adults have cared for their parents and feel that they missed the season of romance and marriage.

But times are changing. While this cultural norm worked well in an agrarian economy, you have a job and need to support yourself. It's time for you to have The Conversation with your siblings in order for everyone to voice opinions. This should include sisters- and brothers-in-law, especially if they are behind-the-scenes power brokers. Be prepared for someone to voice anger or resentment, or attempt to impose guilt on you for trying to redefine the family relationships. When you redefine your relationship with your mother, there will be a chain reaction in your siblings' relationships.

Remember, long after your mother's death, life will go on for you. The decisions you make now could either enhance or hamstring your own social and economic future.

12. My mother is a recent widow and wants to pal around with me. How can I tell her that I want to be her daughter—not her pal?

With families now composed of fewer adult children who are increasingly mobile, you may end up as a *de facto* entertainment director for your parent, especially if that parent needs help with transportation or has health problems. Certainly you will have practical insights for your mother's transition to singleness, although she may be reluctant to define herself as "a single adult."

In some instances, a now-single parent and an adult son or daughter can become friends, but both parties have to want this level of relationship. You will need some boundaries. Resist any false guilt your mother may attempt to lay on you—"So-and-so has time for his mother . . . but don't worry about poor, lonely me. Go ahead. Have a good time. I'll be fine." This issue definitely merits The Conversation.

13. My mother keeps saying, "If you would just lose some weight, the men would come around and . . . " How can I respond to her?

One of the greatest luxuries is unconditional love. All of us want to be loved "*Just as I am,*" in the words of a great hymn written by a single adult. Too many single adults have been sentenced to a weight yo-yo that is tied to an emotional/spiritual yo-yo because of the interpretation of numerals on a bathroom scale. The terms of this sentence declare that, when my weight is under "control," I can live; but should I gain back some of the weight, my life skids out of control.

You know the turnoff impact of BO (body odor) on romance. But few appreciate the pressure of dealing with FPO (five pounds over), especially for women: "Get those five pounds off, darlin', and you'll be dating." Meanwhile, Junior has *dunlop* disease. His belly has "done lopped over his belt buckle," but he gets no hassle. The weight issue is definitely sexist. Ironically, some women can lose weight only by not dating. Dating involves eating out, which means calories and pounds.

Weight does offer some people an excuse for their singleness. But even if this sounds familiar, remember that altering your appearance will improve only the way you look. As Greg Flood insists, "Trying to ease your loneliness by altering your appearance is like trying to save a burning building by redecorating the lobby." He offers sound advice when he suggests, "Before deciding how you want to look, you must first decide who you are. Then, if you still desire a change in appearance, you will be bringing about that change for the right reason—to express who you are, not to change who you are."[1]

Simply put, your attitude about your weight is more important than your weight. Your weight is only digits on a scale. How long will you let numbers control your life? If your weight poses a health hazard, do what you need to do about losing weight over the long term.

Single adults who obsess about weight, either their own or that of those they date, are not healthy marriage candidates. Remind your mother of that reality, and tell her how her comments about weight sound to you.

14. My father thinks that because I am "still" single, I should be under his authority. He wants a key to my apartment and insists that I follow his advice on everything, from cars to men. Even if I am single, am I not an adult?

Lots of family disagreements have been stirred up by parents who do not want or know how to cut the apron strings. Or when you cut them, they race to retie them. In many conservative religious families and in some cultures this is a significant issue because of the misinterpretation and abuse of the Scripture, "Honor your father and mother" (Exodus 20:12), one of the first of the commandments we learn. Most of us grew up assuming the phrase has an exclamation mark. However, that admonition was intended for underage children—not adults!

This issue becomes clouded when single adults move back home or accept financial support from parents. Seldom are there "no strings attached" in such circumstances. These faint or invisible strings can be the strongest. Sometimes memories of conflict in adolescence ricochet through a single adult's mind, particularly if there were few options other than to move home. Old control conflicts can be easily reignited.

Parents and even grandparents have a right to opinions about our decisions, and in some cases, to verbalize or express those opinions, if asked. However, because you are an adult, a parent's opinions remain just that—*opinions* or *options*. Some parents possess wisdom, and it's important to recognize the distinction. One single adult who has faced this issue suggested his strategy: "I hear my father out, then I do what I need to do."

If you are a single parent and accepting your parents' assistance, you need to seriously consider their concerns, but regardless of the situation, do not be afraid to rely on your own wisdom and experience.

CHAPTER 3

Single and "Friends"

15. How do I keep from resenting my friends/roommates because they date more than I do?

Ah, the old ADF (*average dating frequency*) rears its ugly head! Last month my friend had 2.4 dates per week, while I . . . well, it's too depressing to be specific. This experience resembles those "left out" feelings we have when everyone else is devouring the guacamole and chips while we munch raw carrot sticks. I remember one friend who tired of "always being a roommate and *never* a bride!" because she had seen so many roommates and friends marry. (She didn't even bother to attend wedding rehearsals anymore.) "Why can't I find someone?" she groaned. "*Anyone!*"

I say, more power to those who are dating. Yet the issue becomes complicated when you have a roommate and have to hide out in your bedroom to avoid intruding on steamy romantic interludes going on in the living room. Or when you become receptionist for the calls, "Is Susan there?" or "Could you take a message for Susan?"or "Do you know where Susan is?" You want to snap, "No, I am her roommate—*not* her mother!"

It gets sticky when you suspect that wedding bells are in the offing, and you are going to have to cough up money for showers and Tupperware and face interviewing and breaking in yet another new roomie (or move if the lease is in your roommate's name).

The issue gets more complicated if there are sleep overs. Many non-dating roomies have stumbled through their dark apartment, hunting a drink of water, only to stumble across a stranger and ask in alarm, "Who are *you?* And what are you doing in *my* living room at 3 a.m.?"

It's really tense when your roommate wants you to "disappear" for a few hours (or days). They may not even see it as an imposition. After all, "Nothing personal. Two's company and three's a crowd!" This situation may lead you to come back with, "You know, I pay half the rent around here!" and before you know it, you're quarreling. If it is full-blown resentment (slammed doors, broken dishes, or loud music) whenever the "guest" is around, you need to find either a therapist or a rental agent.

16. I have friends who insist on telling me all the details— and I mean *all*—of their dating lives. That only makes me, a non-dater, feel left out. I feel like someone on a relational diet or on a romantic fast!

You could say, "Excuse me, but you mistake me for someone who cares," but the refined readers of *Singles Ask* would never say such a thing. But you might think it. Sometimes friends regale us with the rehash of their romantic lives because they want to include us in their good fortune. "Aren't you happy for me?" Occasionally, they want our honest appraisal. But too often, friends rattle on, telling us more than we want to know. "And then he . . . " We feel like voyeurs. Yuk!

When this happens, it's time to escape. On the phone, you can say, "Well, thanks for letting me know how it's going. Would really like to hear more. Gotta run . . ." (to scream or stick your head in the refrigerator for some therapeutic grazing.) Then at least a ten-minute report does not turn into an epic three-hour diatribe.

If you feel "left out," you may be sending subtle distress signals in your response to the conversation. You need to do some reflecting. Say this word with me, single adults: *jealousy!* Ask yourself, What's going on here? What's really pushing my buttons? And remember, all single adults have lean dating periods. Some just last longer than others.

17.   A friend wants to share an apartment with me. My friend is very emotionally needy. I am concerned how living together might affect the relationship.

Nothing tests a relationship like living under the same roof and sharing a bathroom and a microwave. In many urban areas, high rents and safety concerns make finding a *rentpal* a necessity, especially for housing that nurtures the soul. However, there is a big difference between needing a rentpal—someone to share living expenses and space—and wanting a roommate or housemate—someone with whom to share your home and daily experiences. As that great single adult philosopher, Anonymous, observed, "Familiarity breeds contempt." With a needy roommate, it breeds quickly.

Talk out your likes, dislikes, expectations, and neatness demands with any potential rentpal, because these will become the raw materials for disagreements that can make the walls swiftly close in. If your motivation is economic, be upfront about that. If you want a therapist, look in the yellow pages. And remember, there *are* roommates from hell! And roommates who have dates from hell!

Lots of friendships have been negatively impacted by sharing the rent and the remote. On the other hand, some single adults have found rooming together to be an incredible friendship-building experience. Lifelong friendships trace back to sharing housing together. Again, invest in lots of conversation before you sign the lease (and make sure both of you have thoroughly read the lease). Be sure you have adequate renter's insurance. Here are some key questions to ask yourself:

- Do I want to be a roommate? To share space?
- Do I need a roommate financially?
- Do I want or need to be a roommate with *this* individual?
- Am I willing to risk losing this friendship as a consequence of being roomies?

18.   I'm tired of being only a "friend." I want this to develop into something more.

I once received a Valentine's card that read, "Being around you . . . brings out the want in me!" Many of us are tired of "lite" platonic relationships. We note the magic phrase "something more" in the personals, as in "First a friendship, then *maybe* something more." Some of us knock ourselves out to be available for a relationship, hoping the thick fog will lift and our "friend" will discover that we have been there all along. We volunteer to be something more than a pal as impatiently as a child wanting to be picked for a team at school: *Me. Me!*

To love someone who doesn't love you or to love someone who doesn't love you as much as you love him or her is one of the most painful realities of singleness. I've been through that as both the want*er* and the want*ee*. Sometimes, however, we end up "only a pal," because we didn't clearly communicate expectations during the early foundational stages of the relationship. Some of us dress down around a friend. We get physically, verbally, and emotionally sloppy. Indeed, some women downplay their femininity in order to be "one of the guys."

The reality is that wishing—even hinting—won't make it happen. If you want something more than friendship, you will need The Conversation. However, be forewarned: Your friend may not want to redefine the boundaries. As far as he/she may be concerned, you can only be a pal. Sometimes, after that discovery, it takes a cooling off period to restabilize the relationship to accommodate friendship. Sometimes things are never quite the same.

It's tempting to ponder, Why am I not enough for this person? There may be no good answers. Singleness has its mysteries that defy analysis or explanation. Karen, for example, hung in a relationship for a long time, hoping for something more. Not until her friend came "out of the closet" did all the pieces fit. The potential for the "more" that Karen wanted did not exist.

Some single adults have discovered that you have to initiate the redefining. That begins with redefining (not lowering) expectations. Then ask yourself: Is it possible for this person to see my potential? Sometimes a crisis, such as a major move, loss of job, or illness, can open our eyes and we see someone on the margin of our romantic lives in a different light. You have to decide how long you are willing to wait for this. However, "forever" is not a reasonable answer.

19. How can I share that I want to be a friend without the other person thinking that I want to date?

Honestly verbalize your interests. "There's something I want to talk to you about. . . " You may begin by merely mentioning the idea to test the initial reaction before saying more. If you take the direct approach, the other person may feel pressured or put on the spot. Talk and listen it out so that each of you understands the other's interests and intentions. Ask questions, or restate what you hear, to clarify things. "Correct me if I am wrong, but I hear you saying . . ." When things go wrong in relationships, it's usually because one person fails to understand the hidden relational expectations or longings of the other. Sometimes one person changes his or her feelings without informing the other. These relational faux pas are often the subject for sitcoms, since men and women interpret events, comments, gestures, and silence differently. The harder you work to communicate your wishes and intentions, the better.

20. If friends of the same sex spend a lot of time together, won't people think we're gay?

"Hanging out" can lead to commentary and speculation, particularly by people who have no one to hang out with. This culture is much more willing to allow women to develop close, intimate same-sex friendships without snooping for the hints of homosexuality. Men risk being grilled: "You and John spend a lot of time together. You're not gay or something, are you?" Rampant homophobia and *homoprejudice* keep males from developing strong peer friendships with members of the same sex; that's why most men have only acquaintanceships. That's why romantic breakups can be so emotionally devastating for men. They seldom have intimate, close friends to "nurse" their romantic wounds.

Many younger single adults, however, seem to so appreciate friendships with members of the same sex that they ignore the "wonder if they are gay?" speculations. (Besides, for many, "gay" is not a pejorative term.) "We're "buds" (short for buddies) may be the most accurate answer to questions about your same-sex friendships. Remember, solid same-sex relationships are a vital necessity for any healthy single adult.

And the reality is that it takes time—*a lot of time*—for two people to build significant friendships, especially for same-sex friendships.

21. Who has stronger friendships: men or women?

Men have great difficulty making and maintaining friendships. The phrase "the friendless American male" expresses the relational reality of millions of men, single or married. In the grief groups I lead, I have discovered that many widowers have been hit with a double whammy: their wife was their best friend. So when his wife dies, the man also loses his best friend.

Rarely do married women identify a spouse as their "best" friend. Rarely does a man *not* identify his spouse as his best friend—in many cases, his *only* friend. This is why divorce can be so difficult for a man— he *thought* his wife was his best friend. Divorce, like death, deals men a double loss: spouse and best friend.

Women have stronger friendships because they have such keen communication skills, especially intuitive skills. Women freely invest emotion in their relationships. Research by investigators like Warren Farrell demonstrates that women tend to have better listening skills, which foster better communications which in turn, foster better relationships.[1] Women are more likely to listen to what is said and also to what is *not* said. Women tend to be "*and*" conversationalists, who support and compliment rather than contradict. They reinforce and add on to a conversation: "*And* I think you're right . . . " Men, on the other hand, tend to be "*but*" conversationalists. They listen until they hear something with which they disagree, and then they interrupt with, "*But* that's not true. (The *Packers* won the Super Bowl in 1977?)"

Fortunately, many single adults are learning how to invest in both same-sex and male/female friendships, particularly in the workplace. Some of us are learning that a man and a woman can develop and maintain incredible friendships without having or acting on sexual attraction.

CHAPTER 4

Single and Wanting a Relationship

22. What are some components of a healthy adult relationship?

Healthy adult relationships are a vital part of making the most of the single season. Good friendships are essential for emotional health. Amazingly, by investing in and nurturing a friendship, some single adults have discovered romance as a by-product. Here are a few components of any good relationship, romantic or otherwise.

Good relationships are strengthened by mutual attraction. It does take two to tango romantically.

Good relationships are strengthened by commitment. Some adults are reluctant to commit to a relationship because the other person might move—perhaps across the country—or might move up—perhaps into a new economic bracket or social network. Or they might marry. (Despite the assurance, "Oh, we'll still be pals," marriage does change friendships.) But the risk of commitment is worthwhile. In a committed relationship, single adults do not have to conceal what is troublesome or annoying. In a committed relationship, the "You" barbs are eliminated: "You know what *your* problem is, don't you?" In a committed relationship, adults do not insist on their rights.

Good relationships are strengthened by giving. Giving is a basic component of any healthy, thriving adult relationship, and there are plenty of opportunities to give: items, time, considerations, and opportunities for second chances. There has to be give and take.

Good relationships are strengthened by sharing: When acquaintances step aside, the friend steps in to share it all, the good, the bad, and the ugly. Sometimes a friend necessarily shares things that you do not want to hear. A friend may hold up a mirror into which you may be less than anxious to peer.

Good friends defend. The healthy friend guards information that might hurt or threaten the friendship. At times, I have defended the integrity of a friend who has made a colossal faux pas. A good friend will not allow "open season" on your integrity.

Good friends confront. Healthy adults do not say, "Ignore it and it will go away." Friends know that if something is ignored, it becomes more complicated and can compromise the relationship. Sometimes a healthy friend has to say, "You know this choice you've made or are making troubles me . . ."

Good friends invest emotion. Tears build relationships as well as laughter does.

Good friends support. One celebrated friendship in Hebrew literature is that of David and Jonathan. Their friendship was tested when Jonathan's father, Saul, tried to kill David. An incredible verse defines their friendship. "And Saul's son Jonathan went to David at Horesh and *helped him find strength in God*" (1 Samuel 23:16, italics mine). Good friends help us find the strength to face any crisis or circumstance. They are there for us but also *with* us.

23. What is the secret to making long-distance relationships work?

If you mean, what is the secret to getting the long-distance relationship to result in a *healthy* marriage, the odds are against it. However, if you don't want to get too close but want some dating excitement in your life, a long-distance relationship (LDR) can definitely provide that. It's best if you share the same area code, and preferably the same zip code.

Admittedly, LDRs are common in this mobile, rootless culture and can provide a sense of high drama when they last: "*Our* relationship worked against all the odds." A good relationship with potential for healthy marriage (not *merely* marriage—anyone can get married. Having a healthy marriage is another issue) needs lots of time together before the "I do–ing." LDRs certainly boost the profits of the airlines and long-distance phone carriers. But talking on the phone—even for hours—is not the same as being together and experiencing non-verbal conversation on a more regular basis.

Moreover, when a couple in an LDR spends time together, both want the limited time to be quality time. So they conspire to overlook relational warning signals or distressers. It takes two extraordinary individuals to make a long-distance relationship work.

24. I'm very confident and decisive, and I intimidate men. Should I try to change this, or should I not worry about it?

Many men are threatened by confident, assertive, decisive women. Other men are attracted to these same qualities. They may be in the minority, but they do exist. As an assertive person, I would strongly discourage you from trying to change or disguise your personality traits in order to attract, let alone please a man. Women who do that and then marry often find that when conflicts arise (as they do in even the best marriages), their real personality traits reemerge. The result can be a marriage crisis, physical abuse, even divorce.

Whether you're an assertive person or not, don't put all your hopes for a happy life on getting married. Singleness has advantages, and many single adults live happy, fulfilled lives. While being single has its struggles, it's a whole lot better than jumping into a bad marriage.

25. My friend makes little snide barbs about my body. Should I just ignore the comments?

Take the comments very seriously. Such remarks are icebergs: ten percent visible above the waterline and ninety percent below the surface. What your friend is saying reveals what he really thinks and isn't saying. For your own mental health, you need to ask, "Is there a molecule of truth in what he is saying?" Then ask, "Is this person likely to help me or encourage me in changing or dealing with it?" Certainly not with snide comments.

Pull the plug on this relationship and move on!

26. Is a Christian singles group the best place to look for a marital partner?

Since there are such incredible variations in single adult groups, even in Christian settings, one has to carefully evaluate the safety of any group. Christian single adult groups can be a good place to meet people. But meeting a potential marital partner should be a secondary benefit in participating in a singles group. More importantly, a single adult group can also help you read the maps of this place called Singleland. Be alert, however. Unhealthy "crazy makers" and sexual predators or "sharks" prowl these turfs, sometimes going from group to group, looking for their latest relational "hit."

27. What complications does one encounter in dating someone from another ethnic group?

It's hard to believe that less than a generation ago, interracial marriage, especially between black and white people, was illegal in most states, particularly in the South. While enormous change in "expressed," or public attitudes toward interracial dating and marriage has occurred, suppressed attitudes are resilient.

In some families and social networks, the issue is abstract until you begin dating a person who is "different." Initially, some of your friends may think it is "cool," but if the relationship becomes serious, you may experience a chilling lack of enthusiasm. In fact, you may lose some friends, and relationships with family members can become strained.

The response from your friend's family may also be less than favorable, ranging from caution to outright hostility, and that can add lots of stress to the romance. One single friend was stunned by the hostility of his Asian date's family toward him. His first-hand encounter with prejudice—as a recipient—was an eye-opening experience.

Be alert to the fact that the motivations may be confused. Why are you dating this person? Curiosity? Rebellion? Do you have an agenda? What might either of you gain socially in the relationship? Can this help you to deal with the difficulties you will face?

The interracial couple can expect slights, stares, and innuendo. These days, an unhealthy "polite" racism often lurks below the surface. Your love will be tested, but the testing can strengthen your love. Listen to your heart rather than to the prejudices of those who claim to know "what is best for you." Admittedly, in some families, it is going to take time to get used to the idea of an in-law from another ethnic group; in fact, love for that in-law and for any children you might have together may be constrained, and it will rarely be unconditional.

It should also be noted that African Americans, for example, bring different body-evaluation and appreciation to relationships. Research indicates that African American males are far more accepting of a large female body and less like to value the "thin ideal" of American culture. Wide hips and round buttocks are generally perceived by African Americans as sexually attractive, and are definitely not a turnoff.[1]

You may find real freedom as well as emotional stretching in dating or marrying someone from another ethnic group. Thankfully, in America, you can now choose from rich variety in the human pool.

28. Can you offer a better term than *boyfriend* or *girlfriend?* I find the terms juvenile.

Join the club. The choice of many is my *significant other* or *male/female friend*. Some senior adults prefer *gentleman* or *lady friend* if the individual does not contradict the term. Naturally, some friends and family want to know just how significant your "other" is or is likely to be. It's up to you to either further define the relationship or smile and ignore the question.

If asked, "Is it serious?" you might want to respond, "You know I can appreciate why you would ask that question. But, (dramatically pause) I hope you can appreciate why I do not want to answer that question." Then smile. Real friends will change the subject.

29. What about dating persons from other faiths?

Most single Christian women are well aware that there is a shortage of eligible single men who take Christian faith intentionally. As a result, some Christian women date individuals affiliated with other religions. But Christian men also date people who follow other religions or do not identify themselves with any particular religion.

If you are dating with the intention of finding a mate, then you need to consider your choices. The Christian faith has traditionally discouraged interfaith marriage, based on 2 Corinthians 6:14, which says that believers should "not be harnessed in an uneven team with nonbelievers" (The Inclusive Version). That analogy loses something in our high-tech culture; think of it in terms of your Mac computer being incompatible with a Windows-oriented PC. The same can be true in marrying someone from another religious perspective (even within Christianity). Many couples have experienced great emotional pain because they share so little spiritually.

According to Pastor Arthur Rouner, a relationship as precious as marriage depends on shared values, and faith is the ultimate shaper of one's values.[1] The time involved in dating and engagement offers one an opportunity to closely observe the faith of a partner, particularly under stress.

Be careful. Dating exposes your heart and can leave you vulnerable to hearing what you want to hear. On the other hand, in a faith-diverse culture such as America, dating could help you gain insight into another faith such as Buddhism or Judaism. Remember that there can be fine divisive nuances in a religion, such as the current conflict between Orthodox and Reform Jews.

Certainly, not all dating by single adults is or needs to be marriage-oriented. Dating can be a form of recreation, provide companionship, and be a source of friendship, self-knowledge, and self-development. In fact, when these are the primary focal points, dating may allow a gradual romantic interest to bloom.[2] *Single adults who take their faith seriously, intentionally guard their hearts when dating persons of other religious persuasions or persons who have little interest or intentionality about faith.*

One must also be aware that religious developments in other nations may impact practitioners of that faith in this country as well. For example, the growing fundamentalist movements in many world religions give cause for concern, particularly in their treatment of women. Before you marry, it is essential to understand the commitments you may be asked to make to raise children in a particular religion.

30. How do you recognize infatuation?

Infatuation is often the first wave of romance. Ray Short, a sociologist, equates romantic infatuation with "romantic love" or "being in love." Infatuation is a strange blend of sex, romance, and emotion, with a little anxiety thrown in for good measure. [1]

Infatuation is a big reality in Singleland. "To be swept off our feet" is one of life's most delicious feelings. Life is good when someone loves *you!* However, when single adults declare, "We're in love," it usually can be most accurately translated, "We're in infatuation."

Some single adults, aware that infatuation can be explosive and destructive, also know that infatuation can lead straight to bed (no passing *Go* and no collecting $200). So some opt for a short engagement or a quick marriage. But feelings of infatuation (sometimes described as "warm and fuzzy") will not last and *cannot* support a marriage. Short dismisses infatuation as "false love" and says it is the emotional equivalent of quicksand. [2] Little wonder we say, "head over heels in love."

The reality of infatuation can be reduced to a cliché, "Here today . . . gone tomorrow!" Some of us are good at launching romantic projects but not at finishing. Lots of single adult infatuation addicts are on the prowl. Individuals get turned on or temporarily freed from the boredom of singleness by a brief romantic fling. It is when the hard business of relationship building begins that some people look for the next exit and the next *infatuee.* Admittedly, real love can evolve out of infatuation, but it takes time. Unfortunately, time is a commodity too many single adults think they do not have or will not invest.

In the throes of infatuation, a single adult idealizes the other person and tends to be verbally expressive: "I can't get enough of you." We're like the six-year old devouring the candy in her Easter basket in one sitting. Infatuation can be dangerous and disarming. Some single adults, regardless of their age, kid themselves into thinking that they should go ahead and act out these intense feelings and sexual urges. After all, "we're *both adults!*" Or, "I may never have another chance."

31. How do you let someone know you are interested in a relationship without sex, without sounding "holier than thou?"

Look that person straight in the eye and say, "I want a chance to get to know you—the real you. I want you to have a chance to get to know me—the real me. And there's no way we can do that if we have sex without commitment."

Simply put, sex befuddles the evaluating. Some individuals have been known to be "led around" by their hormones. Ellen Fein and Sherrie Schneider insist, "He must fall in love with your soul, your whole being, not just your body. So the less you do physically, the better. Besides, it's easier to stop something if you don't let things get too hot and heavy right away."[1]

Your date may counter, "Oh, sure, I want the same thing" but then try to persuade you to redefine the sexual boundaries of the relationships to permit more physical contact. "Couldn't we . . . ?" Many men want the sexual equivalent of consolation prizes.

Someone observed, "Prevention is so much better than healing." Too many single adults let a relationship control them, or give in too freely to the partner's redefining process. Here are some ways you can stay in control:

Know what you want. When hungry, I often ask myself, "What do I want?" That's a better alternative than looking at someone else's plate and saying, "Oh I'll just have what she is having" or later saying, "I wish I had that." Ask yourself: What do I want in a relationship?

Know what you do not want. If you don't want premature sex to sabotage a relationship, then make choices that will reinforce your decision.

Communicate your thoughts. Be honest and open about what you think. It may take some rehearsing, and it may trigger initial misunderstanding. Certainly it may take more than one conversation.

Make sure your date hears you. On topics like sex, it is easy to focus on what we are going to say or how we are going to respond. So we do not hear what the other person is saying. Your friend may feel personally rejected: "It's *me*, isn't it?" No. You are rejecting not the person but a level of physical or emotional relationship with that individual.

Suggest the physical limits. Otherwise, you'll end up continuously renegotiating sexual boundaries. Don't get talked into anything that makes you uncomfortable or places you at risk of abandoning your decision.

Confront the "holier-than-thou" accusation. Today a more conservative sexual ethic is common, even among people who do not consider themselves religious. You are far less likely to be labeled a "puritan" or teased about your sexual views, because even the contemporary magazines and "experts" are revaluing abstinence. You can always say no. If the person is long-term good for you, he/she will respect your wishes and will not try to override them.

A clear "no" can keep the relationship from going too far, too fast and burning out.

Simply put, you have the right to take your time. If your date really cares about you, your boundaries will be respected. In fact, they may prove intriguing.

Give yourself a hand for being self-asserting and for standing up for what you want.

32. What is crucial for making a relationship work these days?

A positive, growing relationship is based on a decision: I choose to nourish the growth of this relationship. I choose to invest myself in this relationship, and I will spend the time necessary to make this relationship work. I choose not to participate in any "make do" or "tide me over" relationships while waiting until love comes along. It's disheartening to discover that just as we have "temps" in the workplace, some people are or want emotional, romantic, even sexual "temps." Without saying so, this declares: "You'll do until something *better*—or something with long-term potential—comes along." Unfortunately, the delay of marriage into the twenties or thirties has encouraged romance to be little more than a "series of shifting emotional attachments,"[1] some of which leave wounds, scabs, and scars.

33.   **What are qualities of a good adult relationship?**

Quality 1: Trust. You have to be able to trust each other. Today, married couples spend less time together, particularly those with demanding, dual careers. People frequently find themselves in situations where relational, even sexual temptation is a factor, particularly if they do not handle loneliness well. Our culture has glamorized "on the side" relationships or "flings," making it easier to rationalize, "We're adults. No one will get hurt." But someone always gets hurt. With the cultural pressure to have sex and with the realities of the STD (sexually transmitted disease) epidemics, there's no substitute for being able to take someone's faithfulness as fact. Your partner's choice in a moment of sexual weakness could have lifelong consequences for you, as well.

Quality 2: Affirmation. Growing couples take pride in each other and in their relationship. Wise couples work at establishing a positive atmosphere in which one compliment leads to another. They develop the habit of building each other up instead of criticizing one another. They look for things in a partner to praise and applaud.

Quality 3: Loyalty. Commitment to the relationship is more than a one-time, taken-for-granted promise. There must be a daily investment or recommitment: I will choose today to act toward you in loving ways, even if I don't feel romantic toward you. How can I creatively pay attention to my commitment?

Beware of the person who is always gazing over their shoulder for something "better" or more interesting. This individual will have you talking to yourself in the mirror: *If only I try a little harder I can be enough.* Loyalty means you *are* enough. Loyalty means that past relationships have been extinguished, that old flames are not still "waiting in the wings" for your relationship to crash.

Quality 4: Humor. You need to laugh frequently and laugh together. A good sense of humor can be a creative "wild card" in a relationship. Most romances need big doses of laughter, including self-deprecating humor. "You make me laugh!" is a compliment.

Quality 5: Spontaneity. Open those DayTimers and see if you can wedge in some time for romance. Busyness and boredom threaten healthy relationships. Are you boring? Overly predictable? Bound to your schedule? Your chances of having a satisfying, long-term relationship will be greatly enhanced if you regularly add some variety and spontaneity to your life and your dating. Some single adults become "old poops" before their time; some of us, quite candidly, get rather set in our ways. So, "zestize" your life!

Quality 6: Relaxation. A couple needs to deliberately make quality time for each other, time that is not shared with a TV set or spent as another "graze-and-gaze" video night. If someone spends large amounts of time "glued" to the tube, ask yourself why would that change after an "I do." It's important to develop a pattern of making and appreciating quality time together now, before you make a commitment. Watch out for the workaholic who can be physically present with you but mentally at the office. In this epidemic of stress, you also need quality time alone or "down time" for yourself and for being together quietly rather than "doing" a multi-level date—meal, event, post-event coffee—that seems more like an endurance contest.

Healthy, growing relationships are never instant. They take time, energy, and patience.

34. What is the best way to end a romantic relationship without hurt feelings?

Terminating a relationship is not a once-and-for-all amputation! If there are no post-romance hurt feelings, there could not have been much of a relationship. It takes incredible maturity by both parties to grieve the loss of *what might-have-been,* to adjust to the change and still maintain a friendship. It may take a lot of time to nudge the new "only-a-friendship" along. The degree of difficulty connected with a breakup depends greatly on who makes the decision—you, your friend, or both of you together. If the relationship just stops, like a car out of gas, or if someone aborts it suddenly ("I'm out of here!"), the grief is compounded.

Here are some guidelines for "pulling the plug" on a relationship.

Communicate. Talk. Honestly explain your feelings. Even though your friend may have difficulty hearing you out (let alone understanding what you are saying), you need to verbalize why you are breaking things off. Point out that you are rejecting the relationship—not the person.

Avoid accusations, digs, slashes, and "I want to get one thing off my chest!" conversations. By exit time in a relationship, frustration may tempt you to "clean house" emotionally; to assign blame for the failure of the relationship to meet *your* needs; to point the finger at the other person and engage in a "you" oriented verbal attack. Ill-timed, ill-chosen, or ill-delivered words can destroy any possibility of transitioning from a romance into a friendship.

Don't manipulate or threaten. Don't let yourself be manipulated or threatened to staying in the relationship, and don't use those tactics yourself. If you resort to remarks like, "You'll be sorry, buster!" you could be tossing a boomerang that will come back on you.

Some people prefer to let a relationship slowly strangle itself. Others prefer the big bombastic "Blow Up," which leaves blood and guts everywhere. You need to ask, Does this relationship deserve the energy it would take to change or convert it into a friendship? Remember, if you have had sex, you have severely limited the chances of remaining friends.

I would rather see someone yell, scream, and protest the injustice of love than merely shrug their shoulders and take a hike into the sun set. Too many single adults suppress their anger and hurt, then retreat into a private woundedness that may never completely heal. Unexpressed hurt will simply fester and have a negative effect on the next relationships. What do *you* do with the hurt?

Whatever you do, don't go rushing into another relationship to make up for "lost" time spent in this one. Healing is a process that takes time—lots of time. You are investing in your own emotional well-being when you cooperate with the process.

35. How can a single adult get over a relationship?

The older I get, the more I believe that one does not "get over" a loss but rather *reconciles with* loss, or "befriends" loss. Noted grief specialist, William Worden, urges grievers to decide to "emotionally relocate . . . and move on with life."[1] He also reminds us, "One never loses memories of a significant relationship." The cliché is accurate: "Life goes on." Part of the task for the single adult after a loss is to organize a world in which this once special person is either totally absent or no longer integral.

Reconcile Principle 1: Give yourself time to mourn the romance. You need time to adjust to the loss and to accept healing. The last thing you need to do is to rush into a new relationship to replace the old one.

Reconcile Principle 2: Decide to reconcile with the romantic loss. Ending the relationship *is* a decision. If it's really over, forever, and you know it—move on. Vacate the relationship.

Reconcile Principle 3: Focus on the positive memories. Ignore the temptation to replay the parting scenes in slow motion, frame by frame, peeking through your fingers: "Ohhhh, that hurts *so good!*" Instead, concentrate on the positive memories of the relationship.

Reconcile Principle 4: Catch up with your social network. Simply announce to friends, "I'm back!" (the details are not essential right now). During intense romances, we ignore other people, especially friends. Ironically, you may even have neglected yourself and your living environment. Now is a good time to reestablish priorities.

Reconcile Principle 5: Don't focus on the pain. Recognize the pain of the romantic loss—definitely. Exaggerate—no way! Yours is not the greatest romantic loss of all time, of the decade, even of the year. Yes, it's tempting to sit at the bus stop, Forrest Gump-like, and bewail our tales of romantic woe to anyone who will listen. If you are determined to verbalize your hurt, be accurate and honest, no more. Why not cut out a large paper purple heart and attach it to your dress, suit, sweater, shirt, or computer? When people ask, "What's with the heart?" you will get to share your story.

Reconcile Principle 6: Honestly critique the relationship. Conduct a "romance post mortem" to ponder what went wrong. To what degree am I responsible for failure of *this* relationship? Did this relationship ever have a chance? What is the life lesson I can learn from this? *Every* romantic ending has a lesson to be learned, although it may be hidden. In order to learn it we need to ask the right questions and to listen to answers that emerge from the deep recesses of our hearts. Have you learned anything from this loss about yourself or about human nature that can help you in future relationships? If you have, then the experience has not been wasted.

Reconcile Principle 7: Pamper yourself. "Get thee to a mall!" Dig into your comfort food, whether lasagna, chicken soup, cheeseburger-and-fries, chocolate, or ice cream. Get away for a long weekend for reflection (not brooding). Send a bouquet of flowers to yourself at the office; act surprised but offer no explanations.

Reconcile Principle 8: Seek professional assistance. Trained counselors can help us or come along beside us in our romantic loss and help us learn from it. Turn to Chapter 20 for information on how to find a good counselor and to profit from the experience.

William Worden suggests that the "benchmark" of a completed grief reaction is when you are "able to think of the [individual] without pain." There will long be a hint of sadness "when you think of someone you have loved and lost, but it is a different kind of sadness—it lacks the wrenching quality it previously had."[2] You are no longer paralyzed by the loss.

36. I am attractive and yet still single! What's wrong with me?

"Mirror, mirror, on the wall—Why am I *still* single?"

Still single! are two words that strike fear into the hearts of most single adults. Remember, nothing's "wrong" with you. It shows maturity that you are not just speeding in the express lane to get past your singleness.

Women must consider that there are more eligible women than available men. Statistically speaking, it isn't possible for every woman who would like to get married to do so. Tragically, this culture still distributes the false message that we can "have it all," that "Anything the mind can conceive, you can achieve." *Just try harder!* Some Christians have edited scripture to read, "Seek [a spouse] and you shall find. Hallelujah!" Such statements reflect a totally unrealistic view of the world. Too many single adults have bloodied, exhausted souls from their overzealous search for marital bliss.

There's nothing wrong with wanting to be married. There's nothing wrong with being unmarried. There is, however, a lot wrong with desperately lowering your standards just so you can get married. Here are some things to keep in mind:

Happiness should be based on who you are, not whether you are married. "Must-centered" (I must be married to be a whole adult) living is destined for frustration, heartache, and heartbreak. If a naked ring finger annoys you, put something on it. Roy Fairchild is right to remind us, "One dominant goal or relationship cannot take over a person's life without impoverishment and pain."[2]

Concentrate on being the unique person God intends you to be. Don't let all your time and effort be sidetracked into postponing life while pursuing the elusive romance. You will not only stunt your emotional growth and make yourself a less interesting person, you will possibly scare off a prospective spouse.

My nephew's favorite phrase, "Give it a rest!" is wise. Take a relation-hunting sabbatical or a siesta. Grant yourself a romance "leave of absence."

Nip the bitterness. Bitterness keeps you from seeing the good things you have going for you. Ask God to give you a positive, thankful attitude. When you hit the pillow, hum a little Irving Berlin, "And I fall asleep, counting my blessings," not your romantic losses! Don't be like the bitter single adult who died and insisted that all the pallbearers be females. "If no man took me out while I was alive," she snapped, "I am not about to have six men take me out when I am dead!"

Instead of concentrating so hard on getting married and expending too much energy on looking for the right one, concentrate on *becoming* the right one!

On my refrigerator door throughout my singleness have been these anonymous words: "I have a nightmare of waking up, having avoided all of God's challenges for a Cinderella dream that never came true." Maybe that belongs on your refrigerator, too.

CHAPTER 5

Single and Wanting a Life Partner

37. Is there a foolproof method for finding "the right one"?

As long as marriage is a union of two imperfect people, there will be no "foolproof" system; single adults will continue to be foolish, to be "fooled," and to be made fools of. But here are six basic principles to guide you as you set out in search of the "great mate."

    1. Know what kind of person you want to marry.

    2. Know what kind of person you do not want to marry.

    3. Keep reminding yourself of the difference between 1. and 2.

    4. Spend time with persons in category 1.

    5. Relax. Impatience leads to a poor choice, poor marital adjustment, and ultimately a reality called divorce.

    6. Be patient. Give "the right one" time.

38. What about advertising in the personals?

Many single adults use "the personals" as a way of meeting people. "Video dating" services, computers, and the Internet are an increasing part of a creative dater's repertoire. In a high-tech age, why not use high-tech resources for cyber-matching? Your classified on the Internet could be read not only by single adults (and married adults) in your city, but by that single cowboy in Montana or the single woman in New England who owns a bed-and-breakfast. You can "market" yourself for pennies.

Although there are risks and limitations in personal ads, focus on the advantages. People who place personal ads are less likely to be looking for a quick one-night stand than those who maintain a permanent seat in a singles' bar.

Placing or responding to an ad is worth a try. You might not meet Prince or Princess Charming but you will meet some interesting people or gain new insight into human nature. Expect some distortions of reality in the ads, some generous exaggerations, perhaps well-intentioned. Expect to encounter a few mild-to-serious neurotics (they are everywhere). As the cliché says, "Nothing ventured, nothing gained."

Over lunch one day Dave and I were trashing the classifieds. Then Dave pulled out his wallet and started flashing baby pictures. "Cute kids," I responded. "Met their mother through the personals." Wouldn't you know it! He carries a laminated copy of the ad he had placed five years earlier. See, some ads work!

If you decide that an ad is a worthwhile investment (and an *investment* is what many single adults consider their personals), then the ad and the phrasing of the key elements should give a clear idea of what kind of person you are and what type of person you are looking for. If you decide to go "to print" remember:

• Be honest.

• Be creative. Challenge your reader to put down that remote and call.

• Be brief. If you are too wordy, readers will wonder what you are compensating for.

• Be realistic about the response. Don't expect to build up your arm muscles from lugging in all the mail.

• When you get a response that sounds promising, arrange to meet the individual in a well-lit, public place such as a restaurant. *Never* give out your address until you know that you can trust this person. Never initially meet at either residence and always arrange for your own transportation.

• Do not correspond with prisoners of the opposite sex unless you are a corrections officer.

• Never hesitate to say, "I don't think so . . . " especially if the person sounds weird, angry, rude, or insensitive, or wants you to meet Mother on your first date.

• Verify phone numbers, in case a parent, lover, or spouse answers. Not all "singles" who run ads are single; some just want to be single.

• Listen to what responders tell you and what they do not tell you.

• Let someone know you are meeting this person, telling them the time, name, and place. You may want to be in the media, but not as the victim of a sociopath.

39. How do I know it's the right one?

There is not only one "right" person for you in Singleland. There could be several or even many. The real question is: How do you know whether this is a person with whom you can make a lifelong commitment and with whom you have a good chance of having a successful marriage? How do you know that this person will honor their commitment to you, especially in those inevitable "poorer," "worse," and "sickness" situations the vows mention?

Good marriage prospects come on slow and not like gangbusters. You get to know them gradually, over time. Eventually you discover that deep within you, your hearts and lives (not just your hormones) fit together in the dance of life. Don't be in any big hurry to give your heart away!

Make sure you agree on the basics that can make or break a marriage: faith commitments, finances, children, male/female roles and expectations, friends, career priorities, relationships with in-laws, and these days, politics. Sociologist Ray Short offers this helpful guideline for determining whether your love will stand the test of time: "If you love someone so much that you want that person to be happy, even if you are not the one to make him or her happy, then you really love that person."[1] Remember, you haven't met "the right one" until you can promise to stand by that person as long as you live—no matter how much more "right" someone else seems later on.

Remember also that you are marrying your assumed "right one" *as is*—not for their potential.

40. When I have found the right person and we are planning to marry, how long should we wait to marry?

Many single adults believe that the major purpose of an engagement is to plan the wedding. They spend their time leafing through *Modem Bride* and scheduling appointments with florists, caterers, photographers, and ministers. Some couples get so wrapped up in the details of planning and pulling off a wedding that they fail to heed little warning signals en route to the "I do." An engagement is an opportunity to:

• See your future spouse in everyday situations over a period of time;

• Become better acquainted with each other's families;

• Create an "amorous monogamy" in which "old flames" and romantic rivals are eliminated from the romantic landscape;

• Gain insight into each other's responsiveness;

• Discuss the realities of marriage, especially jobs, money (particularly indebtedness and credit card patterns), traditions, parenthood, and illness;

• Arrange financial affairs and gradually assume the economic realities of marriage;

• Test the roles of husband and wife in decision making and learn some of the "ropes" of the evolving relationship;

• Stabilize the relationship. [1]

If you haven't completed these essential tasks, postpone your wedding. By not rushing into marriage, you make it much more likely that you will have a 25th anniversary to celebrate (and one that is *worth* celebrating). Too many divorced single adults confess that at some point during their engagement they knew they were making a mistake or had strong doubts. Why, then, did they go ahead and get married? "We were too far along. . . . we already had mailed the invitations, etc."

During the dating before an engagement, couples prefer to look at their relationship through "rose-colored" glasses. When an engagement is a whirlwind race to the altar (especially if this is a rebound relationship), you miss an opportunity to confront and work through issues that will greatly influence your future and the future of your children.

Single adults get engaged for the same "wrong" reasons as teenagers: (1) to justify sexual relations; (2) to get away from other problems (romance can be a great anesthetic); (3) for personal security;

(4) to rejuvenate a stagnant relationship that has dragged on too long; and (5) because friends are getting engaged or married. These are bad reasons to get married.

41. Why do all of my dates go wrong!?

You may be dragging around unrealistic expectations. Many single adults are clinging tightly to fists of non-negotiable items on the check-list that "the right one" must possess. Instead, focus your energies on what you can do to *become* the right one!

Remember, for every item on your list of qualifications, you eliminate thousands of potential individuals.

Suppose these items are on your non-negotiable list of desired characteristics:

1. over six feet tall

2. black hair

3. never married

4. religious

5. professional

6. non-smoker/drinker

We start with the basic pool of 34,278,000 single males.[1]
Eliminating all males under 6', the pool of eligibles drops to
    27,000,000.
Eliminating all without a college degree, the pool of eligibles
    drops to 18,500,000.
Eliminating all without black hair, the pool of eligibles drops
    to 10,300,000.
Eliminating all smokers and drinkers, the pool of eligibles
    drops to 7,300,000.
Eliminating all non-religious, the pool of eligibles drops to
    4,600,000.
Eliminating those in prison, the pool of eligibles drops to
    4,510,000.

Eliminating those uninterested, the pool of eligibles drops
to 3,670,000.

Eliminating those in separation/divorce, the pool of eligibles
drops to 1,376,000.

Eliminating those who live with their mother, do not bathe, are
in serious therapy, want a traditional "Yes dear" wife, or
belong to a wilderness paramilitary group, the pool of
eligibles drops to 300,000.

String together too many "must haves," and mathematical probability works against you. You will end up with one eligible male: a Peace Corps volunteer working with an obscure tribe in sub-Saharan Africa whose e-mail is broken.

Sometimes it is wise to take a "time out" from dating and to do a serious audit of your romantic expectations. What do I want? Really want? Have my friends/family been right in saying, "You're too picky!" An audit is a serious look at the *you* that is dating. Put your relationships under the microscope and take a serious peek.

42. How can I make this dating relationship into something with potential?

The healthy goal in dating should be getting to know the person you are seeing. Getting someone to make a commitment or to "pop the question" is a by-product of knowing the individual and loving what you know without ignoring some characteristic that you cannot love or live with. If you shrug and say, "He'll/she'll do . . ." you're overlooking reality. Take your time. Hasty, premature commitment threatens any stage of a healthy relationship. Barbara DeAngelis has identified four stages of romance formation.

Stage 1: Commitment to be sexually/emotionally monogamous
Time frame: Up to three months
What do I call this? "My new relationship"
Option: Say "goodbye" and exit
Question to ask: "Do I want to continue to see this individual? Do
I want to see someone else? You *and* your partner mutually

decide that this is your one and only intimate and sexual relationship (sex covers everything from kissing to intercourse).

Stage 2: Commitment to work toward a partnership
Time frame: Three to six months
What do I call this? "A developing relationship"
Option: "So long . . . it's been fun."
Question to ask: Do we agree that this relationship is special and, therefore, worth nurturing and pursuing?

Stage 3: Commitment to spend your future together
Time frame: six months to time needed
What do I call this? "A relationship with a future"
Questions to ask: Are we creating a healthy relationship? Do we want to spend the immediate future together?

Stage 4: Commitment to spend the rest of your lives together
Time frame: You have had a solid level three commitment
What do I call this? "A committed relationship"
Question to ask: Have we had sufficient experience to believe that we are "right" for each other? [1]

Each stage requires increased commitment, not to marriage but to investing fully in the current stage and exploring the next stage. Hence, as a couple you are not "just dating" but are exploring a deepening relationship.

CHAPTER 6

Single and Female and Curious about Single Men

43. Is there a man for every woman?

One man for every woman may have once been Eden's ideal design, but war, disease, lifestyles, and the recognition of sexual orientations have radically changed things. Why isn't there a man for every woman?

Factor 1: There is a statistical imbalance of 7,400,000 more single American females than males. [1]

Factor 2: According to Laurel Richardson and other researchers, as many as 14 percent of single adult males may be homosexual (14 percent of single adults, not the entire population). [2]

Factor 3: Some men are not good candidates for marriage. The infamous Bennett-Bloom Study found that only 78 percent of women with college educations will eventually marry. A woman's commitment to a career or the demands of fast-paced professionalism may limit the number of eligible men who will support her priorities. Also, many men are reluctant to marry a woman with strong feminist views (what you think of as strong and what he defines as strong could be quite different) and are more likely to marry a "traditional" woman, in other words, a woman comfortable with being "the little lady." [3]

While these factors influence the whole population, they do not accurately indicate the chances a *particular* woman—with her own set of characteristics and circumstances—has of marrying. One friend enthusiastically says, "There are 33,300,000 single men out there and I only need *one!*" [4]

44. Why are so many men not dating?

Years ago the etiquette of dating was simple: man asked woman out; woman said yes, no, or maybe; man planned the date; man paid for the date. The system, although not flawless, worked—otherwise most of you would not be reading *Singles Ask.* Today, in light of changes like healthy self-assertiveness brought on by the women's movement and an apparent surplus of eligible women, everything seems up for grabs.

Why aren't more men dating?

Many men are rejection-phobic. Fear is a powerful motivator. In the celebrated age of *mucho macho,* some men still have poor self-images. They fear being compared with others (especially the Chippendale dancers and daytime soap opera hunks) and ultimately found "wanting," if not outright rejected.

Dating is expensive and requires risk venture capital. Dates are often evaluated on the basis of money: "So, how much money did he spend on you?" or less directly, "Where did you go? What did you do?," which answers the first question. For a single man in a low-paying job or with child support or alimony, or for the single adult with large educational debts, even basic dating can be a luxury. True, some men prefer to spend their money on cars, trucks, and motorcycles (and insurance). But dating is truly troublesome for single-agains, who have as much difficulty funding dates as finding dates. That's why many men are in such a hurry to get past the preliminaries and settle into a *NCPR* (nice, cozy, and predictable relationship). That way they don't have to impress anyone.

Some men are angered by assertive women. These men want the old system back. Rather than mount a futile protest, they take a "time out" from dating. Admittedly, it may be a long one, because the new rules are not going to disappear. A major social shift has occurred.

Some men have unresolved conflicts with women. It may be difficult to determine the root source of their annoyance—their ex, their mother, their first-grade teacher, women in the workplace, the women of NOW, a prominent female politician or leader, or all women in general.

Some men avoid dating to avoid sexual temptation. Some single adults are against nonmarital sex (especially those whose abstinence is fear-motivated) and yet cannot imagine dating without sex; so they will not date. They figure, no dating, no temptation. They are saving themselves sexually for the right one—and you're probably not the right one. Some add religious language—they are saving themselves "for the one the Lord will bring along."

Some men don't date because they see dating as superficial. For some single-agains, someone hit the rewind button and sent them back in time into a second adolescence—this time, fortunately, without zits! A few see dating as the equivalent of purgatory. If a man didn't like his first adolescence, he probably won't like the new adolescence.

Some men don't date because they are interested in sex, not in relationships. With so many places to find easy no-commitment sex (with cyberporn they don't even have to leave their apartment), these men don't want to waste time or money in socializing, which may or may not produce the expected payoff: sex.

Some men only date never-married women. They fear being compared to an ex, having to hear "war" stories, or involvement with someone else's children.

Some men are commitment-phobic. Dating leads to involvement, expectations, and complications—stated or unstated—particularly with single women who hear their biological clocks ticking away.

Some men date with an agenda. Many, if not most, formerly married men want to get married ASAP. Some have overlapping "temp" relationships while waiting for their divorces to be final. A high percentage of men remarry within eighteen months of a divorce or the death of a mate. Many perceive singleness as a prison sentence to be served, with time off for good behavior. They consider dates as marital "replacements."

Some men just don't want to get married because it is too complicated to get unmarried. They just want the accoutrements of marriage without the risks. Some want what Eric Fruge calls *"pseudo-marriage."* [1]

Some men's first allegiance is to their mothers. These are the classic "Momma's boys."

45. What is the difference between Mr. Perfect and Mr. Right?

There are no Mr. Perfects out there (except in their own minds) but there are lots of Mr. Rights! Every single adult has strengths and weaknesses. We hope the one you marry will have more pluses than minuses. Unfortunately, it is often only after marriage that the romantic fog lifts and you discover Mr. Perfect is, well, to say the least, less than perfect.

46. Why do men insist on using physical standards— shape, sex appeal, clothes—to measure the worth of a woman?

Men bring their own culturally-shaped perspectives and their own personal insecurities to their relationships with women. They have been influenced by friends, family, and previous understandings of their masculinity, and they have been shaped, perhaps wounded, by past sexual and romantic experiences. Some are affected—if not hamstrung—by their exposure to pornography.

Deep within each of us are particular attraction factors. Some men are attracted to women with large breasts. Other men are attracted to legs or buttocks (and a few are attracted to brains and a few to financial assets). The intricacies of biological attraction are incredibly diverse. A man may not fully understand them: "That's just the way I am." In my grandfather's day, a woman was viewed as attractive according to her physical stamina and domestic skills like cooking, baking, and sewing; after all, she was going to be part of an agricultural partnership. Could she drive a team of horses? Granddad wanted to know. On a farm she needed to be tough, strong enough for repeated childbearing. Looks were secondary to strength.

Men use physical standards to shore up their fragile egos. When a man dates a gorgeous woman, a "physical knockout" or a "looker," some of her beauty enhances his pals' appraisal of his masculinity. Men who are struggling through mid-life crises often overemphasize physical standards as a way of compensating for their struggles with change. He doesn't feel "old" or "over-the-hill" if he has a "babe" in tow, particularly if she causes heads to turn.

Certainly, many men do appreciate a woman's inner qualities. Those who do, enhance their chances of having a long, happy marriage. Beauty fades, while inner qualities endure or are even enhanced over time.

47.   Do men prefer traditional or liberated women?

It depends upon the man and his point in life. Single adults are caught in the crossfire of rapidly changing cultural values. Some men want a "traditional" woman, which explains the renewed popularity of arranged or "mail-order brides." (Asian women are particularly "prized" because of their assumed subservience.) Other men want a *somewhat* liberated woman. Some want to marry a traditional woman but date liberated women, because they assume that translates into easy sex.

Many men seek a woman who combines the best of the old and the new. But the issue gets complicated by economic realities. Today most men want their wives to work so that as a financial partnership they can afford "the good life," which requires two healthy incomes. Moreover, after marriage or the birth of children, many couples discover that it is difficult to shake the male's expectations. In short, he wants *superwoman*. As a result, many women work two full-time jobs—in the marketplace *and* at home!

So it's Superwoman's market. But as women gain power and status in the workplace and become more independent, many are less willing to bend to a male's unrealistic or antiquated expectations. So the stage may be set early for confrontation. Whose career is going to have priority?

Connell Cowan and Melvyn Kinder contend that when it comes to love, single adults—male and female—want the same thing: "someone to enjoy life's experiences with, someone to make us laugh, someone who understands our fears and sorrows, and someone to make us feel good about ourselves."[1] Eventually, a man asks, "Which woman in my life is most likely to provide that?" Both traditional and liberated spouses can do that equally well.

The best time to talk about roles and expectations is now, before you marry or remarry. Remember, a man may date one woman but love and ultimately marry someone who is quite different. In second (or subsequent) marriages, many men have different expectations than they had earlier. After divorce, a man may be financially strapped or starting over again, and want a woman with a career and $$$$. Or, if he was married to a careerist, he may now want a more traditional woman.

48. I am a professional woman with graduate degrees and a great career. Why do I scare off so many men?

Smart women turn off a lot of men. It's hard for most men to deal with women who are smarter than they are. A number of men will be happy to date you, as long as you downplay or even hide your intelligence. Two friends who are oncologists explained that they got dates as long as they told men that they were "in grad school." If they said, "med school," prospective dates vanished.

Increasingly, men have to deal with smart women at work. But in the social world, it's another matter. So what starts out as a childhood game—Deny your Brains!—ends up a lifelong preoccupation. Ironically, men are greatly impoverished by not getting to know the real you, by letting one part of you—your professional achievement and ambition—outweigh the rest of you.

So take good care of yourself. Don't dumb down to go out with a dumb male. Carefully investigate any man's attitudes toward you, because initially, he could mumble, "Oh, no problem." Initially. However, in the long run, your profession could become a wedge between you, particularly if your career takes off or your income exceeds his.

49. The guy I am dating doesn't have a lot of money but won't let me pay for anything when we go out. How can I convince him that it's OK for me to pay my share?

The hardiness of a man's ego when it comes to money may vary from that of a rhino hide to an egg shell. Many men believe that one key element for ego maintenance is the ability to provide, or at least to pay their own way. Your man knows the meaning of the phrase, "married well." Unless he is a complete cad, he probably won't be overly excited—even in this liberated age—about you paying the whole tab. He will appreciate you *offering* to pay, however.

Couples may split fifty/fifty. As one woman explained to a confused date, "We can go out twice as often if I pay my share." Or the individual with the larger income provides for the "niceties" and the little extras.

You will not be able to change this particular man's attitudes easily. It may well take lots of time and dialogue and some bruised feelings. Be cautious of making comments that contradict your intention. Try to understand how a man hears, "Rob took Karen to (the most expensive restaurant in town) and she thought it was fabulous. He sure treats her like a queen!"

Think about some of the places he wants to take you. Is he trying to impress you by wining and dining you? Wining and dining is wonderful when both people enjoy it and if there is no hidden agenda.

Start with gradual or occasional sharing of the tab. Look out for the man who keeps an "open tab" of what he spends on you. He may expect you to reciprocate sexually for "showing you a good time."

50. Why are men such sports nuts?

Sports gives men a safe venue to communicate with other men. A man can walk up to almost any man and launch something of a conversation with a simple question like, "How about them Braves? Think they are going to win the pennant?" In most cases, sports is a "safe" topic (except during the playoffs).

Think seriously before getting into a relationship with a sports fanatic, especially if he wants you to run a snack service during the game or demands that you sit silently so he won't lose concentration. (Tomorrow someone might ask, "Did you see the big play?" and *because you distracted him,* he would have to tearfully say—despite the replay—"No, I missed it.") If this sounds familiar, remember, there will always be some "big game" or championship to consume his time; you will always have second place. And it's not only the big game—now, sports fanatics have to watch the pre-game and the post-game shows. Watch out when his team loses! Some men take losing very personally, and some react violently, especially if betting is involved.

Again, think twice and then some more before you commit to a sports freak. You will not (I repeat, *will not*) change him. Ask any "sports widow."

51. Why do so many men organize their lives around their jobs?

One of the first questions a man asks a stranger is, "What do you do?" or "What kind of work are you in?" Assessment immediately follows. If a man answers, "I drive a garbage truck," the assessment is "blue-collar." But what a difference if he answers, "I am the executive vice president of the First National Bank." Title has clout. In these days of downsizing, many middle-aged males hedge, "Ah, I'm in sales . . . marketing" and change the subject.

Historically, the man was expected to be a provider. Fathers of brides demanded, "And just how, young man, do you intend to keep my daughter in the lifestyle to which she has become accustomed?" Indeed, many women still want husbands who can "deliver the goods" economically (as well as sexually). Women are advised not to marry "beneath themselves." Women are complimented, "He's *quite* a catch!" which translates: ca$h and a high ceiling on the credit cards!

These days, the corporate world that many men (and women) inhabit wants not just your sweat but also your soul. Corporations want "team-players" who are available not just for forty hours but for whatever it takes to do the job. Work for an insane, workaholic, goal-driven boss with no clue of "family values," and you must play by insane rules. Many single adult males think of work as an arena: It's dog-eat-dog, or "do unto others *before* they can do unto you." Needless to say, this *really* cuts down on free time to date and pushes people to date under great stress.

Success talkmen fill auditoriums, offering the latest "How to be a success" seminars. Yet job security remains an oxymoron for most single adults. In most corporate settings, you can be on the street with your résumé and memories without any warning! Indeed, many fathers are now realizing and lamenting that they gave their companies the best they had. While they provided things and trinkets for their families, they lost the best years of their lives *with* their families because they were too busy! Corporations no longer break backs but souls.

This culture values workaholism; men love to brag about the impossibility of their schedules: "Can't do it . . . how about the 4th?" Men display cramped DayTimers as badges of honor. For some men it's the sweet smell of a deal. Or the *next* deal, if this one didn't satisfy. For many men, it's a matter of identity: "If the corporation or my professional network says I am somebody, then I *am* somebody!"

Yet even successful men can't relax; some eager beaver is waiting to shake the ladder of success if they lighten up. Whether they buy into the values of workaholism or not, the reality is that for most men work is a demanding and jealous mistress, especially if credit cards are maxed out or if there are children from a previous marriage (and an ex with a lawyer tough on child support).

The corporate world hopes that men's jobs will provide their families enough security and trinkets to force them to go along with the grueling time demands. One underlying cause for high divorce in this country is corporate attitudes toward the family. How can you (or your children) have a concept of place or community if your company has transferred you twenty times in eighteen years? How can you date when you lug home mounds of emotional stress when you leave the office or plant? How can you make long-term plans and commitments when you do not have job security?

52. I like this guy but he is such a nerd! Especially the way he dresses. How can I "revamp" him a little without hurting his feelings?

You really want to change the man, beginning with his wardrobe. Many who have tried would respond, "You can't change him!" or "You're wasting your time trying!" A man wants someone to love him *as is*. Yet you want to tinker with the packaging, perhaps so that he doesn't reflect on you. "How did she get hooked up with him!" Or to avoid the subtle criticism from your friends, "Can't you do something about the way he dresses?!"

Never forget, it's what's on the inside that counts. You can have a sharply-packaged, well-groomed, well-dressed man with no character or integrity. You may think, "Clothes make a man!" But no, character makes a man! Barbara De Angelis sounds a note of warning: "He didn't ask you to help him, fix him, [dress him] or rescue him."[1] He asks you to love him.

If, however, he asks you for advice or help with clothing, then (and only then) offer options or suggestions with all the skills of a career diplomat.

53. What gives with this midlife crisis business? Isn't it just an excuse to mess around or be irresponsible?

We live in a youth-oriented, age-conscious society. No one wants to grow old. Mid-life crisis is a man's awareness that he is leaving young adulthood behind and moving toward old age. Midlife gets a man's attention the first time he cannot get an erection! Hello! Or when his body aches after a pick-up basketball game with younger guys. Or when a young adult calls him "sir." Or when he notices that his balding spot is spreading. In zillions of little ways he gets reminded: You are getting older! And someday you will be *old!!!* "Too old to cut the mustard" begins resounding like timpani.

A man's attitude and the attitude of his support network will determine whether midlife is a problem to be solved or an opportunity to be experienced and profited from.

For some single adult males, the crisis is primarily sexual; for others, it is spiritual. For a few, it is emotional, especially if a man realizes that he may not achieve certain long-held goals. Should a peer or friend die unexpectedly, a new awareness of mortality hits: "It could have been me! Time is running out for me to fulfill my dreams!"

Sexual change threatens many men. As much as we joke about "being over the hill," it does take longer to become sexually aroused (or re-aroused) as we get older. Some men have difficulty getting or maintaining an erection; some men are taunted by those memories of early adolescence when erections were seemingly continuous. At midlife a man begins paying attention to his prostate.

In midlife many men compare their wives or dates with women ten to twenty-five years younger. Some men turn to younger women, especially if they blame their sexual concerns on their wives. Thus, a mid-life affair may be an "experiment" of sorts. Men seek affirmation through a little "sexual sampling" or perhaps a full-blown affair, which often leads to divorce and hasty remarriage and eventually to second divorces.

Other pressures are also common to midlife. With the onset of the "empty nest," some couples look at each other and realize that they have little in common. Their marriage focused on the children, who were the delicate cement that held their fragile relationship together. Marital sex has gotten stale, predictable, and boring. Some ask themselves, "Isn't there more to life?" First they wonder, then they wander.

For never-married single adults, midlife can be especially trouble-some. Some ask, "Who will want me *now*?" Some reduce their expectations for a mate, shifting from physical attractiveness to other factors. However, midlife can be a time for growth if adults reflect on questions such as, "Who am I? What do I really value? How have I spent my life so far? What have I done with the talents and gifts (like sexuality) that God has given me? Am I alive? What direction do I want the rest of my life to take?"

Be cautious about dating (let alone marrying) men going through mid-life crisis, particularly those separated men who are trying to "find themselves." I don't think we "find" ourselves, but rather we *decide* our-selves. A midlifer with high testosterone may use you like an elixir to rekindle the flame of life (and love). Occasionally, they come to their senses and go back home. Then you end up romantically high and dry, with only emotional souvenirs to show for it. Even if they don't reconcile with their spouses, middle-aged, recently divorced single adults are high risks as potential marriage partners. Some are almost like kids in a candy shop, making up for what they consider time lost in a dull marriage. Some are sexual samplers: "I want to try this, and I want to try that, and . . ."

Guard your heart or you may be used and discarded by the man "trying to find himself." You and his ex might end up with something in common: You've been wounded by the same man. Mid-life men who are pondering this question might consider these great questions developed by psychologist Sidney Simon:

Question 1: What do I want to do with the life I have left?

Question 2: What do I want to experience?

Question 3: What do I want to witness?

Question 4: What do I want to learn?

Question 5: What do I want to be part of?

Question 6: What do I want to change, shape, leave better than I found it?

Question 7: What do I want to do with the rest of my life? [1]

54. There's a separated man at work who keeps asking me to go out. Any advice?

If he's married, he's unavailable. That means *undateable.* Date a married person—and legally a separated person is *still* married—and you volunteer for pain. Particularly if you volunteer to be a therapist or sounding board for his domestic problems. He may not have a lot of cash to entertain you with. Expect that every so often guilt will overwhelm him—perhaps immobilize him.

Some coworkers will view you as a "home wrecker." It is one thing to be friends. But the fact that you dated him before the divorce was final is what they will remember.

You could make the mistake of assuming that by "separated" he means, not *legally* separated, but no longer with his wife, or no longer trying to work things out, or merely no longer sleeping with his wife. Or you could be only a transitional relationship to help him bridge the gap from married to single again. You could be jettisoned after the divorce becomes final. Finally, before becoming the "other" woman, ask yourself if there could be another "other" in his romantic life, especially if he travels in his business.

Think carefully before saying "yes" to this coworker. Why volunteer for pain?

55. How can I be sure the divorced man I am dating isn't comparing me to his ex?

One friend read this question and answered, "You can't, honey!" He *is* comparing you—especially if you are having sex. Comparison is a common irritant in second marriages whether they follow divorce or death. In fact, some people choose to remain single out of fear that a second marriage won't be as good as or better than their first one. Many men have difficulty establishing a positive new relationship because of old patterns from a previous, disappointing marriage or emotionally traumatic post-marriage dating.

If your friend doesn't talk at all about a previous spouse, or only talks negatively (or goes crazy with rage), that's a warning sign. He may repress some strong feelings, such as anger or resentment, until something ignites the well-soaked wood! Ugly feelings may erupt at the most unlikely moment. Remember, the longer his first spouse has been out of the emotional picture, the more selective his memories will be. He will remember only what he wants to remember. If he verbally compares you to her (or hints at comparison), talk it out.

Definitely expect him to compare you sexually to previous partners. Especially if you say "no" to particular sexual requests or respond with less than hearty enthusiasm.

56. Why do men have such a hard time showing and sharing their feelings?

Men are trained to douse their emotions. Emotional constipation begins at an early age for most males. Boys and young men are applauded for emotional control and humiliated or teased when they lose control and cry. Comments like, "Stop crying or I'll give you something to cry about!" or "Big boys don't cry!" or "Take it like a man!" discourage males from displaying (sometimes even discovering) emotions. Many males are afraid to show *any* vulnerability—it might invite emotional invasion or attack or disrespect. "*Crybaby!*" is an incredible taunt in this society.

But there's good news. More men are shedding their emotionally restrictive macho-jocko molds to pursue Shakespeare's direction, "To thine own self be true." Men are learning that while it may not be masculine to cry, it is definitely human. More single men (particularly if divorced) are becoming healthy as they explore, express, and embrace their emotions. They are discovering that there is freedom in the richness of their emotions.

Females who witness rare male vulnerability must guard the confidences that men share. Vulnerability requires an "apprenticeship" for many men; they will need lots of support and encouragement to make it part of their lives.

57. Why are men so afraid of commitment?

Men's fear of commitment is primarily economically rooted. Men fear losing control of wallet and checkbook and stock portfolio. The phrase "taken to the cleaners" ricochets through men's psyches, reinforced in stories about "the poor guy who had the house in the 'burbs, the 2.3 kids, the boat, and a dog named Spot, who now eats Rice-a-Roni six nights a week and shares a crummy apartment with four other guys." Men love the well-worn myths that lead to a warning conclusion, "I'd be *very careful* if I were you." Men also love their well-worn myths about the stalking female opportunist on the loose in Singleland. Watch out for her!

Moreover, considering the rapidity with which too many single adults enter into marriage, many people make too many commitments knowing precious little about the other person. Who is this person that I am volunteering to share bed, bathroom, and body fluids with, hopefully for the rest of our lives? "Getting to know you, getting to know *all* about you . . ." should be the theme song of single adults. Too much of so-called commitment is premature commitment.

These days, women also express commitment anxiety. Historically, the wedding vows included, "with all my bodily goods I thee endow," and the law does support this. More women, particularly professional women marrying in their late thirties and forties, need to be cautious and need pre-nuptial agreements. Divorces increasingly require therapists and accountants.

58. What's a stalker?

The song says, "I'm going to wash that man right out of my hair," but these days, that may not be so easy. Some men (and women) won't go quietly or completely. They won't accept "no" or "NO!" as final. Stalkers distinguish themselves from the merely romantically hardheaded or wounded by threatening you and refusing to accept your viewpoint:

- "I'm going to hurt you as much as you've hurt me."
- "You can't get rid of me so easily."
- "I'd watch my back if I were you."
- "You're going to be sorry."

The stalker's ultimate reality is: I want what I want—control over you! In this sense, stalking is the premarital equivalent of domestic violence, and it can be terrifying for the object of the stalker. Stalking may end up in violence—emotional and spiritual, if not physical. Typical stalking behavior includes the following:

The stalker persists in an inappropriate manner with the relationship. For you it may have been only one date, for him it was just the beginning.

The stalker is overly attached to symbols—photos, tickets, and other trinkets of the relationship. These "linking objects" or items sentimentally and symbolically connect you to him.

The stalker was violent or abusive during the relationship.

The stalker is uncontrollably jealous or possessive after the relationship ends. You have asked him to leave you alone, yet he persists in calling or coming to your home, work place, or place of worship.

The stalker demonstrates obsessive behaviors: making increasingly demanding or threatening phone calls or e-mails or showing up unexpectedly or uninvited at places you frequent.

If you have never been stalked, it's difficult to appreciate the emotional pain and stress the stalker can generate. However, stalking is not always easily legally proved. You will need physical evidence (such as tapes or photos) or witnesses to collaborate your story. The police often initially dismiss this as a "lover's spat," not to be taken seriously. They may patronize: "I wouldn't worry. He's just a sore loser. He'll leave you alone when he meets someone else." The problem is, this guy is not going to meet someone else. You are his romantic bull's-eye! Some stalkers even manipulate with religious terminology, "God wants us to be together" or "It's God's will."

59.   How can I protect myself from a stalker?

The best protection may be preventive—know the people you date. Always honor your intuition. Don't initially disclose where you live. Meet someone in a safe place for first dates. If you are stalked:

Consider a second but unlisted phone line. Use the answering machine on your first line to record harassing calls, "no one there" calls, repeat unwanted calls, and threats.

Consider upscaling the security of your home or apartment (moving will not deter the determined stalker).

Vary daily routines so that you are not predictable: what time you come home from and go to work, where you park, shop for groceries, grab a quick snack, etc.

Inform the local authorities and seek a restraining order.

Keep detailed records of all incidents involving the stalker. Use a tape recorder, answering machine, camera, or video camera.

Make certain that the police officially record incidents to establish a "trail" of abuse that will stand up in court.

Ask family, friends, and coworkers not to give out your personal information, especially if the person says something like, "I'm trying to get in touch with her and was wondering if you could give me her new number." The correct answer is: (1) "Who is this?" and (2) "I will give her a message that you called." [1]

Any stalker should be taken seriously. Share information about the stalker with others. Some adults are "polite" stalkers. Friends may doubt your allegations, especially if the stalker is a woman. But polite stalkers push boundaries and annoy without stepping over the legal line.

60. Why do men date and marry younger women? Why do women date and marry older men?

Men date younger women *because they can,* and because historically society has encouraged them to. In fact, most men date and marry women younger than themselves.

However, women who marry much older men have to contend with a label like *"gold digger"* or worse. Women become romantically interested in older men because of their (1) money, (2) power, and (3) prestige. The man thrice-blessed is not going to be lonely for long. As a bachelor, Secretary of State Henry Kissinger's active social life troubled President Richard Nixon, especially because Henry dated beautiful Hollywood starlets who did not support Nixon's policies. Had Kissinger been merely an overweight Harvard professor or a truck driver, dating starlets would have been much tougher, if not impossible. As Henry explained, "Power is the great aphrodisiac!" [1]

61. Why do men want sex so much? Why can't men touch and caress? Why can't men be intimate or tender?

This culture prizes virility, whether assumed or demonstrated. Men have to keep proving that they are sexually "with it." Intercourse is the male way of proving oneself, or, in the male vernacular, of "scoring." Sex is, after all, a game. These days men are more sexually anxious since their partners can leave them for someone else. A sexual partner may not be shy in verbalizing sexual performance expectations or in critiquing sexual performance. No wonder impotence is on the increase, and not just among older men. Browse the sports sections of most metropolitan newspapers, and you'll find ads for impotence clinics. Try to find out how the Lakers did last night and you find some sad sack and an 800 number and the ad copy, "Call today."

Intercourse is intimacy for most men. To put it bluntly, most men make love with their allegedly "ever-ready" penises—not with their bodies. Consequently, anything like a vasectomy or a below-the-belt hit strikes fear in mens' hearts and produces a sympathetic groan. Men are generally conditioned to focus on one goal: intercourse. Intercourse is "it," it's the real thing. Every other sexual act is an appetizer, an opening act for the headliner. "Going all the way" or "scoring" terminology for sexual expression discloses the reality that sex is a game for many men. Men are so out of touch with their bodies, particularly as they age, that they have no idea that the entire body is an erogenous zone. Because they have had no exposure to healthy and creative sexual touch, they have only one selection on their menu—the main course, intercourse.

No wonder browsers see the word *cuddle* in so many personal ads. If more men knew the delicate art of touch and cuddling, they wouldn't be home alone with only the remote control in their hands.

62. Why are so many men having second childhoods? Some of these hormone-driven fifty-something single males act like sixteen-year-olds!

We live in an ageist culture. The fear of growing old sends men into either depression or hair styling salons, toupee outlet malls, and gyms. Some are even dabbling with plastic surgery (and not just for sagging skin under the chin or eyes). For most, the fear of age is a subtle fear of death. Men fear the loss of sexual attractiveness or performance, especially given the obsession with the sculpted male chest and "washboard abs" described in commercials and ads. Surf cable and you'll quickly find someone trying to sell you some machine that will not only revolutionize your body but also your lifestyle! With a little work, your body can look like the one demonstrating the machine, without even working up a good sweat.

Men have a deeply rooted fear of being dismissed as "an old fart," or "over the hill." As Grandma Walton used to say, "There's no fool like an *old* fool!"

Indeed, if men could become comfortable with the reality that one can age and still be sexually attractive, most men would not act so relationally foolish at times.

63. I am dating a great man. I enjoy being with him, but I don't feel any tingle-and-glow. Definitely no fireworks. Should I hang in there or bail out?

Lots of single adults keep their romantic skills in use by hanging out in "You'll do *until* something better comes along" relationships. The modus operandi of too many single adult relationships is, a bad date is better than *no* date! Wrong!

On the other hand, perhaps your friendship is worth nurturing into something more. OK, some single adults do not exude excitement, charm, charisma, or pizazz. You may need to revise your "Has to have . . ." list. So, he's not Mr. Personality or Mr. Excitement. Underneath the veneer may exist some incredible characteristics that would guarantee a long-term nurturing relationship. Some men's best attributes can only be recognized and appreciated with time.

64. What about dating a younger man? I mean *really* younger.

If you are "robbing the cradle" and want my approval, think again. But some men are attracted to older women. Men may believe older women are less enamored with or empowered by the feminist movement. The older woman, they assume, is more likely to fit the "whatever you say, dear" mold. Some men are looking for mother-figures (perhaps grandmothers). Some are recruiting nurses for their future old age. Some men fall in love with women who happen to be older.

What counts is your love for each other. Certainly you will have to deal with the social commentary: "Why she's old enough to be his *mother!*" Relationships with his mother may be initially, even permanently strained, especially if Momma acquires step-grandchildren from your previous marriage in the process. But increasingly, birthdays are just numbers on a piece of paper or a state of mind.

65. The wedding vows say "forsaking all others." Does this include a mother? My fiancée's mother has him wrapped around her little finger. She says "Jump!" and he asks, "How far?" He insists that everything will change after we are married.

Unfortunately, Momma has a decisive head start and may use her "home court advantage" to the max. Some mothers will not easily abdicate their place in their son's life. Some pathological mothers will consider you a rival to the throne. If your fiancé jumps when Momma says "Jump!," does he cancel plans with you to respond to Momma's call? Does Momma have "something" of a health problem that is always "acting up" and requiring his immediate attention? What is the long-term plan for Momma's retirement years and care? Is he considering you as a future caregiver for her?

Look closely at the relationship. A genuine Momma's boy means heartache and heartbreak. He may be one to "love from a distance," especially if Momma prefers another candidate for her daughter-in-law. "When a young man marries, he divorces his mother," says the Jewish proverb.[1] The traditional wedding vows, based on the words of Jesus, contain three key elements: (1) *to leave* father and mother (Matthew 18:5); (2) *to cleave* to the spouse; and (3) *to weave* the one-flesh relationship. The traditional wedding vows' "forsaking all others" definitely includes Momma.

66. Why do there seem to be so many "Momma's boys" in Singleland?

Smaller families. With smaller families, many mothers have had more time to emotionally invest in sons. When a marriage starts going stale, mothers invest more emotionally in their sons than in their husbands. The increasing number of female-headed households adds to this phenomenon.

While a great deal of attention is focused these days on sexual or physical incest, little comment has been made on emotional incest—a mother creating a one-flesh emotional bond with her son. Many sons relish their mother's praise or their mother's access to financial resources. So a strange relationship develops between mother and son. In single-parent families a son often becomes "Momma's little man." Or the son becomes a surrogate spouse or confidant in a dysfunctional marriage.

Some mothers have sabotaged normal, full, heterosexual develop-ment by suggesting that women are Eves—temptresses and seducers who will lure the son away from Momma's well-plotted career course and her relational plans for him. Some mothers want a clear answer to the question, "Who loves you the most?" "You, Momma."

Momma's boys can be great achievers. They will go to whatever lengths are necessary to make Momma proud. Franklin D. Roosevelt, J. Edgar Hoover, and General Douglas MacArthur were classic "Momma's boys." Many mothers long to hear a son quote Abraham Lincoln, "All that I am, or hope to be, I owe to my angel mother." [1]

67. What's with all these angry men in Singleland? They seem to be mad at all women. What did we do to them?

The conservative swing in this country has focused on male-female relationships and the feminist movement (or its dreaded *agenda*). When women started moving upward in their professions and tapping on the glass ceilings of the "good ole boy" power domains, men longed for traditionalism: "When men were men and women were women!" Men muttered that women were snaring jobs that belonged to men. Little wonder that the Congressional sweep in 1994 was attributed to angry white men voting Republican. Lots of men feel emotionally threatened by strong, independent women who are "movers and shakers" in the financial and political arenas. In fact, men commonly dismiss aggressive, competent women as "bitches" or "*ball-busters*" or lesbians! What an incredible admission of fear and vulnerability. Why not *heart-buster* or *back-buster*?

Admittedly, some men do have significant romantic and financial wounds as a result of divorce. Men like to moan about being "taken to the cleaners," although economic impoverishment is a more likely consequence of divorce for women.[1] Rarely do men bother with statistical validation of their myths. One man says it in a locker room or on a radio call-in, then the host "spins" it into reality, and by nightfall it is "masculine" gospel.

Basically, it takes two incomes or 2.3 incomes to have the "good life" in this country. So some men are angry that women who "won't cooperate with the plan or the man!" are glitching the good life for them. Men assume the world would be so much safer for them if women would not be so "uppity" and would stay in "their place" (which of course is defined by weak men).

What I find particularly troublesome is not the blowhard who loudly espouses his opinions, even if no one is asking or listening. I worry about "nice" men who nurture anger that smolders beneath the surface. That anger can eventually erupt in outrageous acts of violence against women. It's true that, if challenged over their words or attitudes, many men respond, "I'm only joking" or "Nothing personal," but today's male conversations about women can tend to be troubling.

The anger in some men is fueled by a nostalgic pining for the good old days, when they imagine that romance and relationships were simple. Well, it's time for them to wake up and smell the latte! It's a new world out there, and bravery, not anger, is necessary for survival. I have never been threatened by a woman. Never! From a faith perspective, I want women to be everything they can be. "The pie" is not reduced if women get a generous share!

68. While looking for a video of mine at the apartment of the guy I am dating, I found porno flicks. When I confronted him, he said it was "no big deal" and that lots of men watch X-rated movies. Is that true?

Pornography is a multi-billion dollar industry in the United States.[1] Apparently lots of men watch X-rated porno movies and read porn materials. But it *is* a "big deal," despite your friend's protest. One cannot be exposed to pornography without some mental and sexual residue. Suppose I drink milk out of a glass, and I drink it all. Because of the thin milk residue on the glass, I won't pour diet cola into the glass until it is washed. Pornography leaves a filmy residue on the soul of the viewer and those with whom he or she has relationships. Porn tints sexual perspective and scars the sexual imagination.

Many men who view pornography—not all—carry the attitudes of the pornographer into their sexual relationships. Hence, they may initiate or demand sexual repertoires that you consider offensive. You may feel like sex is following some script. Guess what? It is. The sex flick becomes real, with you as the actors. Your partner is both the director and "the star."

The plot lines of pornographic material are never conducive to the development of healthy male sexual attitudes. The plots are rarely about joy or laughter or intimacy. The man has to "deliver," even if the woman does not want sex. Porn tends to reinforce sexual stereotypes. Porn is about performance and orgasms rather than tenderness and affection. Often, the male viewer becomes a voyeur, peeking in on sex. Some men become enamored of, if not addicted to, particular porn repertoires or themes.

Many men use porn to jump-start or heighten their masturbatory experiences. Some have become conditioned to quick orgasms, which leads to a rushed, "get it over with" orgasm with a partner. Given the refinement of the VCR technology and remote control, men can also use the milder sex scenes in R-rated movies as a resource for masturbation and for developing sexual attitudes and fantasies, while still self-righteously condemning porn. The rewind and replay functions can be hazardous to the development of a healthy sexual attitude.

Sadly, such sexual rehearsing makes sexual encounters less wonderful in marriage. When men get used to a particular repertoire, it eventually fails to deliver the desired kick, so they escalate to a new level of porn.

Pornography that was once sold in seedy looking "adult" book-stores is now instantly available through computer access. Future high-tech advances will elevate interactive computer porn to an art form. A man with a computer, sitting at a keyboard, literally directs the woman on the monitor what to do sexually. "Teledildonics," a new technology, simulates sex with sights, sounds, and tactile feelings of the real thing. Companies plan to facilitate safe high-tech sex between people anywhere in the world through the use of special body suits that will stimulate the body "convincingly." Thus, in the distant (or maybe not so distant) future, prostitutes "will sell their wares by telepresence." Or you and a boyfriend or Internet lover could have telesex while in bedrooms on opposite sides of the world. It's not just a brave new world, it's a frightening new world! [2]

Some men will invite you to watch a video with them as a way of reducing your resistance to particular sexual acts. "Come on, just try it." Be concerned when the man dismisses porn as "harmless" or if he tries to talk you into sexual practices that make you feel uncomfortable. Never let a man talk you into a sexual act that hurts or degrades you or reduces sexual intercourse to simply a bodily function. Never let a man talk you into an unsafe sexual activity. Any sexual behaviors that damage or bruise the humanity God has given as our sexual birthright should offend the single adult.

69. My boyfriend used 900-sex numbers a lot before we met. He says it was just a way of relieving stress, and that once we get married, he won't even be interested.

Stress reduced at $3.99 a minute gets expensive and habitual. What he may not have told you is that he may have been doing more than chatting; he was masturbating. There are a lot of kinky (by anyone's definition) 900 call numbers out there. In fact, these sex lines rake in between $750 million and a billion dollars in this country each year. [1] Any night of the week, between 9 p.m. and 1 a.m., an estimated one million Americans dial a number for commercial phone sex. According to one provider, 75 percent of the callers are lonely and basically want conversation. However, "the ease, the anonymity, and interactive quality of phone sex explains its commercial success. " [2]

One woman who paid off her fiancé's $1,000 monthly phone bill naively explained, "He promised it wouldn't happen again." It did. And it continued. He never did "forsake" his friends at the 900-sex lines for the real woman in his life. I don't think this is what Alexander Graham Bell had in mind when he invented the telephone.

CHAPTER 7

Single and Male and Asking about Single Women

70. How can you say no to a sexually aggressive woman without losing her or having her think you're gay?

Women are more aggressive these days. Some women enjoy a role that has traditionally been reserved for men. Increasingly, men are faced with the "no" etiquette—How do I say no? Clearly many men are threatened by the sexually or romantically aggressive woman.

What to do? Follow your convictions and simply say no. You may lose her, but if you do, she's worth losing. You will have a much happier relationship if you look for a woman who can respect and share your values. Of course, you will try to say no in a way that it is neither a put-down nor a surprise. You are saying no to a premature sexual relationship—not to the person. In a study of midwestern male virgins, researchers found that leading rationales for male no-saying were "It is against my religious beliefs" and "I believe that intercourse before marriage is wrong." Clearly, not everyone says yes (or Yes!) [1]

If she wonders whether you are gay, let her. Having sex with a woman doesn't prove that you aren't homosexual; a significant percentage of males have had sex with both women and men.[2]

Talk it out. Explain your convictions. A well-said no could open the door to a better or lasting relationship. Regretting a no is far better than regretting a yes!

Saying no to a premature sexual relationship could allow you a romantic future.

71.   What is the biological clock?

The term *biological time* clock refers to the growing awareness by women in their late 30s and early 40s (and their mothers) that their ability to conceive a healthy child is diminishing. Changes in fertilization technology and ethics may impact the biological clock in the future. Consider the sixty-three-year-old woman who gave birth to a healthy child. (In this case the eggs were donated by another woman and fertilized by the birth mother's husband).[1] The biological clock may be of particular concern for women who have concentrated on their careers and have postponed marriage, especially if they have parents who pressure them about providing grandchildren.

Experts at the New York Fertility Research Foundation say that at age thirty-five a woman has only a 90 percent fertility rate; thereafter, the rate declines, particularly for those who have been on the Pill. So in order to have a birth child, many women have to marry by their mid-thirties. Increasingly, many discover that simply going off birth control and having sex does not instantly lead to pregnancy. Since women are born with their full complement of eggs (while men manufacture sperm daily), the likelihood for birth complications increases the older the woman is at the time of pregnancy.[2] Moreover, infertility is more likely if a woman has had a sexually transmitted disease.[3]

Men who marry later in life generally marry younger women and are more likely to have a family. Women who marry "late" in life have less chance of having children of their own. This reality may lead to a desperate, or biologically-driven romance, entered into basically for the purpose of having a child before the clock chimes. This has prompted some men to ask, after a short marriage and a subsequent divorce, "Did she want me or my sperm?" At this point in life, a woman may enter a marriage with the attitude, "If it doesn't work out, at least I will have a child."

72.   Do women pay as much attention to men's physiques as men do to women's?

Photography, films, television, beauty pageants, even pornography have stimulated our culture's intense obsession with physiques and attractiveness. We shamelessly ogle beauty contestants. *Playboy* magazine established its niche in the hearts of men with its airbrushed "girl-next-door" centerfolds, not its interviews. But when *Playgirl* hit the newsstands, suddenly American men felt insecure. Chippendale's and other clubs featuring male stripteasers sprang up around the country; male strippers strutted on the afternoon talk shows. Male "hunks" brightened up calendars; beefcake on the soaps enhanced the scripts. Women cheered, "Turnabout is fair play!"

Now the hunks are the stars. John Wayne, James Cagney, and Jimmy Stewart would have trouble landing parts in movies today if reading against Tom Cruise, Jean-Claude VanDamme, Patrick Swayze, Denzel Washington, Arnold Schwarzenegger, or Alec Baldwin. For generations, men sat on beaches and by pools ignoring the water to gaze at the babes, punching one another and saying, "Get a load of that!"—thus reducing a beautiful woman to a sex object, a *that*. Now, women respond, "Two can play *that* game!"

The brainless male "bimbo" is in. Check out the movies, sitcoms, and ads—even TV weathermen and news readers have to be "hunkable." Soap manufacturers used peekaboo shots of well-sculpted men showering to hawk their wares; customers stampeded supermarkets—it was one of the most successful soap marketing campaigns in years.[1] One commercial for a shower fixture, featuring a muscular hunk shown from a variety of angles, became an ad "winner." A particular perfume has turned the nude sculpted body into an art form on billboards and magazines. Increasingly, ads are nearly as steamy as R-rated movies and have become what some consider soft porn. In this culture, skin sells.

Researchers Glen Wilson and David Nias asked men to identify which parts of a man's body they thought would most excite women, then asked a group of women the same question. The men answered: muscular neck and shoulders (21 percent), muscular arms (18 percent), large penis (15 percent), and height (13 percent). Wrong! The women reported buttocks (39 percent), slimness (15 percent), and flat stomach (13 percent).[2] Today "beefcake is becoming as important as cheesecake in the advertising world and men have joined women in an obsessive preoccupation with looking better, as evidenced by the growth in men's skin care products and hair colorings."[3] Clothing specialist Richard Martin explains, "It's reflective of a growing objectification of the male body in our culture,"[4] an objectification predominately perpetuated by women.

73. Isn't "beefcake mania" going too far?

Oh, no!, protest women long tired of the breasts-and-buttocks obsession of men. Yes, say body-anxious men. Actually, the demand for male beefcake followed women's rebellion against cheesecake. "Men started thinking about appearance when women started asserting that they should not have to. Women's outrage at being treated as sex objects freed men to become sex objects."[1] Psychologist Naomi Wolf notes, "We're waking up to the myth that women are not visually stimulated. That's nonsense. Women are just as aesthetically engaged in looking at men as heterosexual men are engaged in looking at women."[2] Some women ogle daringly. One man whined, "I felt like she undressed me with her eyes!" Times have changed!

Nias and Wilson's research on women and the male body has been verified. Many women seem to be very interested in men's behinds The comment from a woman, "Nice buns"—with or without an exclamation mark—has left a lot of males confused. Indeed, "the male buttocks for women have become the psychological and conversational equivalent of the female breasts for men. Women now seem to have the same compulsion to comment on men's [buttocks] as men have to remark on women's breasts . . . In the culture of gender affirmative action, it's become *politically correct* for women to cast an appraising eye on the male body."[3]

Beefcake is good for the economy. Men now spend millions for skin care products. Men join health clubs and schedule facelifts and penis and pec enlargements. They apply Rogaine and have hair transplants. They order gym tools that promise to turn a flabby belly into those desired tight abs! Given the number of baby boomers approaching midlife, the "goldrush" is on.

It would be fun to go back to the good old days but it won't happen. Male beefcake sells the products and sets the trends. Younger single adults were asked, "Now that men are being depicted as sex objects in underwear ads, etc., how do you respond?"[4]

	AGREE WITH STATEMENT		
	Total	Male	Female
It's a sign of more equal footing between the sexes	46%	47%	45%
It's emasculating to most men	5%	6%	3%
It puts more pressure on men to look good	31%	36%	27%
No one should be depicted as a sex object	18%	11%	25%

Beefcake mania has significant consequences. Although 38 percent of women in a national study reported being "dissatisfied" with their bodies and looks, surprisingly, 34 percent of the men reported dissatisfaction (double the amount found in earlier research). Men identified these areas of concern: midtorso (50 percent), weight (40 percent), and muscle tone (32 percent).[5] In a study of younger single adults, men identified the following as sources of dissatisfaction: stomach (48 percent), weight (25 percent), muscularity (45 percent), buttocks (14 percent), chest (30 percent), penis (14 percent). It is significant that these subjects were young single men, who one would expect to have more attractive bodies.[6] Maybe it's time to put down this book and head to the gym for a few reps.

74. So, what do women today really want in a man?

No answer would be true of all single women. But some factors seem significant for many single women.

Communication skills. Women generally don't enjoy having to read a man's mind or interpret his silence. They value men who can be intensely loyal and transparent. The strong, silent type is out, because all those suppressed emotions eventually erupt. If a man doesn't communicate while dating, he won't after mumbling an "I do."

Attraction. A man should have some physical attractiveness. He doesn't have to be a hunk, but muscle-heads and nerds are not overly valued as romantic grand prizes.

Charm. A sense of humor and good manners can compensate for what a man lacks in communication skills and physique.

Sex appeal. Two words say it all: "He's sexy!" But of late, the most subjective criterion is not so much sexual *chemistry* as it is sexual integrity. Does he have a healthy sexual attitude and a healthy sexual history? Has he been sexually responsible or has he been at the mercy of his testosterone? Will he be completely honest about his sexual history? How will he model sexual values to children? This does not mean that he hasn't made some sexual mistakes and doesn't have some sexual regrets. It means he owns up to them and has learned from them.

Balance. A man who has an interesting perspective on life is a valued date. He is more than what he does for a living, or the possessions and toys his work style has allowed him to accumulate (car, house, guns, boat, stocks, computer, etc.). He has interests, hobbies, pastimes, and friendships.

Maturity. Most women don't want to marry a "Momma's boy" or a man who spends incredible time and energy acting out the mucho-macho-jocko routines he thinks manly. Sustained emotional stability is a prize. Women want to marry a man, not a kid. They are wary of the man who hasn't quite grown up yet.

Independence. An important element of attraction is the ability to stand alone as well as together. An independent man is not controlled by peer pressure.

Healthy self-esteem. If a man is in touch with himself, he is far more likely to enhance and affirm a woman's own self-esteem (and not be threatened by it).

A willingness to commit enthusiastically. Many single women insist that man who has a commitment to commitment can be quite an attractive catch.

75. How can I tell a woman I want only to date her, not marry her?

You may be one of those single adult men that women are constantly complaining about: the commitmentless *homo sapiens malus singularis*—playing the field and not hearing the ticking of the biological clocks in Singleland. Here are some suggestions:

If you are not ready to get married, or commit to marriage, say so.

Say so and say so often. Like some medicine, "repeat as often as necessary."

Use a "broken record" approach in repeating your expectations. Saying it once may not be enough. You may even want to preface it with, "I know you want more, but this is as much as I can give."

Don't have sex. Sex changes any relationship. Some single adults will use intercourse as "bait" to manipulate a person into some level of commitment. You will be safer emotionally and spiritually if you stay out of bed.

Some women use "presort" dating. That means they only date men they would consider prime candidates for marriage. "Others need not apply." So your offer or acceptance of a date may have been intended merely as a way of having a good time, or getting to know the other person better, but the woman's motivation can be far more serious.

If it's not her, tell her. Some people are like chameleons—they will try to change to be whatever another person wants them to be. If there is something specific about the woman you are dating, which, if changed, could enhance your relationship (like her not seeing her ex, even socially), tell her. Your vague answers may mystify your date. She may stand for hours in front of a mirror pleading, "What's wrong with *me?*" If the answer is "It's not you," tell her.

Be honest. Say what you mean and mean what you say. Be aware of how your truth may sound to her.

Be prepared to end the relationship. If she is not listening to what you are saying, one or both of you will get hurt. It's not unlike missing an interstate exit. Sometimes you get so far down the interstate after an missed exit that there are no easy returns. As the sign says, "Exit now!"

Clarify the status of previous relationships. If your previous relationships are not over, why are you dating? Is this relationship little more than adult babysitting to tide you over? "No one wants to invest time and emotional energy (and cash—might as well be painfully honest) establishing a relationship that could be terminated with a simple, 'I've gone back to my old girlfriend (or spouse).'" [1]

Your date may be coaxing you to do a quantum leap from level 1 to level 4 with a "we can get to know each other once we're married." Give your relationship time. If the woman is in a hurry, it's time to say, "Maybe I'll see you around."

76. If a woman has had sex with other men, even if she was married to them at the time, won't she compare me to them, especially sexually?

Of course she will compare, just as a man would. One single woman explained, "We always do, but we always lie and say we don't. One thing an experienced single woman quickly learns is to never damage a man's ego or you'll crush a heart and a relationship."

"To know" is the verb the Old Testament often uses for intercourse. Knowledge includes memory. Intercourse is such a significant, memory-laden human experience that it cannot be described as only a genital experience. It is mental, too. We do not "delete" or erase the video or disc of our sexual experience. Memories of other sexual experiences have ways of invading our current thinking without warning or apology. We are profoundly influenced by sex. That's the way it's supposed to be. It is not just another bodily function. The memories, particularly of peak sexual experiences, draw us back to our partner again and again.

So many men are performance-oriented when it comes to sex. The question in many male minds these days is not, "Was it good?" but rather, "Was *I* good?" Especially with all the current emphasis on sexual techniques and skills. And "Was *I* good?" means, is she comparing me to other sex partners? If yes, then how did I rank?

Moreover, women these days chat about men's sexual performance over coffee. It's acceptable polite conversation. Among many women, "Is he good in bed?" is a standard question for starting a conversation. Eavesdrop on chats between friends over cappuccino in cafes. Lots of subtle double entendre humor in everyday conversation relates to sexual performance and sexual anxiety.

Yes, there is a place for technique, and some people are "good in bed." But a more solid foundation for a good sex life is the character, integrity, and trustworthiness of the two people making love. Sadly, given the sexual résumés of many single adults, the question has now become, *Was I as good as* _____ *or the last dozen sex partners you've had?* Lots of men in these liberated times wonder, but do not dare ask, "How do I rate?"

Even if your partner is widowed or divorced and has had only one partner (say an ex or a deceased spouse) you may have to discipline your comparisons, expressed or unexpressed.

77. The woman I am dating is constantly reading these romantic novels—steamy stuff! The kind with a half-naked hunk on the cover. She says lots of women read them.

Many women do enjoy their romance novels. It's an 800 million dollar industry with some 1,800 new titles every year.[1] (I have friends who trade them by the grocery sack!) However, overexposure to that style of hype romance can foster a lot of notions that cannot be healthy for real-life relationships. It can become the equivalent of overweight people sitting around reading cookbooks or "browsing" in bakeries.

On the other hand, ask yourself about why the "half-naked hunk" on the cover irritates you.

CHAPTER 8

Single and Balancing Sexuality and Faith

78. Why has God not answered my prayer for a mate?

It's possible that God *has* answered your prayer. Your prayer may have been answered in the way that God answers many prayers: God may have said, "No" or "Not yet." You may not like God's answer and may not understand it, but even a no is still an answer.

Many single adults approach prayer only with an attitude of "Give me . . . give me . . ." and then fill in the blank, as if ordering from Home Shopping Network or a mail-order catalog. Some believe that by praying with a particular formula or intensity, they can obligate God to answer favorably.

Prayer is not a way to get things, particularly a mate. It is a way to get to know the giver, God. By open, candid, and regular communication with the Creator, you prepare yourself for the kind of spiritual depth that is so important to successful singleness or marriage.

God answers prayer in six ways:
sometimes with yes, sometimes with no;
sometimes now, sometimes later;
sometimes with less than we ask, sometimes with more.

79. Does God have only one potential mate for me?

People have traditionally wanted God to be a matchmaker. Many sincere Christians will assure you that God "has someone picked out for you." The image that comes to mind is God playing a marital chess game to get you and your one "right" person into checkmate. But what if you miss that one person? Are you doomed either to singleness or to a "runner up" marital prize? Too many marriages begin with one (or both) of the partners considering the other as something of a "consolation prize." "Oh, but she has such a great personality" is burdened with hidden meaning. My friend, Lizz Curtis Higgs, who married later than the norm, described her experience: "The ladies at my church were always fussing over me, trying hard not to feel sorry for me, though they obviously did. 'A-w-w-w-w,' they'd say, 'No husband? No children? Poor thing!' More than once, they intoned, 'God has a man for you.' (To which I always said, 'Hey! He knows my address, what's the holdup?')" [1]

While "waiting for the one God wants to bring into my life," many singles live on hold. It's as if they assume the right spouse will appear magically if they just sit at home patiently until the UPS deliveryman asks, "Where do you want him, lady?" Or they long for that moment when, "Across a crowded room, and suddenly you'll know . . ." (or hope or decide).

The idea that there is *only* one perfect marriage partner doesn't come from the Bible. It may come from the Greek philosopher, Aristophanes, who declared that human beings had once been round, had four hands and four feet, and one head with two faces, looking opposite ways. But the gods were afraid of these beings, so they decided to cut them in half. Now everyone is searching for their "other half." [2] Hence the hackneyed introduction, "Meet my better half . . ."

Some Christians have unknowingly misinterpreted Genesis 2 to accommodate pagan philosophy and make many single adults feel miserable. Genesis actually says that because the first woman, Eve, was created out of the rib of the first man, Adam, whenever a man marries a woman, they "become one flesh" (2:7, 24). It doesn't say anything about there being only one, "right" potential spouse for every single adult—and if you miss it, too bad.

When we bring the individual we want to marry to God and ask, "What do you think?" God may well respond, "What do *you* think?" God is not going to strong-arm you into his choice for your mate. "And you're going to like this, buster. Got it?!"

A single man or single woman is a whole person, not half a person. The New Testament clearly teaches that wholeness is found not in marriage, but in relationship with Jesus Christ (1 Corinthians 7). "See to it that no one takes you captive through hollow and deceptive philosophy, which depends on human tradition and the basic principles of this world rather than on Christ. For in Christ all the fullness of the Deity lives in bodily form, and you have this fullness in Christ . . ." (Colossians 2:8–10).

We should be willing to ask God and our religious community for direction and guidance. Traditionally, engagement vows were made in church to give communal recognition to the seriousness of the commitment. In many parts of the world today, notices or "banns" of a wedding must be put up in a church to give congregants the opportunity to offer a response. Yet the spirit of rugged individualism leaves little room for questioning when it comes to romance in America. Here, marriage is viewed as a choice between two individuals, and the father or mother is informed of the couple's decision, rather than asked.

We are always on shaky grounds, expecting God (let alone family and friends) to "rubber-stamp" our selection. We must be prepared to listen if God tells us, "No" or "Wait" or "Not this one" or "Not at this time."

The testimony of good marriages is, "I'm glad I didn't leap at the *first* one I thought was God's will." Many adults can only hum the "Doxology" in thanksgiving when they think of the disastrous marital choices they might have made when they *thought* it was God's choice for them.

80. How can I pray for a future spouse?

We can pray about whatever is on our minds. We ought also to ask for:
- *patience* to avoid saying, "You'll do! Let's get married."
- *courage* to risk really getting to know this individual before the "I do"
- *strength* to pull the plug on or to exit a bad relationship
- *wisdom* to see the individual and the relationship accurately

Maurice Lamm offers excellent prayer guidelines for single adults to consider:
- Talk in your own language, the way you would to a friend.
- Do this when no one is around (otherwise, you'll censor).
- Don't feel guilty for neglecting to do so up to now.

- If it's hard at first, keep trying. Practice makes perfect.
- Ask for help—that's what God is there for.
- Tell God everything. Besides, he already knows.[1]

Telling God everything means *every thing* and includes our longings for marriage. The individuals we choose to date and the one we choose to marry are good subjects for prayer.

81. Should I actively look for a mate or just wait for the right one to come along?

Do everything you can to determine whether marriage is a good option. Consider your own personal strengths and weaknesses as well as what you sense God is calling you to do with the gifts and abilities you have been given. Hormones and loneliness are an inadequate basis for choosing marriage.

God has promised us many things, but the certainty of marriage or a lifetime of marital bliss is not one of them. The difficulties of married life are revealed in the vows themselves: "for better for worse, for richer for poorer, in sickness and in health—whatever—to love and to cherish." Marriage is not a necessity for a good life. Historically, researchers and commentators have noted a high rate of mental illness and high mortality rates among single adults. But researchers are reexamining both the concepts and the populations these conclusions were based on. Recent research has now established that "mature single women are beginning to report they perceive advantages and opportunities for single adults, such as personal autonomy and growth, that have made 'flying solo' a psychologically rewarding experience." [1]

If, after a careful inventory of your own traits, in-depth conversation with friends and counselors, and diligent prayer, you conclude that you are a good candidate for marriage, great. But now what do you do? Avoid both of the options you mentioned in your question. Actively looking for a mate—"leaving no stone unturned"—is counterproductive. On the other hand, simply "waiting for the right person to come along" reflects a misguided view of how God works in our lives. Just "hanging out" relationally sounds pretty dull.

Put your thoughts of marriage on the back burner and choose to enjoy the adventure of living as a child of God. Make the most of the season called "single." Don't let opportunities for fun, work, adventure, service, and meeting new people pass you by because you are preoccupied with not being married. In the romantic meantime:

Pray for insight into any negative signals you may be transmitting in Singleland. Work on your personal weaknesses.

Pray for patience. The more frantic and panic-stricken (*desperate*!!!!) you are or seem to be, the less appealing you will be as a person and as a potential date or mate!

Invest yourself in something, some cause, some institution, some ministry, bigger than yourself. Happiness comes more though giving than through getting.

Guard yourself against opportunities for "easy" sex as a "consolation" prize. Choose not to settle for any "discount" relationship.

In other words, be good to you.

82. What is abstinence? What is celibacy?

Abstinence is the absence of sexual relations or sexual relationships, and may be either voluntary or involuntary.

Celibacy is abstention from sexual activity by choice. It is a conscious and deliberate decision. Most Roman Catholic and many Protestant thinkers contend that celibacy precludes all sexual activity, including masturbation. Other Protestants would broaden the definition to allow for solo masturbation—although the more accurate term would be *partial celibacy.* Some would argue that celibacy is the absence of all genital activity intended to produce orgasm.

83. What motivates single adults to be celibate?

Religious celibate single adults including priests, nuns, and some lay people do not have sex because of the requirements of their church or holy order. Jesus talked about single adults "who have renounced marriage for the sake of the kingdom of heaven." (Matthew 19:12).

Frightened celibate single adults think that with all the sexual diseases in Singleland, celibacy makes a lot of sense. In one study of single adults, fear of contracting AIDS or an STD ranked third and fourth as motivators for remaining a virgin. [1] One university's webpage, entitled "Decisions About Sex," asks students to ponder, "What will I do if I or my partner gets a sexually transmitted disease?" Then it turned serious by noting that some STDs can be fatal.

Dr. Art Ulene, in *Safe Sex in a Dangerous World,* contends, "If you can't be sure that you've got a safe partner, abstinence is the only sexual practice you can consider safe . . . I believe that complete abstention from sexual activities with others is a choice that deserves serious consideration in the age of AIDS." [2]

Fearful celibate single adults choose not to be sexual for fear of being emotionally hurt or rejected, again. Remember charm bracelets? Some of us carry mental charm bracelets: "Oh, this one reminds me of Paul who hurt me, this one of Jason who *really* hurt me . . ." Some of us fear that we won't find safe partners—not only *physically* safe, but emotionally and spiritually safe as well.

Burned out celibate single adults have seen it all and done it all sexually, and now find themselves sexually numb.

Jealous celibate single adults feel like they have been placed in "quarantine," but they covet the sexual behaviors of others.

Angry celibate single adults follow the letter of the law but not the spirit: "I am celibate, but I am not very happy about it!"

Pharisaical celibate single adults know how to reach orgasm a half-dozen ways and yet take pride that the fragile gem of virginity remains intact so long as coitus is avoided. One theologian contends that such thinking "has helped open the floodgate to a tidal wave of noncoital promiscuity." [3] Ira Reiss, a sociologist, labels these celibates "technical virgins" who honor the letter of the law but not the spirit of the law. [4] Orgasm, yes; penetration, never!

Situational celibate single adults are celibate with the individual they intend to marry or assume they will marry. Sadly, given the remaining double standard, men have been permitted to fool around with someone else in the meantime. Thus, "You'll do until . . ."

The traditional Christian teaching is that *all* unmarried single adults should remain celibate. That's hard for some single adults to live with these days, particularly given that dating is encouraged from an earlier age and adolescence is prolonged, for many, into their twenties. That's a long time to "just say no." And lots of single adults have undeveloped or rusty "no" skills. But there are positive reasons to be celibate:

• Many people choose celibacy because they believe it gives them more power and control over their lives.

• People who are celibate have more time to devote themselves to other aspects of their lives.

• Individuals struggling with sexual addiction issues find that a period of celibacy is the only way to regain sanity in their lives, sexually and emotionally.

Some healthy individuals see celibacy as a self-imposed "time out" and certainly not a penalty. It is a way of restoring sanity and reducing sexual pressure. "The choice of celibacy," note authors Evelyn Eaton Whitehead and James D. Whitehead, "must be a decision not against, but *for something*." [5]

84. What do you mean by "say yes to the best?"

Celibacy isn't beneficial to you unless you have freely made the choice not to have sex. If you were marooned alone on an uninhabited South Sea island, technically you wouldn't be practicing *positive* celibacy because you would have no choice but to abstain. If you are too frightened by diseases or if you are afraid of being hurt or rejected, you are making your decision negatively. Celibacy is the freedom to choose what is sexually wise. Thus, one of my themes with single adults is, "Say yes to what is best."

Clearly, celibacy or abstinence has to be more than a bumper sticker or a family values slogan such as, "Pet your dog, not your date!" or "Control your urgin'; be a virgin." [1] Cute slogans sell T-shirts, but rarely influence decision making.

Celibacy is not a once-and-for-all decision. It is a resolution made and perhaps remade: *Today* I will not nurture any sexual invitation that harms or hurts me or you or that devalues sexual expression or that vetoes my values.

Celibacy is not repressing our sexual drives, but rather choosing not to act on them. Celibacy does not make condemning pronouncements on others but rather says, "This is what I have chosen."

85. **Is there a relationship between prayer and sex drive?**

The cliché says, "Prayer changes things." Prayer does change things—often it changes our attitudes toward our circumstances. Sometimes the Creator changes the circumstances; at other times our perspective gets stretched, and we see the troubling issue in a different light.

Christians have often had problems with the intensity of the sex drive. The key shaper of the New Testament, Paul, lamented, "For what I want to do, I do not do, but what I hate, I do" (Romans 7:15). Lots of single adults respond, "Been there/felt that!" Sadly, some single adults have prayed—make that pleaded—for God to take away the wondrous sexual endowment he has given.

Recently, the Heaven's Gate cult made headlines with their mass suicide. The males had themselves castrated to be rid of sexual urges and desires. This is nothing new. The great theologian Origen took the scripture "if part of your body offends" to mean that he should be castrated. He believed that "the elimination of sexual functioning was the foremost of living sacrifices pleasing to God." [1]

We should pray about our sexual "opportunities" and wonderings and longings. Sex is always an opportunity for reflection and for obedience: What does *this* act mean? To me? To the person I share it with?

86. **How do you pray about sex?**

Matthew Kelly suggests that we begin by asking "Jesus for help and guidance the same way you would ask any friend. Sit with the Lord and say, 'Lord, I have this problem. This is the situation . . . These are the circumstances. What do you think I should do, Lord?' Explain the problem to Jesus as clearly and completely as you can, and then listen." [1]

Ask God to give you courage to honestly confront your sexual drives, desires, fantasies, and wonderings, and the insight to make good, healthy, long-term decisions. Pray before facing sexual crossroads, when a decision to escalate or de-escalate the sexual tension in a relationship must be made. Otherwise, you will be paraphrasing Augustine's prayer, "Make me pure—*but not tonight!*"

Sometimes we pray in awkward moments and situations: "I need help, *now!*" Part of praying is paying attention to those small voices within us that say, "This is not the best choice. Find an exit." Don't be prudish in composing your prayers. After all, we are dialoguing with the Creator, the One who thought up sexuality.

Rather than praying to God to take away your sexual desires, your sexual orientation, your sexual realities, or your sexual scars, pray for insight, courage, and wisdom.

87. Isn't it God's will for all people to be sexually satisfied? If God made us sexual people, why would he veto sex for single adults?

If by "sexually satisfied" you mean orgasmically satisfied, no. Americans have gone overboard in misinterpreting the opening words of the Declaration of Independence, which declare that all people are endowed by God with certain inalienable rights, to include a "right to orgasm." We generally think of our right to "*the pursuit of happiness*" as a right to happiness. Far too often, single adults assume that the right to be a "happy camper" is the same as the right to the pursuit of happiness.

Some readers have heard a spouse saying, "I just want out. I'm not happy. I want to be happy. You know it's my constitutional right· life, liberty, and the pursuit of happiness." So you found yourself divorced, perhaps a single parent, sorting through chaos. This culture's bedrock is now "me first, if you please" and with "my rights" (which in light of this question, means my orgasm!).

While healthy, meaningful sexual expression is a great element of our humanity, it has to be kept in balance. When sex is pursued as an end in itself, it becomes shallow and distorted. Partners become an "it" rather than human beings. "Oh, please, let me be your *it*, tonight!" as a lot of sexual groupies apparently plead with professional athletes.

Too many single adults assume that marriage will bring them endless orgasmic bliss. Hardly. They need to take a good, hard look at the divorce rate and the marital unhappiness rates.

Even in marriage, there are going to be times—lots of times!—when your sexual needs cannot or will not be met by your partner. You may have to give yourself a hand, so to speak. The needs of children, illness, shift work, or workplace stress will redefine your sexual repertoire and douse sexual drives. Learning to accept reasonable limitations *now* helps prepare you for a level of sexual commitment you will need if and when you do marry.

88. Is it God's will that we should not have sex before marriage?

Three New Testament passages teach that premarital sex is less than God's ideal: 1 Thessalonians 4:3–8; Mark 7:20–21; and 1 Corinthians 6: 12–20. It's hard to be any more direct than: "What God wants is for you all to be holy. God wants each of you to keep away from sexual immorality; and learn to control your own body in a manner that is holy and honorable, and not be mired in passionate lust like the Gentiles who do not know God; and in this matter no one should wrong their neighbors or take advantage of them" (1 Thessalonians 4: 3–6).

89. Did Jesus have to deal with sexuality?

Jesus—the Son of God, single adult—had genitals! This fact has made religious people nervous for about the last 400 years. So nervous that they had artists retouch the great artwork of the Renaissance to cover Jesus' genitals. Now as those great works are being restored, loincloths have started to disappear.[1] Remember, in a preliterate culture, you couldn't just tell people Jesus was *fully human*—you had to show them!

One early heresy was Gnosticism, which tried to divide the spiritual Jesus Christ from the earthly carpenter, Jesus. The Gnostics argued that Jesus was only *quasi*-human, certainly not "flesh like our flesh," let alone "genital like our genital." Repelled by the idea that God could be joined to something as "unspiritual" as a human body, the Gnostics said that Christ only *appeared* to be human and did not really suffer and die.

Since then, many Christians have been so busy protecting the divinity of Jesus that they have never examined his humanity. Since he was circumcised on the eighth day, obviously he had a penis; moreover, Scripture states that Jesus was "made in human likeness" (Philippians 2:7). Some readers will be enraged to hear that Jesus had erections. But if he was *fully* human, as the Bible clearly says, then Jesus had erections.

While it is not clear what he did about his hormones, he did not sin. But on any day of his single season, he could have.

I wish the Gospels were not silent about Jesus' adolescence and early adulthood. We read about him as a babe in Bethlehem and as a young boy in the temple, and then the Gospel writers fast-forward over the next eighteen years (when most men are high-hormoned) to the launching of his ministry. Those years might really be insightful to us as single adults.

The full humanity of Jesus was affirmed by the author of Hebrews, who wrote years after Jesus' death. "He had to be made like his brothers *in every way,* in order that he might make atonement for the sins of the people. Because he himself suffered when he was tempted, he is able to help those who are being tempted" (Hebrews 2:17–18). Jesus certainly had the capacity for sexual intercourse but chose not to use it. A neutered Jesus without hormones or sexual temptation cannot understand me, let alone help me. Jesus cannot possibly expect single adults to be celibate if he used his supernatural powers to resist sexual opportunities and temptations. Jesus was human, biologically fully male, yet he chose to be celibate. Some single adults would argue, "Sure, Jesus was tempted . . . but *not* the way I am tempted. Or not as intensely! My urges are like surges! No way!"

Can temptation be authentic if there is no possibility of saying yes? Scripture does not say that Jesus was a eunuch, but that he rejected marriage and said that some would reject marriage "for the sake of the kingdom of heaven" (Matthew 19:12). Surely Jesus struggled with his sexuality as a single adult; it was no cakewalk.

90. Didn't Jesus say that anyone who even looks at a woman has committed adultery?

The phrase "undressed me with his or her eyes" illustrates Jesus' point. Jesus thought that the rabbis had been too lenient in teaching that good intentions were counted as good deeds, "while bad intentions were counted against you only if you succumbed to the temptation."[1] Jesus rejected such shallow thinking and modeled a respect for women that was radical for his time. The passage you alluded to (Matthew 5:27-30) takes on a new meaning when you hear it paraphrased by writer

Tim Stafford: "When you deliberately look at a woman (or a man) strictly as a sex object, dehumanizing her (or him), then you're as guilty of sexual infidelity as someone who actually goes ahead and acts out the plan." [2]

Jesus was urging his hearers (and us) to discipline our eyes and our minds and to take a high view of the word *neighbor,* to avoid using our gaze or our stare to make people uncomfortable, to avoid dehumanizing people as sex objects, to be used and discarded as so much is in this age of the disposable and the one time-use.

Jesus' teaching has often been misinterpreted. Avoiding lust does not mean that we refuse to recognize the biologically obvious. But if I visually drool over someone or replay what I see in slow motion, saying, "How can this person's body lead to my pleasure?" then I have lusted. If I evaluate this person solely on the size of their bust or their buttocks or whatever my point of attraction is, then I do not see them as a whole person. I have devalued one of God's creations.

91.   **Is thinking about sex the same as lust?**

Webster defines *lust* as "intense or unbridled sexual desire." Lust refers to those thoughts that focus on getting pleasure and getting sexual satisfaction. We lust if we fantasize about a particular person in bed or in specific sexual positions. Lust reduces another person to an object to be exploited, used, and often discarded as a means to our own gratification. Many single adults (and their leaders and counselors) are overly frightened by their sexual thoughts and feelings, which compose the "shadow" or dark side of their personalities. Some resort to fantasy when they masturbate (or even during intercourse) because they cannot accept or honor their own body's feelings of pleasure. It is too threatening.

Essentially, lust is the insistence on having your own goals met: me. Me! Me!!! Lust is really the desire to do what I want to do regardless of what God wants or what a partner wants. We lust when we reduce intercourse to "Just this once, baby" or "I need it so much." Our modern consumer-oriented, permissive culture says, "Why deny yourself? Go ahead. Have it your way." No wonder that, sexually, many of us say,

"I want what I want, and I want it now." Sadly, some single adults are so desperate to hang on to any romantic possibility, that they say yes to another's sexual agenda and discount their own.

92. Is fantasy wrong?

All of us fantasize about one thing or another, and most of us fantasize about sex. What we do with those fantasies can complicate our lives.

We are the only creatures than can mentally anticipate sex. The ability to imagine sexual experience is part of our arousal system, as is the ability to remember past sexual experiences. God was determined that the human race was going to survive, but he did not just leave it up to the hormones. He linked sex to our brains and our imaginations and our creativity, which are our great sexual organs.

Fantasies become troublesome when they are selfish or self-centered, when they dehumanize the individual. They also become counter productive when they too narrowly focus, say, on specific parts of the body or on sexual repertoires or scripts that degrade the individual.

According to Dr. Arch Hart, a psychologist-theologian, fantasies have three functions:

1. Fantasy creates and supports sexual arousal; it adds pleasure to sexual activity. That's why romance novels emphasize the settings as an enhancement to the sex.

2. Fantasy serves as a substitute for the real thing (or person) not yet available.

3. Fantasy rehearses sexual experiences and provides a safe outlet for sexual experimentation. So you read about something, and then you experiment with it in your mind before you actually try it.[1]

Rather than let fantasy harass you, be glad for the sexual feelings and the stirring beneath them. Sexual imagination is a wonderful gift from God, but like all of God's good gifts, it's wise to discipline it. Clearly, some sexual behaviors are best tested first in the theater of the mind.

Some fantasies frighten us or lead us to wonder, "Am I normal?" Fantasies generally fall into a common range. two thousand single adults were asked, "Have you ever fantasized that you were having sex with . . . " The following percentages responded yes: [2]

	Men	Women
A friend or acquaintance	27%	18%
Another lover	21%	17%
An ex	17%	16%
A celebrity	19%	7%
A stranger	10%	5%
A fictitious person	8%	6%

Also, some fantasies are more oriented around situations rather than persons. If fantasies are troublesome for you, explore them with a professional counselor. After a significant study of male fantasies, Bob Berkowitz concluded, "By examining the context and texture of male sexual fantasies . . . we can come up with a better understanding of who he is, what he wants, and why he does what he does." [3]

93. My friends say that if I were just more "spiritual" I wouldn't struggle so much with sexual issues. Are they right?

Our culture has an obsession with genitals and sexual abilities (just look at all the magazine headlines in the grocery store checkout lanes), and fails to understand the link between sexuality and spirituality, which go together like a pair of gloves. It is not either/or. You are more than your sexuality. You are a human being with a magnificent sexual endowment. four thousand years ago the Psalmist declared, "I praise you because I am fearfully and wonderfully made; your works are wonderful, I know that full well" (Psalm 139:14).

Too many single adults spiritualize away their sexuality; they see no way to integrate or balance the two ingredients into wholeness. It is either/or instead of both/and. Some of us have grown up in spiritually abusive traditions that have demonized God's incredible gift, or have urged rigid control of the body and the appetites—the flesh! So we're afraid to acknowledge our sexuality—to say nothing of our gratitude for the capacity. Others go the opposite direction and become so hypersexual that they cannot integrate their spirituality with their sexual realities. As a result, when the need and the pleasure have passed, "we are left gratified rather than grateful."[1] In the right circumstances, we can be gratified *and* grateful. Paul wrote, "You must know that your body is a temple of the Holy Spirit, who is within you—the Spirit you have received from God. You are not your own. You have been bought with a price. So, glorify God *in your body*" (1 Corinthians 6:19–20, New Inclusive). What would it mean to "glorify God *in/through* your body"? Few of us have ever given it much thought. Some of us have only heard those words in an abrasive *Thou shall not!* manner. We've never heard the free, positive, empowering side of those words. I am somebody because I am God's temple!

Paul could be paraphrased simply, "glorify God *in your sexuality*." Or *through* or *with your sexuality.* Paul calls single adults to be deliberate stewards of this marvelous gift. Paul lamented those who had an imbalance in their sexuality and faith. For although they knew God, they didn't give God honor or praise and never even said, "Thank you." When was the last time (if ever) that you deliberately thanked God for your sexual abilities, mysteries, and capacities? God says to single adults: Pay attention to your sexuality and to your spirituality.

CHAPTER 9

Single and Wondering about Touching

94. Can you suggest how we women can help the men we care for to be emotionally intimate with us?

Men have the same emotional needs as women do: to be loved, to be cared for, to be admired, to be nurtured. However, many men do not understand that emotional intimacy is a prerequisite for satisfying these desires. Unfortunately, we have no equivalent of driver's ed for intimacy. It's still a live-and-learn (or regret) process.

Stuart Miller studied one thousand North American and European males and found that "most men clearly admitt[ed] they had no real friends [with] most of the rest pretending or thinking that they did when they did not." [1] Men often have a number of pals or buddies, but they have far fewer deep friendships than women do. So men frequently have to be emotionally "jump-started." Here are some suggestions:

Treasure any hint of tenderness. Men are often reluctant to be tender for fear that their masculinity will be questioned. They don't want anyone to think of them as wimps or sissies or weak.

Praise them for emotional growth. "I like it when you are this way, when you open up and share with me."

Introduce them to touching, softness, and caressing. Most men need to learn that a tactile "invasion of the Third Brigade" is not what most women desire.

Listen. When men talk about their feelings, don't interrupt. Assure them of your confidentiality. Listen with your eyes *and* your ears.

Give clear signals. If you drool over Brad Pitt or Antonio Banderas or Dom DeLuise (our readers have a diverse range of ages), yet you encourage your man to "open up and be vulnerable," he will have trouble reconciling these mixed messages. If you want the rugged macho man, say so.

Guard the data they share. Men share facts first, then perhaps feelings. Men fear betrayal, particularly after a messy divorce or breakup. They disclose personal information in installments. If you repeat what a man shares with you to two or three dozen of your closest friends on e-mail, you hurt him and reduce his chances of being vulnerable in the future.

Encourage men to open up. Most men hesitate to be emotionally intimate and habitually suppress their feelings because they lack positive role models. Recall the jokes when President Bill Clinton told voters, "I feel your pain." Men will not easily abandon their culturally induced restrictions, even though they rob them of the rich experiences of genuine intimacy. The most effective tools for helping them are time, gentleness, and lots of reassurance.

95. As a single adult, how can I satisfy my need for touch?

It isn't intercourse that many single adults miss after the death of a mate or a relationship, but the touching and the cuddling. They miss reaching out on a cold night, or after a bad day or a bad dream, and finding Someone—and not just anyone—there.

Your biggest sexual organ is your skin. God created us to touch and to be touched. More than 60,000,000 sensors cover our bodies, from head to toe and in between, delicately tuned to capture the gentlest touch or to sense a threatening touch. Sadly, many single adults know only about two to three thousand of them. Babies can die without touch, without receiving sensations of love and affirmation through these "touch receptacles."[1] So what happens to single adults who are not touched? Who do not touch?

Many of us are touch-starved. Remember being told, "You're too big to be held?" No one is ever too big to be held or touched. But because of cultural roles, single men are unlikely to touch in healthy, caring ways. That's why many men have "Roman" (roaming) hands and "Russian" (rushing) fingers on dates. They are trying to make up for the touch deficiency. One could accurately say that most men are touch *challenged*.

Mention the word *massage* and listen for the snickering. For many men, massage has strong sexual connotations. Many confuse licensed therapeutic massage with "massage parlors." True, when massage parlors first opened, many were fronts for prostitution. Yet researchers were stunned to discover that the clients were not primarily seeking sexual services. They wanted to be touched and listened to.

Thankfully, therapeutic massage is losing its stigma, and more and more trained licensed massage therapists are available to offer safe, healthy therapeutic touch. Massage is always an investment with wonderful dividends.

Most of us have been overly intimidated by the great, unspoken Eleventh Commandment: "Thou shall *not* touch!" Certainly, touching has its risks. If one person is more comfortable with one level of touch than another, clear communication will be necessary to avoid misunderstanding; make clear what you mean when offering a "back massage."

Be on your guard about inappropriate touching. Some single adults might misinterpret your intentions. Moreover, inappropriate touch in the workplace could get you more familiar with sexual harassment guidelines or even terminated. Lots of people are "touchy" about touch.

96. What are some healthy rules for "good" touch?

Know what feels good to you. Find mutually accepting ways to incorporate nonsexual touch into your friendships.

Learn to hug well. A hug can make a world of difference in how a day goes. At times, when you can't find the right words, a hug speaks with an eloquence all its own.

Pamper yourself. If you don't have anyone to hug, hug yourself or a tree! It's not quite the same, but it will help. Take more baths and fewer showers. Join a health club; after a vigorous workout treat yourself to a hot shower, sauna, or long, hot soak. Buy body lotions and baby your skin. You are definitely worth it. Give yourself or others a gift certificate for a massage.

Be alert to the hug-aholic. Some people are always volunteering for a hug, but you quickly sense that they have more in mind. A side hug, hip-to-hip may be the best. Beware of the single adult who continually whines, "I need a hug."

97.   What level of intimacy is best for single adults?

According to researcher Robert J. Sternberg, a healthy adult relationship delicately balances three elements: passion, intimacy, and commitment.[1] Relational problems develop when one component dominates the other two. Some couples, for example, can bear their souls to each other but have little vested in passion or commitment. What they really have is a high-grade friendship. Some couples allow passion to overrule either commitment or intimacy. What they have is an affair or a fling; in some cases, the relationship is little more than duo-masturbation. They share the body but not the soul.

However, when you pay attention to and balance all three elements, the relationship prospers. By investing commitment, passion, and intimacy into a relationship, you allow love to grow safely. Single adults in relationships should periodically take stock of the boundaries of their relationships by asking, "Are we overemphasizing one or two elements? If so, how can we bring the relationship back into a healthy balance?"

The Bible calls for a strong connection between sexual intimacy and commitment. God wants to protect us from unnecessary pain and emotional suffering and so has given the gift of sexual intimacy within a loving, committed-to-permanency relationship. When sexual intercourse takes place in the context of lifelong commitment it is consistent with God's best. Complete physical intimacy—intercourse—is healthiest when there is a solid commitment, a commitment not just to the moment but to a shared future.

Some single adults browse the New Testament seeking a list of sexual "dos" and "do nots!," hoping to find out "how far they can go." But they won't find one. God has endowed us with the gift of sexuality, linked with responsibility (Galatians 5:1, 1 Corinthians 10:23–24). God is not a passion-douser but an intimacy-enhancer. So to examine your practice of intimacy, make an audit of your sexual behaviors, fantasies, and longings by confronting the tough ponderables.

• Are you really as committed to this individual and to the relationship as your behavior suggests?

• Do you have "appropriate vulnerability." [2] Is the level of sexual expression commensurate with the level of commitment and vulnerability?

• What do you mean when you say, "I love you"?

If you have been sexually intimate:

• How will you respond if the relationship ends? Or if there is a pregnancy?

• Are you fully informed about the risks of AIDS and other sexually transmitted diseases? Do you fully implement that knowledge?

• Are you aware that some infected people are asymptomatic—that it could be years before herpes or HIV makes its presence known?

Sexual intimacy is a wonderful thing, all but impossible to capture in words. But God has more than fabulous orgasms in mind. He wants you to have not "safe sex" but *safe intimacy,* which replicates the relationship of the Garden couple: "The man and his wife were naked—and they were not ashamed" (Genesis 2:25). I translate that, "And the man and woman were vulnerable." How vulnerable are you in your relationships? Is your partner vulnerable? What would it be like for you to be emotionally naked and unashamed? For those of us battling mid-life physical realities, what would it be like to be *physically* naked and unashamed? What would it be like to bring "all of me" into a relationship? What would it be like for you to have someone who could love you as you are—with those love handles? the twenty extra pounds? stretch marks? surgical scars? the less-than-centerfold-breasts? the less-than-Chippendale bod? What would it be like with no agendas to change this or that about each other?

98. Why does a man go to bed with a woman and then never ask her out again?

Men are goal-oriented. In sexual matters, a man's goal is intercourse. Some seek only shallow relationships that provide them with opportunities for orgasms. Men know that once a woman has said yes to sex, she is more likely to be thinking about the long-term possibilities for the relationship. She starts lobbying for commitment. That is not what these men want.

Some single men are Don Juans. Their goal is conquest, overriding your no. Getting a woman to say yes excites them more than the intercourse itself. These men delight in plotting strategies and in enticing women—through compliments, affection, gifts, candlelit romantic dinners—into bed. But their interest ends as soon as the sex is over. They move on to someone new so they can repeat the chase and capture (although some men juggle multiple partners so they have an established sex supplier while seducing their next supplier).

99. Is it normal not to have too much sex drive?

Some single adults have strong sexual drives, some have weak drives, and most are somewhere in between. Sex drive varies according to stress, illness, and, for women, menstrual patterns. Caught in the middle of a contested child custody battle or a job change, you may not have much sex drive at all (or your sexual needs may be stress-driven). Single parents who are drained by caring for their children commonly report diminished sexual drives.

Although it sounds outrageous, even bicycle seats can diminish sex drive in males. Prolonged riding can douse a man's sex drive, even permanently, through injury to the perineum (the area between the penis and the anus) or prolonged irritation sustained during long bike rides. [1]

Recently, counselors have been seeing single adults (and married adults) affected by a condition labeled *Inhibited Sexual Desire* (ISD). Adults who do not initiate sex may have many of the following characteristics:

- A low rate of sexual activity (including masturbation)
- Lack of desire for sexual activity
- No response to erotic materials
- No wishes for sexual activity
- A failure to notice the opposite sex. [2]

ISD can be either temporary or long-term (without treatment), general (applying to all potential sex partners) or situational (limited to a particular partner). The problem can be linked to depression over a relationship, poor body image, low self-esteem, or power struggles in a relationship. Aside from ISD, however, reduced sexual drive may also result from:

- severely negative parental attitudes ("Sex is dirty!" "Men only want one thing: sex!" "Watch out for that woman. She will trap you.")
- a history that includes rape, sexual abuse, or trauma
- a pattern of constant sexual pressuring
- stress
- gender identify confusion ("Could I be homosexual?")
- inability to talk about a sexual relationship [3]

Some single adults have a *sexual aversion*, a severe fear of sexual activity or the thought of sexual activity, which leads to avoidance. Guy Kettellhack labels this "a frightened celibacy." [4] "You are not supposed to fall into bed with a man you just met—not because it's wrong but because, due to sexually transmitted diseases like AIDS, it's not *safe*." [5]

A parallel condition called *sexual burnout*, experienced by perhaps 20 percent of adults, is "marked by a sense of physical depletion, emotional emptiness, and a negative sexual self-concept." [6] Sexual burnout can happen to single adults who have been very sexually active and promiscuous, since sex can have a numbing effect.

Before you diagnose yourself (not a good idea, by the way) as suffering from one of these conditions, ask yourself what standard of sexual desire you are comparing yourself to. What you fear is a low sex drive may be quite normal.

100. What is sexual anorexia?

Patrick Carnes, a leading addictions specialist, has identified "sexual anorexia" as a radical denial of sexual desire. The sexual anorexic typically experiences the following:

- a dread of sexual pleasure
- a morbid and persistent fear of sexual contact
- obsession and hypervigilance around sexual matters
- avoidance of anything associated with sex
- preoccupation with others being sexual
- distortions of physical appearance
- extreme loathing of bodily functions

- obsessional self-doubt about sexual adequacy
- rigid, judgmental attitudes about sexual behavior
- excessive fear and preoccupation with sexually transmitted diseases
- obsessive concern or worry about the sexual intentions of others
- shame and self-loathing over sexual experiences
- depression about sexual inadequacy and functioning
- self-destructive behavior to limit, stop, or avoid sex (gaining weight to be unattractive) ·
- intimacy avoidance because of sexual fear[1]

Sadly, some single adults are so afraid of their own sexuality—let alone the sexuality of others—they have to be "in control." So they live their life chanting: "Do not do or accept anything that would reveal vulnerability. No chances for mistakes. No chances to be hurt again. No vulnerability! A life stance based on safety. No sex means no terror."[2]

101. Is it possible to have an overactive sex drive?

Yes, but it is more likely that you are just at an age when your hormones are screaming for attention. On the average, a male's sex drive is usually strongest in his teen years and twenties. A woman's sex drive, however, usually peaks somewhat later. Many young single adults feel that they are "oversexed" and tease each other about being oversexed, but most people their age are having similar experiences.

It should be noted that some people have occasional or momentary overactive sex drives. Some experience what Carnes calls sexual "bingeing" or "occasional periods of extreme sexual promiscuity" not unlike food bulimics who binge on eating.[1] Thus, a male, for instance, could be celibate in a relationship, yet compulsively masturbate while watching porno flicks, just as one might eat a normal meal on a date and then go home and pig out on junk food.

102. How far can I go in petting?

"How far can I go?" is the number one question asked in my seminars on sexuality. Some single adults want a Talmud-like clarity: "After date #1 you can do this; after date #2 you can do that." And some single adult leaders have attempted to offer just that—a very specific, legalistic code that tries to cover every situation and every level of relationship. But it's an impossible task.

For the record, "necking" is defined as sex play in which the areas above the waist are stimulated; "petting" includes everything else, except intercourse. In my lifetime, the word *necking* has become archaic. I feel terribly old even mentioning it.

Many Christian single adults believe that as a relationship matures, the intimacy and the commitment are matched; therefore, increasing amounts of physical intimacy are permissible. Some would call this "sexual gradualism."[1] Still, many find it difficult to make these choices and are puzzled about where to draw "the line" of a healthy boundary.

In fact, if not in intention, petting is foreplay. Petting carries sexual arousal to a higher intensity and the body responds by preparing for intercourse. For example, the normal acidity of the urethra in the penis becomes more alkaline to protect the sperm, which it "assumes" will soon be en route; the walls of the vagina lubricate to better accommodate the "expected" penis. Petting is not unlike sending false alarms on your security alarm. It confuses and frustrates your body. "Here we go again!"

"How far can I go?" is not a wise question. "How far *should* I go?" is wiser. Wherever you draw the line, invoke the law of diminishing returns. After a while you will have a greater desire to move on to new areas of sexual exploration.

Many single adults insist that once they cross some biologic threshold, "wild horses" couldn't stop them. This convenient threshold notion helps reduce their sense of responsibility for their sexual choices and their anxiety when they have made unwise choices. For example, in one study of 795 single adults, 6 percent of the men reported resorting to sexual coercion because they were "so aroused that it was impossible to stop,"[2] as if that made their behavior less offensive. It is too easy to rationalize, "We've gone this far, might as well go all the way."

However, I contend that people can always stop (not always easily, of course). We are not locked into some unstoppable physiological process, like a rocket launch sequence. Yes, stopping may be extremely difficult or psychologically unpleasant, even awkward, but no one escapes full responsibility for their sexual choices. "It just happened" is inaccurate; the truth is, I allowed "it" to happen, unless it was rape.

A second myth is that of "The Line"—the notion that there is some magic sexual line that must not be crossed. Once they've accepted this notion, many single adults want to see how close they can get to the line without crossing it. The basic issue of sexual responsibility gets lost in an intense legalism designed to maintain technical virginity. For example, one single man insisted that only full penetration of the vagina by a man's penis constituted "sex." He was very proud that he wasn't like other single adults who "went all the way" (to orgasm).

Tim Stafford points out that Scripture is silent on the issue of petting between unmarried adults; in biblical times, singles were not even allowed the freedom to be alone, unsupervised. Men and women did not always even "date" before marriage. Stafford insists that instead of getting entangled in "How far can we go?" a better question would be: What sexual choices and behaviors are "really helpful in expressing the love and commitment we feel for each other?," [3] and while we're at it, which are counterproductive? What sexual choices and behaviors will best give this relationship a chance? Remember, a lot of potentially stable relationships that might lead to marriage are sabotaged by poor sexual choices.

Obviously, the time to ask and answer such questions is before you get to any magic line. When hormones are at flood tide, the chances of making wise long-term sexual choices will be significantly reduced if you are only now asking, "What to do? What to do?"

You are *always* responsible for the level of intimacy you seek or permit. You may want to be "swept off your feet" so that you can assuage your guilt, but keep in mind that intimacy is a slowly escalating network of decisions, a series of yeses that you give at various levels of relationship.

103. Does the Bible forbid intimate touching and petting to orgasm?

If you want an Eleventh Commandment, "You shall not pet to orgasm!" my answer would be, it's not there. Of course, not everyone would agree. Peter Gomes, a single adult and preacher at Harvard Memorial Chapel, reminds us that "To read is to interpret." [1] Gomes notes, "behind the letter of the law is the spirit that animates it, the force that gave it and gives it life." [2] Sadly, some single adults live by the letter of the law, the "jots and the tittles," as Jesus described them.

Most arguments are not about the whole of Scripture but about the interpretation of a particular passage or theme. For example, take the verse, "For the word of the Lord is living and active, sharper than a two-edged sword, piercing to the division of the soul and spirit, of joint and marrow, and discerning *the thoughts and intentions of the heart*" (Hebrews 4:12). So, this scripture seems to be asking, why do you want to caress your date's breasts? Exploration or exploitation? Is your motivation primarily for the satisfaction of your own sexual needs, your mutual needs, or out of boredom or curiosity?

Here the Bible pushes us further than a straight yes or no answer would. Yet some see the Scriptures primarily as a rule book, a passion-douser, because they believe nonmarital sex really irritates God. In their ranking of the severity of sin, fornication is like a three-star sin (and gossiping only a half-star sin). But as the apostle Paul reminds single adults, "Since you died with Christ to the basic principles of this world, why, as though you still belonged to it, do you submit to its rules: 'Do not handle! Do not taste! Do not touch!' These are all designed to perish with use, because they are based on human commands and teachings [and interpretations!]" (Col. 2:20–22). Paul had been around enough sexuality—and single people—to know that rules don't always work. He goes on to say, "Such regulations indeed have an appearance of wisdom, with their self-imposed worship, their false humility, and their harsh treatment of the body, but they lack any value in restraining sexual indulgence" (2:23). False humility leads to the subtle temptation to be "holier-than-thou" or to go around tattling and gossiping about the sexual sins of others. "Thank God I am not like those who sleep around!"

Think of it this way: the Bible does not specifically forbid cybersex to orgasm. The people in Biblical times would never have even been able to imagine a computer or the Internet or our sexual mores, so the Bible does not specifically address the issue. However, from a deliberate reading of the whole of Scripture and through reflective interpretation, one can formulate a biblically dependent response: Any sexual behavior is sinful if it is predominantly me-centered or violates human dignity or integrity. And that includes petting; certainly petting to orgasm is sinful if one uses threat, force, prestige, ridicule, or threat of rejection to persuade an otherwise unwilling person to participate in it.

Single adults who bask in a false spiritual pride because they don't "go all the way" like *some* single adults, but who would caress to orgasm, are on soft ground. Paul warned, "But watch yourself, or you also may be tempted" (Galatians 6:1).

Ponder these questions:

• Is this level of physical intimacy as beneficial to my partner as to myself?

• Is this level of physical intimacy wise for all single adults? If not, why am I an exception?

• Is this level of physical intimacy reasonable at this point in the relationship?

• Is this level of physical intimacy the best choice for this relationship's future?

104. What is outercourse?

Sex has been so discussed that we immediately understand what "it" means in our music and double entendre humor. But we often think of it as a specific sexual activity—intercourse. In one men's magazine, a sex questionnaire had this caveat, "We'll demurely define 'sex' as vaginal intercourse." [1] So, a single adult could have engaged in oral sex every night for six months, but by that narrow definition still be a virgin or not "sexually active."

Outercourse has been called "all but" or "*almost* the real thing." Outercourse would include kissing, massaging, cuddling, mutual masturbation, oral sex, cunnilingus, and "dry humping"—everything except penetration. Think of outercourse as a staircase, moving from one step of sex play to the next but, by ruling out intercourse, never reaching the top.

Level 1: Making out with lots of "hand" action

Level 2: Grinding against each other, with or without clothes, and with or without orgasm for both partners

Level 3: Extended smooching, humping with rubbing. Could include duo-masturbation. Although couples are semi-clothed, orgasm is the goal.

Level 4: Oral sex, either mutual or one way, with orgasm for receiving partner. [2]

Many couples begin, at least, with a particular plateau of outercourse as the goal or limit, although they may agree to move on to the next level. The goal (preferably a *shared* goal) is to delay having intercourse or to "save" intercourse for the future, either with this partner or another partner. Many single adults find that by defusing the goal (i.e., putting off getting to The Main Event by the most direct route) they can enjoy a great deal of pleasure. "The idea is to remove performance pressure, slow down and start getting to know each other better. The focus is on love play—not foreplay." [3]

Outercourse focuses on touch that does not necessarily turn into foreplay. Again, you will need to ask, What does this particular act of intimacy mean? How comfortable do I feel with this level of intimacy?" How comfortable does my partner feel? Many single adults feel that "almost there" is better than "crossing the line." Keep in mind that although outercourse is a way to circumvent the birth control responsibility issue, outercourse (especially oral sex) leaves you vulnerable to emotional stress and the transmission of STDs.

105. What does it mean to be "addicted" to sex?

Sex and romantic addiction is not just some fad; it is not just something trendy on the talk shows. It is a devastating, relationally crippling reality for many single adults. Sex can become a compulsive need, physically and emotionally. Sexual relationships become increasingly destructive in all areas of an addict's life: career, family, dating, and self-image. These individuals become sex-centric. Their entire lives revolve around sex. It becomes an addiction, not because they need sex more than other people or because they have "high sex drives," but because sex lessens or even numbs the pain of their lives. Dr. Patrick Carnes, a leading authority on sexual addiction, explains that those who are sexually-addicted "use sex to help them control their moods and manage stress and anxiety," although, unfortunately, it vastly complicates their lives.[1] According to Carnes, many single adult sexual addicts cling to three strong beliefs that drive them sexually. As long as the beliefs persist, the behaviors persist: (1) I am worthless and unacceptable to God, myself, and others; (2) others will abandon (hurt or reject) me. I must meet my own needs and look out sexually for #1; (3) Life will never get better, and I am helpless to change it." [2]

Addicts use sex to avoid paying attention to their lives. That may be why some crudely say "I want to get me *some* . . ." or "*a little.*" Just as alcoholics use liquor, just as drug addicts use heroin or crack, so sex addicts use orgasms to deaden or escape their pain. They may verbalize it as "I need some lovin'" but the bottom line is: I need sex! Sexual and romantic addiction brings havoc to the lives of many single adults, directly or indirectly. Indeed, paraphrasing the words of AA, in order to get help, the single adult sex and romance addict must admit, "I am powerless over sex and love addiction" and "my life has become unmanageable." Addiction may lead to affairs and to divorce. Some single adults never marry because of their addiction. Their emotional and sexual needs are entangled in their addictions—no one person could be sufficient or enough for them.

Take a moment and slowly read through some of the character-istics of sex and love addiction as defined by Sex and Love Addicts Anonymous (SLAA).

Yes   No

____ ____   Do you find yourself unable to stop seeing a specific person even though you know that seeing this person is destructive to you?

____ ____   Have you had or do you have sex with someone you don't (didn't) want to have sex with?

____ ____   Do you believe that sex and/or a relationship will make your life bearable?

____ ____   Do you feel desperate about your need for a love, sexual fix, or future mate?

____ ____   Do you find that you have a pattern of repeating bad relationships?

____ ____   Do you feel entitled to sex?

____ ____   Do you feel that your life would have no meaning without a love relationship or without sex?

Yes   No

_____   _____   Do you have sex and/or "relationships" to try to deal
with or escape from life's problems?

_____   _____   Do you need to have sex or "fall in love" in order to feel
like a "real man" or a "real woman"?

_____   _____   Do you feel that your sexual and/or romantic life
affects your spiritual life in a negative way?[3]

What happened when you read through that list? Recognize any
sexual habits? Maybe you thought, "Been there/felt that!" Now go back
through and thoughtfully reread the list, pausing to reflect on any
questions that set off your soul's Geiger counter. Circle or highlight
words or phrases that leap out at you. Answer these questions by
locating yourself on a scale of 1–10:

1				10
This isn't me	*occasionally*	*frequently*	*a lot*	*This is me!*

All of us, at some point or the other in our singleness, have had
some of these experiences, but SLAA would ask, "How deeply does the
addiction run?" in your experience?

You may want to call them at (617) 332-1845 and ask for informa-
tional materials and for the location of a group near you. Sexual
addiction may be a reality for you now, but the good news is that is
does not have to remain a reality. Through "working the program,"
many sex and romance addicts have discovered "a whole new experience
of sexuality as a non-addictive medium."

Be aware that SLAA does not promise a "cure" in one or two
meetings. First you have to admit that you are powerless over sex and
love, then you have to believe that "a Power greater than ourselves" can
restore you to sanity. Eventually, you will have to come face-to-face
with your sexual résumé in order to complete Step 4: "a searching and
fearless moral inventory of ourselves." But the only real chance a sex
and romance addict has for real love is to go through the program.

106. What is date rape? Acquaintance rape?

Rape is often thought of as a guy in a ski mask attacking a woman. That is the stereotypical model, perhaps, but two new models have the same impact.

• If someone you date forces you to have sex it is *date rape* .

• If someone you know but whom you are not dating forces you to have sex, it is *acquaintance rape.*

Here are the key elements: forced, unwanted intercourse (oral, vaginal, or anal) that violates your body and your trust. It is an act of violence. It is a crime. Unfortunately, a lot of women—and some men—can say, "It has happened to me!" In one study of 2,000 single adults, 21 percent (11 percent of the men/29 percent of the women) had been physically forced into a sexual act by a date, a sexual partner, or a friend. However, over 41 percent did not consider the experience a rape at the time.[1]

Other research reveals the following:

• One in twelve men admit to having "forced" or having tried to force a woman to have sex with them.

• 90 percent of all rapes are not reported.

• 60 percent of all reported rape victims know their attacker (92 percent of adolescent rape victims).

• 43 percent of women who had been raped did not initially identify the act as rape.[2]

Many single women do not report rape because they fear humiliation. Or they fear they will not be believed. Or that word will get back to parents, friends, an employer. Admittedly, police, psychologists, and pastoral care givers have had difficulty understanding the nuances of rape, especially date rape. The male charged with rape will want his attorney to explore every square inch of the victim's sexual history if she presses charges, which can pressure her to sweep the experience under the rug. The date rapist may have gotten away with it before— this woman may be only his latest victim. Moreover, because such a high percentage goes unreported, it could be years later before the woman discovers he has given her herpes.

Naturally, police will ask, "Did the rapist use force?" Or to paraphrase the cliché, "Show me the bruises!" Force, however, is not always

physical. The date rape victim rarely has knifecuts or bruises or contusions. The legal definition of "force" includes:
- the threat of violence;
- telling you that "bad things will happen" if you don't consent;
- taking advantage of you when you are too drunk or high to give consent;
- threatening to tell other people that you had sex, even if you didn't;
- saying that they will hurt themselves if you don't give in.

Too many single adults do not take a "no" seriously. Or they are so determined to get what they want, they will not hear a "no." Some men have been conditioned to expect resistance and to surmount it: "I like a woman who puts up a little fight." But "no" doesn't legally require an exclamation mark. Legally, no means no, even if
- you have been making out;
- you have been drinking or taking drugs;
- you agreed at first, then changed your mind;
- you have been going out for a long time;
- you have had sex before;
- your date has spent a lot of money on you;
- you go to a secluded place to be alone together.[3]

Date rape, and all of its emotional, spiritual, physical and legal implications, could be avoided if three questions were asked in the midst of the passion:

1. Do we both want to have sex?

2. Have I said yes clearly enough?

3. Has my partner also said yes clearly?

In an increasingly violent society, more sexual coercion can be expected. Indeed, some men have perfected it to what experts call *aggressive verbal coercion*. "Making someone consent to unwanted sex through verbal coercion may not seem so bad because no overt force or violence is used, but the effect of such an experience can still be very debilitating to the victim."[4]

107. What could be considered sexual coercion or sexual aggression?

- lying about being in love with you;
- getting you drunk or stoned;
- pressuring with continual arguments. [1]

I would add

- placing an uninvited hand on breast or on genitals after it has been rebuffed with "Don't!" (with or without an exclamation mark) or physically moved away;
    - strongly pushing or jerking the head or hand toward the genitals.

In one sample of over 400 single adults, 60 percent of the women and 50 percent of the men reported having been subjected to some coercive strategy. [2] In a recent study of 635 single adults, 77.6 percent of the women and 57.3 percent of the men had been involved in some form of sexual aggression or unwanted sexual interest. [3] "It just goes with the territory called dating, these days!" one woman explained. "You've got to stay on your guard every moment."

108. What are some guidelines for avoiding date or "post-party" rape?

- Avoid parties with excessive alcohol/drug use (75 percent of date-rapists and 55 percent of victims had been drinking/taking drugs before the rape).
    - If you attend a party without a date, take or make a buddy.
    - Don't announce that you're leaving alone or walking to your car alone; ask someone you trust to walk you to a car or taxi.
    - Be cautious about bumming or accepting a ride from a stranger.
    - Avoid anyone who makes you feel uncomfortable.
    - Socialize with people who share your values. [1]

Know your date. Also know that drinking can change a "nice guy" into a date rapist! While, today, women increasingly are revaluing virginity and developing strongly assertive "no" skills, some men will press to challenge and override your no. They may assume you are saying no because you don't want to be perceived as *easy* or that you are playing hard-to-get.

So, practice your "no's." If you think "it can't happen to me!," think again. What would you do if the situation got out of hand? Jeffrey Kelly suggests standing in front of a mirror before a date and rehearsing whatever words you would use *to refuse a proposition for unwanted sex.* These days, it would be wise to practice this conversation with a friend for reinforcement and for critique. You never know when this might come in handy and keep you from being a victim of date rape or acquaintance rape.[2]

109. Any words of warning for men on this subject?

It is *never* OK to use force, or threaten to use force to coerce a partner into sex, even if

- she teases you;
- she dresses provocatively or "leads you on";
- she says no but you think she means Yes!;
- you've had sex with her before;
- you've coughed up big bucks for the date;
- she is under the influence of alcohol or drugs.

She may well be interested in some sexual contact other than intercourse. If you have any doubts, think. Then think again. Then think some more. Ask her. Clarify what she means and what she wants. Some argue that you need a "yes" to each escalation of physical contact.[1]

If date or acquaintance rape is part of your sexual history, it need not forever wound you. Seek professional help. Join a support group. Become more assertive. Know what levels of physical intimacy you want and do not want! Never compromise.

CHAPTER 10

Single and Defining Healthy Boundaries

110: What do you do in a dating relationship when two people have different standards concerning physical intimacy?

Always go with the more conservative standard. That way, even if one partner is disappointed, the other is not pressured into doing something that feels uncomfortable. Moreover, it is easier to change a no to yes, than a yes to no.

Talk. Talk about the reasons, experiences, perhaps even the bruises that have influenced your differing standards. Some of us have embraced our standards after reflection on our experience of the black-and-blue realities of adult dating. Some men come on strong only because they think they should act macho. Talking it through can convince them that their sexual bravado isn't necessary, that they can be themselves. Some single adults are intimacy-challenged and try to make up for time lost in a previous relationship or marriage. Talking about it can defuse the pressure and slow things down.

Third party the issue. You might want to go to a counselor or third party. The purpose is to gain an outsider's perspective.

Question promises. Some partners promise ecstasy and enjoyment and pleasure. Some cajole, "Try it, you'll like it." Maybe you will, maybe you won't. You are an adult. Know your boundaries and honor them.

Reject generalizations. "Everybody does it." Really? If there is only one couple or one individual in the universe that doesn't, the generalization is invalidated. David Scott wisely warns, "Never do something in order to fill someone else's expectations of you!" [1]

Test the level of commitment. Is an escalation of intimacy wise at this point in your relationship? Will it throw one aspect of your relationship out of balance? When a diamond cutter works with a raw diamond, that uncut precious gem is full of possibilities. Yet the cutter knows that one wrong tap with the chisel will mar that potential. When intimacy develops more quickly than the rest of the relationship, it can have the shattering effect of a poorly aimed chisel.

Give the relationship time. Why do you have to have this level of physical intimacy or this particular sexual behavior now? What is the big rush? A person who is going to make a great long-term friend or spouse is not going to override a partner's objections or hesitancy or try to fast-talk them into some sexual act(s) that they are not ready for.

Don't be manipulated or pressured. Ignore pleas (please!) like "Just this *once*" or "It won't hurt you." If the individual pouts or gets angry or abusive because you won't go along with his sexual agenda, little warning signals (like at railroad crossings) should go off in your brain (and in your soul)! You have one self-centered single adult on your hands. By ignoring your own values and feelings to "accommodate" another, you set a dangerous precedent in your relationship. The apostle Paul used a wonderful phrase, which although directed to the topic of getting married, is appropriate here. "But the [single adult] who has *settled the matter in his own mind*" "is under no compulsion but has control over his own will (and hormones) [1 Corinthians 7:37, NIV, italics authors].

111. How do I say no to sex, tactfully yet forcefully, with someone I want to have a good relationship with? He feels that by denying him sex I am denying or rejecting *him*.

No's have to be rehearsed before getting to a "no zone," a situation that calls for a choice. You've seen the T-shirt, "And just which part of no don't you understand?" Some no's need an exclamation mark, because many men have been conditioned to believe a no means either

"Maybe" or "A little more persuasion, please." Some women do play sexually hard-to-get, fearing that otherwise, they will be perceived as "easy." Just remember, you are not responsible for another's sexual needs—only your own.

If a single adult sulks or pouts, that individual is immature.

If a single adult badgers you, that individual is abusive.

If this single adult doesn't call again, the individual was a poor, *poor* marital risk.

But suppose you do see potential in the relationship, and you want to "hold" on to this person. Is it worth it? Does this person see anything in you besides the potential for a sexual good time? Is sex the only thread holding your relationship together? You are setting yourself up for some big-time pain if you use sexual intimacy as a glue.

The key to sexual decision making should be love and respect for the other person. If an adult cannot accept your no, it's time for a speedy exit from the relationship. A study of almost 400 single adults identified these motivations. Do any sound familiar?

• "Often when I need to feel loved, I have the desire to relate to my partner sexually because sexual intimacy really makes me feel warm and cared for."

• "I frequently want to have sex with my partner when I need him or her to notice me and appreciate me."

• "When I need to feel a sense of belongingness and connectedness, sex with my partner is really an important way of relating to him or her."

• "Often the most pleasurable sex I have is when it helps my partner forget about his or her problems and enjoy life a little more."

• "I enjoy having sex most intensely when I know that it will lift my partner's spirits and improve his or her outlook on life."

• "Often when my partner is feeling down on life or is unhappy about something, I like to try to make him or her feel better by sharing intimacy together sexually." [1]

112. Give us some helpful "No" saying techniques.

• Explain that you will say no before you get to the "no" zone.
• Use a "broken record" approach (No. No. No. No. No! NO! NO!!!)

• Be consistent. If you said yes yesterday, your no is going to be confusing today. Your partner could ask, "Well, yesterday we had sex. Why not today?"

• Talk about the reasons and emotions that underly your no.

• Reject the sex, not the person.

• Don't be badgered or worn down. Make it clear that your no is not negotiable.

• Remember "just this once" can have lifelong emotional and physical consequences, particularly if it is risky or unsafe behavior.

• Anticipate some "post-no" blues.

113. How do you deal with a strong sex drive, a really strong sex drive?

Be grateful you have a strong, healthy sex drive. Paul describes ingratitude in Romans 1, where he comments on adults who "neither glorified God nor gave thanks to him" (Romans 1:21) but "worshiped and served created things rather than the Creator" (1:25).

Admit the strength of your desires. Don't pretend that you have quiet, sleepy, shy hormones—whether you are divorced, widowed, or never-married, twenty-six or seventy-six.

Understand your sex drive. When the Psalmist observed, "I praise you because I am fearfully and wonderfully made; your works are wonderful, I know that full well" (Psalm 139:14), most single adults limit that declaration. "Perhaps the whole of my body is 'wonderfully made' but not my capacity for sexual expression." "Who, me?!" says Joe Average Single Adult with a poor mean dating frequency. "Fearfully and wonderfully made? Ha!"

Yet the Psalmist was no prude! The Creation narrative tells us that when the Creator looked on his various works he saw "that it was good" (Genesis 1:25). However, when he created humans, he elaborated on that critique of his handiwork: "God saw all that he had made, and it was *very* good" (1:31). The best translation is French: *viola!!!* God thinks that all of creation is wonderful, including our sexuality.

When was the last time—if ever—that you prayed, "O God, I thank you for these hormones . . . for sexual attraction . . . for my sexual feelings that remind me that I am male . . . that I am female? I thank you for the intricacies of arousal."

Discipline your sex drive. I am constantly on a diet. I have a biological appetite for what I need to keep my body going. Unfortunately, I have a *learned* appetite for donuts, ice cream, potato chips, candy, etc. (lots of etc.). So, every day I have to make reasonable choices about my appetite. That means asking, "Who is in control here: me or my hunger?" Instead of reaching for the Hostess Twinkies, I munch veggies. The same is true with sexual appetites. As a single adult with a full complement of hormones, I have to make daily choices about what to do about those impatient little guys with big ambitions who whine and sulk, "We never have any fun!"

It's common to hear someone say that you shouldn't say no because "suppressing your sexual desires can hurt you." But let's distinguish *suppression* from *repression*. *Repression* is denying your sexual drive, so that all your sexual thoughts and feelings are forced into your subconscious. You snarl like a determined lion tamer, cracking the whip: "Back! BACK! BACK!!!!"

Suppression, however, is when you know you have a sexual drive but you choose not to act on it. Suppression of sexual desires is a healthy, conscious action. Celibacy is rarely fatal—on the contrary. Healthy responsibility requires reflection. I must give honest attention to my sexual needs, interests, and choices. But I also discipline what sexual thoughts I entertain and make cozy. Some choices—even those suggested by friends—are not healthy for me. This goes back to Paul's advice about "settling it" in our "own minds." Paul added, "Do not conform any longer to the pattern of the world, but be transformed by the renewing of your mind. Then you will be able to test and approve what God's will is—his good, pleasing, and perfect will" (Romans 12:2).

Exercise your options. Choose not to use your sexual drives in ways that are driven by short-term motivations. So, some study of sexual behaviors says that 88.3 percent of single adults have done or do what you haven't or won't. Don't say what's wrong with me? Say yes to what is best.

Refuse to play the "Poor Celibate Me!" Symphony. It's too easy to whine, "I am missing out on all those orgasms." Don't be a sexual martyr.

114. Anything else? We are talking a *very* strong sex drive.

Matthew Kelly, who writes for Generation Xers, suggests that we consider making a prayerful "resolve." For example, Joshua, leader of the Israelites after Moses' death, was forced to action because his people were dabbling in the world views (particularly sexual views) of their neighbors. Joshua challenged them: "Choose for yourselves this day whom you will serve, whether the gods your forefathers served beyond the River, or the gods of the Amorites " (Joshua 24:15). In essence, Joshua was giving the old "You-can-do-what-you-want-to-do-but-here's-what-I-am-going-to-do" or the "What I would do *if* I were in your shoes" speech as he declared with great conviction, "But as for me and my household, we will serve the Lord."

I do not want to overspiritualize dealing with hormones and sex drives. On the other hand, I am not willing to ignore the spiritual component of sexuality, either. You have an opportunity to reject what the culture is telling you and to make a healthy long-term decision, a resolution: "This is what I have chosen to do with my sexual options."

Kelly, a single adult, explains the method that underlies his resolve. "Toward the end of my prayer time I try to make one resolution for that day. Sometimes I make the same resolution for days and even weeks. Once I have finished my time of prayer, I ask Jesus for the strength and the grace to live that resolution. Then at night before I go to bed I examine myself in the area of the resolution I made." [1]

I invite you to put down *Singles Ask*. Take a deep breath. Now just reflect back over the material you have read. What's going through your mind? Does this resolve sound a little unreal? Has anything in the text "leaped out" at you or nudged you?

Then pray this prayer or create your own: "Lord, this day, in this particular situation, given the circumstances as I understand them, I pray for wisdom to know your will, courage to do your will, strength to live with your will. But I do need you to remind me that your will is always for my good. Amen."

115. Is it true that, "If you don't use it you lose it!"

No. Many adults who married in their 40s, 50s, 60s, or even 80s—after years of being single—report great satisfaction with their sexual relationships. The old myths about the effects of aging on sexual performance are largely imaginary. While sexual desire in men usually peaks in early adulthood, men and women are capable of full creative sexual expression well into their 80s, unless some medical condition interferes (which could happen at any age). But many still use the myths to their advantage.

In this day, given the reality of AIDS and the connection between multiple sexual partners and cervical cancer,[1] it might be more accurate to say, "If you wrongly use it, you may lose it." And your life as well.

Older readers need to hear these words, "Sexuality for [older adults] is not a slippery slope to sexual inadequacy."[2] Moreover, despite the dis-ease in our culture with sexy senior adults, many seniors have learned the rich vocabulary of an intimacy that is not so frantic and intercourse-centered.

116. I seem to have no self-control. None. Zero. What can I do?

Join the club. Two thousand years ago, Paul wrote on self-control, "I do not understand what I do. For what I want to do, I do not do, but what I hate, I do. And if I do what I do not want to do, I agree that the law is good . . . For I have the desire to do what is good, but I cannot carry it out. For what I do is not the good I want to do; no, the evil I do not do—this I keep doing." Without going into specifics, Paul lamented, "How wretched I am" (Romans 7:15-19). Now you may not exactly feel wretched, but you get the point. You've probably turned over a "new leaf" at least a couple of times.

I doubt that you have *no* control. You can enhance self-control in these ways:

Admit your inability to say no. Hum the song, "I'm just a single who can't say no." Then try, "I'm just a single who *can* say no!"

Join an accountability group. Find some other single adults, or look up Sex Addicts Anonymous (a twelve-step group) who are experiencing the same struggles. Hold one another accountable for sexual choices. What you will find is great strength in knowing that others struggle, too. You are not the sexual Lone Ranger. Locate a meeting of Sex and Love Addicts Anonymous in your community. Many have found these groups to be safe places. Or explore your issues with a spiritual director or skilled counselor.

Commit to realistic no's. For example, if you want to stop masturbating, reduce the frequency between episodes. Extend the intervals between experiences. Alter your pre-masturbatory rituals or repertoires (we tend to be creatures of habit). It's easy to promise—even vow— Never again! But that makes the defeat more frustrating. Set an *achievable* goal and then increase it by increments. Or you can decide, "I am not going to have multiple partners or juggle multiple relationships." That's a physically and emotionally healthy decision.

Rehearse your no's. Practice the how and whys of saying no to sexual temptation *before* you enter the "no zone." To use a food analogy, all my good intentions might wear thin when the waiter waves the dessert tray in front of me and asks, "What will you have?" Practice saying no ahead of the big moment.

Keep trying. So you slip up. Renew your commitment to your resolve. Look at the prayer that Matthew Kelly offers. No one ever said "No-saying" is easy!

Don't beat yourself up. Some of us can get carried away with the "You!" talk. We are harder on ourselves after failing than we are on others. Give yourself a gift: give yourself a break.

117. Will God forgive me if I said yes and later asked for forgiveness? How many times will God forgive me?

Peter—who knew a lot about failure—once asked Jesus, "Lord, how many times shall I forgive my brother when he sins?" He hinted that he thought the answer ought to be "seven times", *max* (Matthew 19:21–22). Jesus popped his little bubble by answering "seventy-seven times." It was Jesus' ways of saying, "an unlimited number of times." If the Lord had such generous expectations of our forgiveness, we can certainly expect the scope of his mercy to be expansive.

Of course, God's grace is not a license for us to do whatever we please. That would be what a single adult theologian named Dietrich Bonhoeffer dismissed as "cheap grace."[1] Instead of worrying about how many times God will forgive us (we know that God forgives all who repent of their sins), we should be asking whether we are willing to request and receive God's intervention in our lives, to live as *forgiven* single adults. Remember, Jesus was toughest on the religious "holier-than-thous."

God wants to empower us to make good, healthy choices, choices with a future. The prayer of the great saint, Augustine (354–430), who lived a pretty wild sexual life, is too common among today's single adults: "Give me chastity and continence (sexual self-control) but not just now." My friend Father Joe Nassal says it this way, "God invites us to be holy *and* to be human." Forgiveness is the mortar for that invitation!

118. Isn't there still a double standard? Aren't men expected to have their "fun" and women supposed to be "Snow White"?

The Double Standard is alive and well, thank you very much, particularly among very religious people and people who perceive sexual issues in black and white! If anything, with the new sexually conservative (or cautious) breezes blowing through Singleland, women are held to an even *higher* standard. In the business world, if a woman is involved in an affair with a subordinate, she will pay a heavier price than would a man. At least among heterosexuals, there really are no male equivalents to taunts like "whore" and "slut," let alone "nymphomaniac." Indeed, the male term would be envious: *stud.*

Healthy relationships have standards—but not double standards. The Christian single cannot embrace a double standard. Paul, writing 2,000 years ago and no doubt aware of Jesus' compassionate encounter with the woman "caught in the act of adultery" (it takes two to *do* adultery—the male was allowed to get away), declared "There is neither Jew nor Greek, slave nor free, male nor female, for you are all one in Christ Jesus" (Galatians 3:28).

CHAPTER 11

Single
and Dealing with the
Past or Pasts

119. What is romantic grief?

Romantic grief, epidemic in Singleland, is the pain experienced when a significant romantic relationship ends. Every loss has an accompanying grief. Every loss requires a choice: Do I acknowledge the loss or do I attempt to ignore it? Most single adults attempt to ignore the grief by jumping immediately into a new romance. But romantic grief cannot be ignored. It's like the Midas muffler slogan: "You can pay me now or you can pay me later."

The romantic griever faces six basic choices.

1. *Recognize the loss.* That initially sounds strange but as Generation X says, "Duh!" Sometimes you are the last to know the relationship is over. There is no negotiating or bargaining; your love has moved on. It's tempting to hold the torch but as the cliché says, "It's time to wake up and smell the latte. This one is over!" Recognizing the loss is also about auditing the loss. We need to attempt to understand the loss, although that will not always be possible, especially when the loss ended in a big fight or verbal blowout that's left lots of wounds and emotional clutter. Some romantic losses remain lifelong mysteries.

2. *React to the loss.* As the spiritual goes, "You've got to walk that lonesome valley. You gotta walk it *by yourself.* Oh, nobody else can walk it for you . . . " You must dance with the loss and the pain,

especially if you are the receiver rather than the decider. Crying, restlessness, depression, and irritability normally accompany loss. You need to find ways to express your feelings; talking to a friend, journaling, and working out are positive choices.

You must also identify and mourn the secondary losses. As a couple you may have had a favorite cafe or restaurant. Now you cannot bring yourself to go there because of all the memories. While your primary loss is the loss of the relationship, the secondary loss is the great coffee. People initially feel the loss of a secure sexual expression with a person they love. Sure, you can find someone to have sex with or to date, but it is not the same.

For many single adults, a break-up brings the secondary loss of predictable dating. In this relationship, you knew your weekends were filled; no popcorn and rerun nights alone for you. Now, like many single adults, you sit by the phone with your DayTimer in one hand, the remote or a book in the other, with perhaps a nice mini-buffet of munchies nearby. Waiting. Waiting . . .

3. Recollect and reexperience the relationship. It is important to remember the relationship and the individual realistically. We tend to remember what supports our perception and not necessarily what really was. Some of us are like Jeff, a single adult described by Armistead Maupin: "Jeff has become increasingly prone to creative remembering. I don't mean that he lies; he just arranges the facts more artfully than anyone I've ever known. In fact, as in his work, he's not so much a writer as a rewriter, endlessly shifting the facts . . . I've learned to take his memories, as well as his projections, with a few zillion grains of salt."[1]

Most single adults practice "selective" memory. But from a more objective vantage point—our eyes red, noses sore, tear ducts depleted—we may be able to put some of the relationship into perspective. We may have pretended not to know that we wanted this individual to "rescue" us from yet another night with the chip & dip and remote control. We may have forgotten the temper or insensitivity or tardiness or insane driving. What habits have you conveniently overlooked?

Some of us hang in mediocre relationships, hoping that it is going to get better. Hoping that the relationship will turn some mystical corner and "Ahhhhhh: Bingo!" Sometimes it takes a friend to help us remember *realistically:* "Well, what about the time . . . ?" Frequently the friends prods us to ask: "What am I pretending not to remember about this relationship? This person?"

Sometimes dreams add a piece of the puzzle. We will need to talk it out with a trusted friend or counselor. After an airplane crash, the FAA conducts an audit asking, "What went wrong here?" so that it can be avoided in the future. Single adults need to do their own audit. Sometimes, remembering realistically is painful because we cannot rely on the luxury of saying, "He broke up with me, etc." We have to ask: What did *I* contribute to the failure of this relationship?

This can be especially difficult for widow/ers. Some marriages were not "that good" in reality, despite the public facade. Some widow/ers feel guilty that they do not regret the death of the spouse or the ending of the marriage. Some grieve for what the relationship was *not.* Remembering realistically is a big step toward healing.

4. *Relinquish your old attachments to the person.* Perhaps it's time to "box up" or even jettison some of the mementos and souvenirs of the relationship. Put away the pictures. Sometimes a piece of clothing or jewelry or some object prompts painful nostalgia: "Oh, I remember when she gave this to me . . . when we bought this." Such items are called "linking objects" because they link us to our romantic pasts rather than to our future.

5. *Readjust or reinvest.* Life goes on—even when you think it won't. Things will never be the same but things can be better. It's time to move adaptively and creatively into the new world without forgetting the old.

6. *Beware of the temptation to use substances or experiences to alter your grief or to numb yourself from the pain of the loss.* Some single adults or newly-singled adults use alcohol, drugs (illegal or prescription), food (particularly comfort food), work, indiscriminate sex, a premature romantic relationship, shopping, even obsessive exercise. *Any substance or experience used to take away the pain or to make you forget the romantic loss only complicates the grief.*

120. Isn't just going out and dating the best way to get over this loss?

Yes, if you didn't get enough "grief" the first time. What you really need is a "time out" from dating in order to do your grief work thoroughly. Even great athletes need a little time on the bench to catch their breath. Don't think of it as a penalty but as an opportunity to reflect, to reassess, and to reposition yourself.

Grief specialist Alan Wolfelt suggests that "women grieve, men replace."[1] That's especially true with romantic grief. The temptation is to say, "I'll show 'em!," to jump into a "making up for lost time" or "rubbing it in" relationship, hoping that friends will report back to your ex, "Oh, she has forgotten all about you. She's dating this incredible hunkman!" or "He's out with a different babe every night." That's hidden-agenda dating, which uses another person for our emotional agendas. It amounts to romantic coercion.

Consider this temporary romancelessness a fasting from dating, a personal leave to do some necessary soul work and heart repair.

121. How can I healthfully deal with this loss?

During this moratorium on dating when you do your pseudomonkhood stint, Dr. Wolfelt suggests paying serious attention to the following tasks.

Express the reality of the loss to someone. All single adults have had a slobbering mini-fit during which we wake a friend in the middle of the night, moaning, "It's over . . . I've been consigned to the romantic junk heap. *Again!*" We've all been comforted by hearing from a friend, "Poor baby . . . " It helps to know someone still thinks we're a valued part of the human race. And it helps to hear the promise, "You'll feel better in the morning (or in six months)." Bartenders have been known to turn into something of an "Ann Landers" for heart-broken customers, particularly men.

Sometimes, we need to express our hopes and disappointments verbally. I had so hoped this one was The One! Now, it's "Go directly to (romance) jail! Do not pass Go! Do not collect $200! Back to square one, romantically." Elizabeth Kuster is right when she insists, "Let's face it: Breakups . . . rank right up there with car wrecks, menstrual cramps, and really bad infomercials." [1]

Tolerate the emotional suffering while nurturing yourself physically and emotionally. "Tolerate?!," you protest. "I've been through four boxes of Kleenex already. My nose looks like Rudolph's!" You've got to tolerate it. Just put up with some level of romantic blues while making good decisions for your future. Sometimes the only way through it is *through* it!

Convert the incidence from presence to memory. While there is value in talking it out, there comes a time when you *have* talked it out—only you just don't know it. Sometimes, our friends are "listened out." The clue is when you check your answering machine, hoping your ex called ("Oh, baby, what a fool I've been . . . take me back!"). Instead you hear your friend's voice: "You've got to move on!!! Get A Romantic Life!!!"

It's like a Walkman. You have a favorite song and hit the play button, then rewind, then play. Over and over. Or maybe it's more like a VCR. You hit the "pause" button and freeze the painful moments on your screen. You advance the loss, frame by painful frame. Day after day, you sift through the romantic ruins, like veteran Detective Lt. Colombo, hoping to uncover a clue to what went wrong, hoping to trip over the missing link of explanation. Yes, the "Woe is me!" thoughts will sneak back, but you can choose not to welcome them with open arms. You set the timer. Okay, I'll give you two minutes. But only two minutes.

Reconcile with this loss. You do not "get over it." Instead, you will look for a "let go" moment in which you say, "What's the life lesson in this?" You reflect on that and you eventually reconcile with this loss. Time may prove that it wasn't you. Hopefully, you will be wiser after this lap around the romantic track. Be good to the now wiser *you* that will enter into the next relationship.

122. I want revenge! Sweet revenge.

Plotting revenge should be at the top of your list of things *not* to do after a romantic loss. Revenge cannot be steered or guided; one never knows its ultimate destination or consequences. Someone said, "Living well is the best revenge." It's so tempting to say, "I want to hurt you as much as you've hurt me." Country music stars have gotten rich singing on that theme. Yet, Hebrew wisdom—and if anyone knows about the temptation to retaliate, the Jewish people do—offers some words of wisdom and warning: "The smallest revenge will poison the soul." [1]

123. How much should I ask about my partner's past?

Sing along with me: "Getting to know you, getting to know *all* about you." Knowing the words to this Rodgers and Hammerstein classic is essential these days. Everyone comes with a past. Admittedly, some have a lot more colorful pasts.

Has your partner been married before? If so, consider talking to the ex(es) or friends of the ex(es). Beware of the multiply-married individual who says that he/she was the innocent victim *every* time. Remember, if two and two do not add up to four, you have a problem. My friend, Diane Swaim, who has counseled many, reminds us, "Past is history . . . unless it affects the present." [1]

Has your partner been forthright with disclosing accurately their financial history? Are you dating someone with a financial history or credit rating that is going to complicate your life? Your dreams? What is their debt? Are they paid up on alimony and child support? Have they declared bankruptcy? If you want more excitement in your life, marry someone with IRS troubles, and then file a joint–financial return, without reading it. Or marry someone who is always bailing out family members. Or marry someone who always has a big deal "cooking" that will make millions!

How much do you know about your partner's sexual past? According to former Surgeon General C. Everett Koop, any time you are sexually intimate with someone, you are sexually intimate with every person they have been sexually intimate with in the last seven years, plus every person those individuals have been sexually intimate with. [2] The consequences may not be AIDS, but herpes, or chlamydia, or human papillomavirus (HPV)—certain subtypes of which increase a woman's risk of developing cervical cancer. [3]

Admittedly, some people have reformed and turned over a new leaf when it comes to sexual choices. They have practiced "safer sex," well, most of the time, or almost all of the time, but maybe not every time!

"Safer sex" guidelines make sense for *sustained* behavioral change but will not work for sporadic change or "just this time."

What do you know about your partner's emotional past? Some single adults have battled substance abuse and addiction. You need time and you need awareness of the issues involved with recovery before you even think about saying, "I do." Ask yourself: Do I have enough data to make a reasonable and intelligent choice? What warning signal or hint of difficulty am I ignoring? I counsel single adults, "Better to have a bruised heart now than a broken heart later." Alas, some did not listen to this advice and now have incredibly mangled hearts. A troublesome past is all the more reason for serious premarital counseling with a competent counselor.

124. My father molested me from the time I was thirteen until I went to college. He told me never to tell and that, besides, "No one would believe" me. How do I forgive him? How will I ever tell a prospective mate that my dad took my virginity?

Realize that you are not the only one to whom this has happened. One study disclosed that 18 percent of women and about 10 percent of men report that they were abused as children (women generally by a family member, men by a nonfamily party).[1]

Realize that someone will believe you, and that forgiveness is not simply ignoring what happened. In some traditions, it has been too easy to forgive—particularly for people who get confused by the meaning of the commandment, "Honor father (for doing the incest?) and mother (for looking the other way?)." You will need to go through a process of dealing with this ugly reality and attempting to find meaning in it before you can experience real forgiveness.

Find a skilled counselor who has worked with abuse cases. Realize that this is not a problem to be "fixed" in three visits. Through a trust relationship with a counselor, you can peel away the layers of this experience and the memory, and slowly, over time, make room for healing.

Pray for courage to initiate the process and the courage to continue in the process. Emotional ups and downs are part of the process. If you confront the perpetrator, he may deny it. So, you may never hear words you want to hear, "Yes, I did hurt you and I want your forgiveness." But by beginning to process your pain and by confronting the abuser, you give him an opportunity to deal with *his* pain. In a significant number of cases, the abuser was also abused. By getting help, you will avoid passing this on to yet another generation.

For some individuals, one consequence of unresolved sexual abuse may be singleness. Some have chosen to deal with abuse by gaining great amounts of weight or being intentionally unattractive to hide their sexuality; others drift into deep depressions and lower-than-low self-esteem. Some can—or will—never trust again. But you do not have to keep this pain in a sealed plastic bag. You can begin the incredible journey to healing. Remind yourself of the Japanese proverb, "the longest journey begins with the first step."

The facts of our losses may never change, but the stories that we make out of those losses do. At some point, you will have to decide if and how to tell your story to a date or a person you plan to marry. This story does impact your sexual interaction or the potential for sexual interaction, and it is only fair for a partner to know some of it, at least.

You may want to consider writing a letter of confrontation. This could be to an incest perpetrator or to anyone who has sexually or emotionally violated you. The letter contains these components:

• A factual account of what happened without any evaluation, from your perspective. It should be as detailed as possible with dates, places, and description of the incidents.

• A description of how you feel about the experiences described. For instance, "I feel dirty; I feel less than a woman/a man."

• A projection of what you want. For instance, "I want you to admit that this happened, to seek counseling, and to ask for my forgiveness."

Mail the letter registered or certified so you will know that it was received.

This type of letter has been helpful, particularly for victims of date rape, because it gives the victim the experience of "doing something constructive" about it. It could give both the abuser and the victimized a whole new perception of how a particular behavior was perceived and the consequences.[2]

125. I want to date virgins and marry a virgin. But everyone I seem to meet is not a virgin.

Are you a virgin? If you "prize" virginity (you said you want to date virgins and marry a virgin), are you able to offer that to the woman you date? There's a lot of hypocrisy about virginity these days, particularly by males who cling to the remnants of the double standard.

By this point in our lives, in our sexual stories, most of us have regrets; some of us have gigantic regrets, one of which may be the loss of virginity or the particular circumstances in which virginity was lost. A dozen times a day we may say, "*If only . . .*" Some of us fearfully keep the secret: "If anyone ever finds out about this . . ." Unconditional love is pretty rare in Singleland. Apparently, you are not willing to offer unconditional love. I have to tell you this: You will miss out on a lot of great non-virgins who could have been a great spouse.

126. What is a "promiscuous virgin?" That sounds like an oxymoron.

"Promiscuous virgin" may sound like an oxymoron, but it is a reality for a lot of single adults, particularly of the conservative stripe. The reality is that, with a prolonged adolescence, a lot of single adults have drawn plenty of "lines in the sand" sexually. Many who consider it their religious obligation to forgo sexual intercourse have mastered a lot of strategies for reaching/giving orgasm *without* actual vaginal penetration.[1]

Many "technical virgins" pride themselves on never being vaginally penetrated (or in the case of males, vaginally penetrating) but wax eloquently about not going "all the way" or loudly espouse the values of "Just Say No!" When I hear that slogan I always want to ask, "No . . . to *what?*" Technical virgins, male and female, know a dozen ways to reach orgasm without penetration and therefore avoid "loss of virginity."[2] Meanwhile, a single adult who said the premature yes and has lived to regret it often feels condemned or second-class because of the loss of their virginity.

The Gospel offers a radical challenge to such thinking by critiquing its emphasis on purity. For instance, the woman at the well (who had a rather checkered sexual history: five husbands and living with a man at the time) was invited by Jesus to taste forgiveness, to be part of his kingdom (John 4). How much more does he want to set us free from sacrosanct, phony, legalistic virginity? To the outright ex-virgin and the promiscuous virgins and self-righteous technical virgins (as well as the insecure types who have to "have" a virgin to marry—particularly hypocritical males who have helped women lose their virginity), to all of these Jesus says, "Go and sin no more" (John 4:1–4), which I think translates, don't let your past ruin a perfectly great redeemed future.

127. What is secondary virginity?

Secondary virginity, second virginity, or neo-virginity are terms describing a growing recognition, especially among single adults of faith, that an individual can take responsibility over sexual choices and with God's help redeem previous poor choices. Admittedly, individuals do not physically become a virgin again, but spiritually and emotionally, they do. When Nicodemus came to Jesus doubting that a person could be "born again," he had the same skepticism as you might in reading this. "Surely he cannot enter a second time into his mother's womb to be born!" (John 3:4) Jesus explained that he was speaking of a spiritual rebirth. So, secondary virginity is a spiritual virginity. One advocate describes it this way, "A sexually experienced man or woman can renew or reclaim virgin status by making the decision to discontinue further sexual activity until marriage."[1] Admittedly, one must define what is included in "sexual activity." Does it mean only no intercourse or does it mean no intimacy leading to orgasm?

128. How does one deal with "unresolved" relationships such as a person not forgiving you? Or not wanting to work things out? What do you do when the other person won't even talk to you?

Many single adults have heard the line, "I don't ever want to see you or hear from you again!," maybe even "as long as I live!" Many of us have had doors slammed in our faces, have heard the thud of a phone in our ears. We have had people whom we once loved, who once loved us (or said they did) turn and walk away from us. We have tried to make amends. We have tried to clean up the jagged edges of our hearts. Some of us have dodged emotional hand grenades tossed in our direction because we wanted healthy closure on a romantic loss. But reconciliation takes two. There comes a time when you have to say, "I've done the best I can" or "I've tried."

Some of us may not *want* closure because that would force us to admit things for which we need to ask forgiveness. Or because we would have to recognize grudges we need to let go of. As long as we believe, "It's *all your* fault!" we are relieved from having to own up to our own relational inadequacies.

One of the hardest phone calls I've ever made was on New Year's Eve to a person I had deeply hurt. I wanted to start the new year knowing I had asked for (and hopefully received) forgiveness. I prayed for courage and that the individual would hear me out. (Yes, I also prayed that this individual would not be home.) I began my conversation, "There is something I need to say to you." Silence. "Are you still there?" I asked. "Still here." I said what I had rehearsed, and some things I had not rehearsed. And I received a gracious forgiveness. I want to believe that rehearsing my words helped. But more importantly, I believe that asking God to help me paved the way for a quantum leap in emotional healing.

Another way is the computer conversation. Sit at a computer keyboard and create a conversation with the individual. Certainly you could manipulate the conversation to benefit yourself or to insert five words: "Forgive me . . . you are forgiven." But if you take this forgiveness exercise seriously, you may get into the head and heart of the wounded person. Amazingly, this works.

Another method is to write what you need to say into a letter. It may be important to let some time pass between drafts. Do you send the letter? Perhaps. Perhaps not. For some, writing the letter is sufficient. Thorough confession is good for the soul. Cleaning up unfinished debris from previous relationships prepares for a new relationship.

129. How much do I need to know about my spouse-to-be's finances before I marry?

Everything, if you want the relationship to work. There are financial opportunists footloose in Singleland and you could have volunteered as the bull's-eye. "Here's my stock portfolio, my savings accounts, my CDs—abuse me!" You don't have to be rich to be taken—you just have to have more money or assets than the opportunist (and be somewhat naive). These days many rely on a prenuptial arrangement, especially when the individuals are older or have significant assets or children from previous marriages or relationships.

• *You need to know about liabilities and potential liabilities.* Litigation, bankruptcy, liens, or real estate may still need to be sold and divided with an ex.

• *You need to know about financial habits.* Has your "good time" dating been floated on a credit card? Then you can expect to help pay off the debt incurred in being wined-and-dined. Love those roses and expensive restaurants, eh? Well, you may help pay those off after you marry if the items were charged on a credit card with a high credit ceiling.

• *You need to know of unpaid child support or alimony or promises.* Promises made to children in a previous marriage(s): I'll pay for your college, I'll buy you a car when you graduate, etc. could complicate your economic lifestyle, too.

• *You need to know about the credit rating and credit history.*

• *You need to know of unpaid or underpaid taxes.* This is especially true of individuals who are self-employed and who pay quarterly.

• *You need to know of insurability, particularly for health coverage.* Marriage should not be a financial grab bag. Financial surprises have ambushed too many. Your spouse-to-be's finances become your finances in the eyes of the law. Creditors and bill collectors can interrupt romantic moods with a "When are you going to pay up?" If you want real excitement, get romantic with someone who owes money to a loan shark or a vengeful ex with a great lawyer. Your money can flow awfully fast into an ex's (or their children's) piggy bank.

There's nothing wrong with being financially black-and-blue, particularly after a divorce or two, or a downsizing, or a business failure. But hiding or failing to fully disclose one's financial picture may be grounds for divorce via fraud. In some states, it is fraud. Guard your heart and your checkbook and be honest.

CHAPTER 12

Single and Asking about Nonmarital Sex

130. What is so wrong with premarital sex between two consenting adults, considering the eroding status and strength of marriage?

Instead of asking, "Why not have premarital sex?" ask, "Why should two adults have premarital sex and thus contribute to the eroding status and strength of marriage?" Why not ask, "What's so right about nonmarital sex?" Once upon a time, as late as the mid-1960s, most nonmarital sex was, in fact, preceremonial, before the big "I do." These days premarital sex is not really the issue. Most sex between single adults is *nonmarital*—sex without a commitment to marry, sex without any intent to marry.

A card passed in to me during a question-and-answer time—"I firmly believe it is possible and natural that sex, regardless of marriage, when conducted with love and respect, should not be condemned." But who's condemning? I am questioning. I get nervous when a single adult wants to "conduct" sex. I have "conducted" research projects, but I cannot imagine intercourse as something you *conduct*. Sadly, some premarital or nonmarital sex between single adults is little more than mutual masturbation: let's "get off" together. It is really not intercourse, which as Webster defines it, is an "exchange especially of thoughts or feelings (communion) or physical sexual contact between individuals."[1] Single adults are rarely *intercoursing*—they're "having sex." It is little more than a genital workout. Maybe that is why the infamous F word has become so common. The spectacular is too easily stripped of the particular. "Communion" sounds too spiritual, too sacred. So single adults have sex and see it as nothing special. One woman noted, "The experience of my generation suggests people rarely get what they are looking for from premarital sex, unless it is purely sexual. When it's too available, sex itself loses its meaning."[2]

You're correct in noting the eroding status of marriage. Too many marriages, these days, are little more than economic partnerships. Many of the bad marriages and divorces that contribute to the high statistics involve people who, a generation ago, argued, "What's so wrong with premarital sex? or living together?"

It is so tempting to sacrifice your future on the altar of the immediate. If Bill and Karen decide to have sex outside of marriage, there is no way Bill can give himself totally, without reserve, to Karen in that moment. Instead of being naked, he's being *mostly* naked, from a spiritual viewpoint. The orgasm—particularly the male's—cannot be held back in such moments. Men willingly give up their semen but not their hearts. It is not "making special" but "making ordinary." Bill suspects—perhaps even knows—that the relationship has no real future; despite her longings, Karen may suspect that the relationship is not going to the make it to the finish line.

So each partner withholds something of themselves, keeps some of themselves "in escrow," in order to have a "starter kit" to launch the next relationship. Even in the moment of sexual surrender, each fights to the hold back feelings or words of tenderness, which could be misinterpreted. Jennifer Grossman nailed it when she observed, "I see a pattern among my girlfriends—when they sleep with men, they cry. Sleeping with a man you've known for a week is such an 'almost.' It's almost what you want—but a chasm away from what you really need."[3] How many times have you settled for an "almost" relationship.

131. So, what motivates single adults to have sex?

Here are some rationales for sexual intercourse:
- to seek emotional valuing by one's partner;
- to express feelings of emotional value for one's partner;
- to obtain relief from stress or from negative psychological states;

- to provide one's partner with nurturance or stress relief;
- to enhance one's sense of power;
- to experience the power of one's sexual partner;
- to experience pleasure;
- to procreate.[1]

Take a moment and reflect on the list. Do you recognize your sexual motives on the list? Rank the list in the order of your own motivations. What other motivations would you add to this list?

These days there are still good reasons *not* to have sex outside of marriage. Ellen Dissanayake, an anthropologist, argues that our de-ritualizing culture doesn't know how to make and keep important things special. We insert the word "lite" in front of everything from beer to cheesecake to sex to ritual. In *Homo Aestheticus,* she insists that we should be "*making special,*" which she insists is a "fundamental human proclivity or need."[2] Lots of us in this single season have made sex pretty ordinary, "no big deal." Yet sex ought to be *special! Very special!*

Nonmarital sex can be enjoyable (according to the orgasm Richter scale). Maybe it can be "conducted" by some without emotional damage. But can *you* engage in it (or be engaged in it) without risk? Is it the best choice for you at this time in your life? Are you tempted to think, "Now *maybe* he will like me? or love me? or commit to me? or marry me?"

Nonmarital sex is less than the best. It separates the physical act of intercourse from the total giving that God intended. It's less than the best because it is clutching after a partial good—a "feel better" orgasm rather than the deep stirring of the soul.

132. If you don't have sex before marriage, how will you know if you are sexually compatible? How do you know you are getting a partner who really knows how to make love?

Sexual compatibility and comparison are two burdens for today's single adults. Skimming through a magazine in the grocery checkout line, you find the results of the latest poll about sexual satisfaction. Headlines on magazine covers promise better orgasms, more orgasms, "Bigger Os in 30 Days!" So how do *you* compare, Mr. or Miss Average Single Adult? We often walk out of the grocery story feeling less sexually confident and even envious of others.

In most nonmarital sex, the participants are "performing" and, in essence, auditioning for a place in someone's life or memory. Going through both partners' minds is an insistent questioning: "*How am I doing? How am I performing? Could I please hear, 'O baby, you are the greatest!'?*"

So they really aren't fully "there," in the present moment. Like contestants in an Olympic event, they await the judges' scores: 8.8, 8.1, 7.3! (or lower). In the process, there also is a lot of angling for the satisfaction of *my* needs or my sexual wants. Sometimes, it's as crass as "you scratch my back, and I'll scratch yours. But, if you don't mind, *my* back first!" So many single adults have a fixation with techniques. As a result, we settle for sexual relations rather than sexual relation*ships*.

Sure, some single adults are "good in bed" (they've had lots of practice) and others may be technique-challenged. But do you really want to be orgasmed by a "technician" who knows "the moves"? Would such a partner even notice let alone nurture your soul?

Sex has the most potential to be satisfying and deeply soul-stirring in a loving, committed relationship. Marriage provides a safe environment in which those less-than-ideal physical experiences (sex can be lousy—you do know that, don't you?) can be accepted as a part of life. So, this night wasn't 9.4—maybe more like 4.9. But, in marriage, partners are comforted by the reality there will be other moments.

No one is always stimulated, always ready, always unstressed, and always in a good mood. Each of those factors can affect sexual experience. Within the committed context of love, forgiveness, and acceptance, a bad day or a bad sexual experience is not the end of the world or the relationship!

Finally, sexual proficiency can be learned within marriage. People in the Jewish tradition recognize the importance of *mekom hanekhama*, or "place of comfort."[1] What most single adults need—and what marriage offers—is a safe place to encourage the full expression of love. I need a *mekom batuah*, or safe place to be me, to be naked, to be vulnerable. Outside of marriage, you seek safety in a dangerous laboratory. I am deeply moved by the words about our first parents, in their *mekom batuah*, the Garden of Eden, "The man and his wife were both naked, and they felt no shame" (Genesis 2:25). I want that same reality for myself and for all single adults, but it cannot happen by stripping sexual intimacy of its specialness and reducing it to ordinariness.

133. Are there any exceptions to "no sex" before marriage? What if you are in love, but have to wait for things to the work out, say, financially, or for the divorce to be final?

You're not even married yet, and you're already asking about exceptions!

A correlation exists between premarital or nonmarital sexual standards and fidelity in marriage. Look ahead a few months or a few years. Will you or your future spouse someday be asking, "What if . . . ?" about marital unfaithfulness? "Of course not!" you answer. But think about it. Why do you feel so desperate *now*? Are you sexually frustrated? Do you feel the need to physically symbolize your love? Every marriage goes through tough times, and so will yours. "Not tonight. I have a headache (or a heartache)" will be part of your marital vocabulary. Yes, it will! What happens when you're pregnant? Or when either you or your spouse finds yourself working in Los Angeles and living in New Jersey? Or when you "fall out of love" for a while? What happens when conflicts, schedules, and illnesses interfere with your sex life? Will you be as certain *then* about your ability to the be faithful as you are now? If you violate one set of sexual norms, you are likely to look for a "Yes, but" exception clause in another!

134. What about living together?

Some would argue that 3.7 million couples can't be wrong. "Living together without benefit of clergy," or cohabitation, is a growing phenomenon. Many believe that the skyrocketing numbers have to be taken seriously: 523,000 in 1970; 1.56 million in 1980; 3.7 million in 1996.[1] Some marriage authorities believe that we have a three-tier premarital system:

dating—engagement — — *living together* — — ? — *marriage*

Still, I strongly discourage living together or "playing married" as a viable option for a healthy future. Couples who live together have the same problems as married adults: they complain about sexual incompatibility, finances, household chores, and fears of pregnancy, but with a heightened—at times, intense—fear of breaking up. Frequently, one partner pushes to marry when it appears that the relationship is threatened. Look at these realities of live-ins.

• Cohabiting couples who marry—even those who already have children—are 33 percent more likely to divorce than couples who don't live together before marriage.

• Live-in boyfriends are more likely to beat their partners than husbands are.[2]

Moreover, the transitory, nonbinding nature of a live-in relationship also breeds all kinds of questions: "Will my partner be there for me? What will it take to push my partner over the edge? Is he/she seeing someone on the side? What if I find myself alone, again?" Does this seem like a relationship that will foster trust?

A live-in relationship may seem like a simple (and financially attractive) solution to the need for intimacy. But it tends to diminish the things that make real intimacy possible: trust, commitment, and vulnerability to another person.

135. Why do we have to get married? What difference does a piece of paper make?

Anthropologist Ellen Dissanayake says that you need to make important things special—including your commitment. Whether it is a church wedding or a tiny gathering in the woods, you need to recognize the deliberateness of what you are doing.[1] You need to create a ritual that says: "What we are doing is serious and we recognize that our relationship has embraced a new intensity." You need family and friends to witness and applaud that commitment.

Marriage provides you with family and community recognition of your commitment to each other:

• for better or worse;
• for richer or poorer;
• in sickness and in health;
• to love and to cherish;
• until death us do part.

In the marriage ceremony friends, relatives, the church, the community, and the state acknowledge your commitment and promise to be there to provide resources to help your marriage, especially in the tough times. Ellen Fein and Sherrie Schneider add one obvious reality: "Living with him may prevent you from dating others and meeting someone you're crazy about, so how smart is it?" [2] You will sooner or later smack your forehead and say: "I could have had a *real* relationship!" If you live together for a period of time and then break up, you will painfully discover what difference that "piece of paper" makes. You will have little protection, little guidance about determining who owns what, little recourse if you get the short end of the deal.

136. Isn't it better to live together until you are sure that you are compatible?

When you have talked to enough people who have been wounded by live-in relationships (or have talked to their children), you discover that a breakup can be as devastating as a divorce. Perhaps it is even worse, because there are few formal structures to offer you support.

Marriage is an unfolding process. The longer you live together, the more you learn about each other. Compatibility is not so much a state of being as it is a decision. You learn to live with inconsistencies and fears, excess weight, bad breath, irritating habits, and a zillion other realities that you don't see in the movies or TV sitcoms. Only marriage offers a level of trust and affirmation that can provide love and acceptance in a sexual relationship in spite of circumstances working to topple it.

No, you will probably not be castigated for living together. At most your parents and grandparents will be somewhat uncomfortable; your mother may not let you sleep together "under her roof." But you will not be saying yes to what is best. You will be cheating yourself out of an opportunity to say and hear "Come grow old with me." That may not seem important at the moment—especially in our moment-centered society—but someday it might. A live-in relationship can never be more than an imitation of the real thing.

Dr. Barbara De Angelis, who has extensive experience counseling live-ins, offers three arguments against living together:

1. You can destroy the relationship by expecting too much from it while it's still developing. "Living together before your relationship has reached a significant level of commitment, maturity, and emotional stability can actually speed up the disintegration of your relationship."

2. You can become emotionally lazy—for example, avoiding conflict to "keep the peace" so that you never confront the issues.

3. You can avoid furthering your commitment to one another. The old saying, "Why buy the cow when you can get the milk for free?" is not inappropriate. "If a man is living with you and enjoying the benefits of domestic life, he has no reason to ask you to marry him." [1]

Two final observations. Sooner or later many single adults will seriously consider living together or will be de facto living together (you leave a toothbrush there, you have lots of clothes and lots of your "stuff" there). You will be tempted to argue: (1) we can save money by paying only one rent (which can help us save money for getting married/reducing our debts), (2) we can spend more time together and not spend so much time commuting, or (3) you can "keep an eye" on your partner, whom you fear losing. Before you so much as move a toothbrush, ponder this: live-in relationships primarily benefit the man. Reread that sentence, please, whether you are male or female. Is imbalance in a relationship really what you want, even if it benefits you?

Before you decide, you need to the have The Conversation about how you see the live-in arrangement: as a test; or as a quasi-commitment toward marriage. Otherwise, sooner or later, you are going to the hear or say these words, "I *never* said I was going to marry you!" If you do move in, set the wedding timer to six months.

If either of you is a single parent, the other will become a de facto parent to the children. You need to carefully think through before assuming this responsibility.

Definitely think twice, no, thrice, about letting someone who is going through a divorce or separation or has lost their job "move in" with you. You are volunteering for major grief. Give this decision lots of time for reflection. Repeatedly ask: "Is this the best for me? For the relationship? If this does not work out, how will I cope?" Never rush into a quick decision to live together.

CHAPTER 13

Single and Asking about Masturbation, Oral Sex, and Anal Sex

137. How common is masturbation?

Few issues have provoked as much debate and confusion among people of faith and single adults as "The Big M"! In hundreds of the question-and-answer sessions I have led, this question has always been one of the three most commonly asked questions. In some settings, I have heard the air sucked out of the room when I read the question aloud. To break the tension, I often answer, "I take a hands-off approach to that topic."

Most people masturbate. Reread that sentence. The question is, how do they feel about masturbating and how do they feel about their typical masturbation sequence, especially if it involves fantasy, or what Jack Morin calls "memorability factors"—those "characteristics which make any erotic event stand out" in the memory. Many divorced or widowed persons, or anyone coming out of a sexual relationship, may recall erotic episodes from their sexual "peak" experiences during masturbation.[1] It's an erotic "remember when."

Research suggests that approximately 92 percent of males and 58 percent of females have masturbated to orgasm at some point in their life.[2] However, these statistics may be low because many people are reluctant to admit to masturbating. ("*What? Me?*")

My one-on-one conversations with single adults indicate that many are shamed by this common occurrence in their lives. Few issues have caused more unnecessary emotional and spiritual grief. Many single adults think "I am the *only* single adult in the whole world who masturbates!" Some see masturbation as some big problem to be fixed or mastered. But masturbation is common, and in the age of AIDS, will become even more common. Five percent of the women and 7 percent of the men in one major study masturbated because they were afraid of AIDS or STDs.[3]

PERCENTAGE OF MALES, BY AGE, WHO MASTURBATE DAILY OR SEVERAL TIMES A WEEK[4]

%	Age
24	under 26
28	27–38
23	39–50
32	over 50

Moreover,
- 61 percent of married men report masturbating (since marriage).[5]
- Of Americans aged eighteen to fifty-nine, 60 percent of the men and 40 percent of the women masturbated in the previous year.[6]
- Seven out of ten men in their late twenties masturbated in the last year.[7] Nearly half of women in their thirties masturbated.[8]
- Lots of married people are masturbating: 85 percent of the men and 45 percent of the women in one major study had masturbated in the past year.[9]

So, it's common. You are not the Lone Ranger.

138. Isn't masturbation a male thing?

No. "If every person who masturbates were to die of shame," Irma Kurtz says, " we'd certainly live on a sparsely populated planet."[1] Women generally begin masturbating later than men; in fact, many do not discover masturbation until after marriage—particularly a marriage in which the husband does/did not pay attention to the sexual needs of the wife. Because so few men have a clue, many sex therapists now recommend that women explore their bodies and learn to masturbate and then teach their spouses or lovers the intricacies of the female arousal system.[2]

In one large study of almost 900 nurses, 92.5 percent had masturbated. However, that study found a significant link between church attendance and attitudes on masturbation. Women who frequently attended church were more likely to report being ashamed to admit engaging in masturbation and to feel guilty about masturbating.[3]

It is not a "guy" thing but many single adults feel it is a "juvenile" thing to be overcome, perhaps because of the residue of unresolved feelings from adolescence—especially those who never anticipated being single at this age.[4]

139. What does the Bible say about masturbation?

Nothing. Some people misquote the ancient story of Onan as a proof-text: "See what happens to people who masturbate!" (Genesis 38:6–10). Onan lived in an era when a male was expected to impregnate his sister-in-law if his brother died (the semen of brothers was considered to be the same because it traced back to the same father). However, rather than fulfill this social responsibility, Onan ejaculated "on the ground"—a socially and spiritually outrageous act for an Israelite. In Catholic circles, the sin of masturbation is called "Onanism," which is one reason you've never met anyone named Onan. In Catholic theology, any sexual act that is not "open to procreation" is sin. For many ex-Catholic single adults, this teaching remains a residual influence in their lives.[1]

Until recently, many Christian traditions have been less than forth-right, preferring a stern or embarrassed, "Don't do it." Some have argued that, since any sexual act outside of marriage is condemned because it is not in a committed, caring relationship, it makes sense to be somewhat condemnatory toward masturbation because the motivation is self-pleasure. In many traditions, the rule of thumb on any human sexual behavior has been, "If it feels good, just say no!"

In previous generations, men who consorted with prostitutes were told, "Well, at least you didn't practice 'the secret sin!'" (a euphemism for masturbation).

Although the Bible does not directly deal "chapter-and-verse" with masturbation, that has not stopped zealous religious leaders from condemning it. In response, Archibald Hart, a psychologist-theologian at Fuller Theological Seminary, observed, "I do not believe that masturbation itself is morally wrong or, to use the language of circles I move in, *sinful.* The biblical references most commonly cited as condemning masturbation are often taken out of context or are cited by those who have other agendas." Simply, "the outright and unequivocal condemnation of masturbation without regard to the circumstances causes more problems than it solves . . . The more we condemn it, the more we keep it secret and private."[2] And the more guilty we feel about masturbating.

140. But don't masturbation and lust go together? How can you masturbate without fantasizing or lusting?

Many single adults insist that they cannot masturbate to orgasm without "props" like fantasy or pornography—either video or still. Others assume that lust is like the booster rockets used to launch shuttles into space—it ignites the arousal process. For some, fantasy is a jump-start, and they assume this is true for all men. There is danger, of course, in generalizing one's own sexual repertoire as typical for others.[1]

More than two-thirds of women and 70 percent of men masturbate "to relieve sexual tension"[2] or because, in the well-worn vernacular of Singleland, they are *horny.* "The tensions they were feeling were the result of their being in sexually stimulating environments in which desire is experienced more frequently."[3] Masturbation becomes the equivalent of stopping at a fast food restaurant for a meal on-the-run when you're hungry. Lots of single adults masturbate to relieve sexual tension or to relax, without any sexual fantasies playing on the big screen.

It's wise to distinguish between sexual desire itself (which is a gift of God) and the lust that Jesus condemned. It is possible to masturbate without lust or sexual fantasy; in fact, it's wiser, because by excluding fantasy or porn you focus on you and on what you are feeling rather than on the actors in your fantasy. You can be more "present" with yourself sexually without visual distractions. In fact, masturbation can help us realize that all of our body is sexual—not just the genitals. Of course, we have to take the time to discover this, and many of us don't. "The practice of rapid, ejaculation-oriented masturbation can be seen as yet another aspect of the male-machine concept. The male who stimulates his penis with the sole purpose of 'shooting off' as quickly as possible is, in effect, treating himself like a machine, a kind of sexual mechanism." [4]

Sadly, masturbation can be particularly guilt producing for widowers and divorcees, who are single after long marriages—especially if there was illness-induced celibacy, and particularly for those reluctant to jump into the fast lane of single life. Some men have sought out massage parlors (not licensed massage therapists) and prostitutes because they believe masturbation is unnatural. While these men have lost their sexual partners, they still have their sexual interest; indeed, their sexual drives may be enhanced.

Inappropriate sexual behavior—including rushing into a premature remarriage—can vastly complicate healing from the loss of a spouse. For many, masturbation is "a helpful and enjoyable way to relieve sexual tensions when no partner is available." [5] Far from being a poor excuse for the "real thing," masturbation is a lifesaver for many single adults who are transitioning between their former married life and a remarriage. It is neither childish nor selfish. In fact, masturbation can keep us from some far more complicating alternatives.

Some argue that nocturnal emissions or "wet dreams" solve the problem. Wet dreams can have intensely erotic scripts, which the individual experiences as troublesome. And many adult males do not experience wet dreams, though they may have erotic-theme dreams with erection but without orgasm. The older the adult, the less likely the dream will result in orgasm.

141. So why do I feel so guilty about masturbating?

People "are more ashamed and secretive about their own masturbating, especially current masturbating, than about almost any other sexual behavior," concludes sex researcher Morton Hunt. [1] Theologian

Richard Foster adds, "No other form of sexual activity has been more frequently discussed, more roundly condemned and more universally practiced than masturbation."[2]

In the *Sex in America* study, about half of the men and women who masturbated reported feeling guilty. Yet feeling guilty did not stop them.[3] Actually, many single adults masturbate quickly to get over the guilt. So let's stop to examine guilt. Is it "real" guilt or pseudo-guilt? Where does it originate?

Residue of parental attitudes. Few of our parents thought masturbation was a discussable subject; if we were lucky, we got a "Here, read *this*." Some information that we got was psychologically and spiritually burdensome and scientifically inaccurate. Who had wise, caring individuals to talk to? I once counseled a seventy-five year old widower, greatly troubled by his masturbation. "Talk to your priest," I suggested. "I can't do that—he's my best friend." I learned that when the man was thirteen, his father pointed out a mentally handicapped man and said, "Jack, *that's* what happens to boys who play with themselves!" All his adult life those words had ricocheted through his mind. Words based on myth can wound even intelligent people.

Residue of peer teasing. Consider the common word "jerk." Its derivation is "jerking off"—slang for masturbation. Some males think masturbation is juvenile, like being a jerk, something a "real" man doesn't have to do. When you say, "You jerk" you are saying, literally, "You masturbator!" Such adolescent teasing leaves a long-lingering emotional residue of shame.

Emptiness. Lewis Smedes, who has written on theology and sexuality, contends that masturbation "always leaves something lacking. A person masturbates with a deep need for another person to fulfill his sexuality . . . (The one who masturbates) needs to learn that the feeling of emptiness after masturbating is not guilt, but only incompleteness."[4] What single adults label as guilt may be little more than emptiness. Emptiness is a first-cousin to guilt. Some of us have been so conditioned to mixing shame and sex, we cannot distinguish between the two emotions.

Audit your own attitudes toward masturbation. Where did your attitudes come from? Do you worry about excessive masturbation, feel it's obsessive? What *is* obsessive? Many would answer "anyone who masturbates more than I do." Archibald Hart, a psychologist with extensive research work in this area of sexual repertoire, defines excessive as "several times a day over a protracted period of time."[5] However, remember that the obsession is the problem—not the masturbation.

142. How do I get over feeling that I have been short-changed in the size of my genitals?

Comparison and competition are the basic themes of adolescence. Growth spurts occur on their own schedule; some mature early, others later. Every teen, at some point or other, has compared penis or breasts to peers, and felt shortchanged or envious. Because of the open arrangement of male bathrooms and common nudity in men's locker rooms, even grown men compare genitals. They tend to tease or ridicule each other. Someone who has a large penis is admiringly described as "well-endowed" or "well-hung." Ironically, men overlook the reality that there is little difference in the length of most erect penises.[1] The use of actors with larger-than-average penises in pornography only heightens the issue. Although men report that they watch porn to see the women, most cannot resist comparing themselves to the male actors—in both anatomy and performance.

Studies of women have found no preferences for large penised sexual partners.[2] However, in less scientific more everyday arenas where the male nude pinup is more common, women have begun openly and daringly discussing their opinions on penis size and making comparisons. Naomi Wolf says that when women began sexually experimenting, one by-product was that "men risked hearing what women hear every day: that there are sexual standards against which they might be compared."[3] Many women claim that open discussion (and any resulting anxiety created in males) is fair play, since women constantly feel evaluated on the size of their breasts. One single adult wrote, "For centuries, women have scrutinized their chests for reassurance of their femininity . . . Just about every woman I know, Christian or otherwise, feels uneasy about her breasts."[4] So women have little sympathy for males who whine about genital comparison and ratings.

The issue has become so complicated that some men explore plastic surgery. Penis enlargement or enhancement, although far from universally medically accepted, is one alternative for insecure men. However, neither the American Urology Association or the American Society of Plastic and Reconstructive Surgeons endorse the procedure. Many physicians first send men who request it to see a psychiatrist. Dr. Abraham Morgentaler, a Harvard urologist who has dealt with many men on this issue, responds, "The best thing I can do is to tell the truth, that I've seen a lot of penises and theirs is great." [5] Given the growing concern about links between breast implants and cancer, one has to wonder if the enthusiasm for penis enlargement is not potentially dangerous and ill-advised.

So what else can you do?

Laugh it off. In a health club locker room, one man commented on another man's large penis: "Wow!" The other man responded, "I'd trade it for one that works." Just as women have developed self-effacing "boob" humor as a defense mechanism, now men must humor up.

Ask yourself: Can I do anything about it? Despite the ads promising bust development and penis enlargement, growth after puberty is unlikely without surgery. Moreover, the whole issue is tainted if you are risking cancer or other complications. Plastic surgery or breast enlargement or reduction is an option single adults can consider but it's expensive. Before you drop the big bucks (few insurance plans will pay for this), talk with a skilled counselor or psychologist.

If you can't do anything about it, change your attitude. As the Commandments remind us, nothing is gained by "coveting," in this case coveting your neighbor's sexual endowment.

Lose weight. The penis you had at a trim and fit age eighteen is "diminished" by the thirty extra pounds of girth now surrounding it. In a sense, it's all about perception.

Don't judge. Judging others—including yourself—by what they look like objectifies them and ignores the value God has given all of us. Many of these superbods can only be achieved by the systematic use (and abuse) of drugs and steroids.[6] Healthy single adults value the worth and dignity of *every* human and appreciate the physical diversity in single adult bodies.

143. What about oral sex?

Oral sex (cunnilingus on women/fellatio on men) is a common part of the sexual repertoire of single adults today. In a survey of heterosexual men in the United States, 75 percent had performed oral sex, and 79 percent had received oral sex, with higher percentages among younger single adults.[1] The Janus Report indicated that 90 percent of their participants had had oral sex, with 88 percent of men and 87 percent of women saying it was either "very normal" or "all right."[2] As Ruth Westheimer has noted, "For many couples oral sex represents just another method for sexual pleasure and the act can climax in orgasm and ejaculation without moving on to [penetration]," which many single adults want to avoid.[3]

There's so much emphasis on intercourse that people aren't given the chance to figure out what else there is and how to be a sexual being without having intercourse. We forget that two people can enjoy each other's bodies—and their own—with significantly less risk through oral sex.[4] In the Christian community, Christians have misused or misinterpreted Scripture to denounce oral sexual practices. Some reject fellatio because it is so commonly used by homosexuals (but that logic would also exclude hugging and kissing). Some Roman Catholics oppose oral sex because it is nonprocreative.

Attitudes toward oral sex are shaped by our attitudes toward our own genitals. Single adults who think their genitals are attractive, sexy, and clean are more likely to engage in oral sex. However, the fact that genitals are used for excretory functions underlies a lot of negative attitudes, even by those who have oral sex. Generally, attitudes are more negative about female genitals than male.[5] Moreover, many women cannot relax sufficiently to enjoy receiving oral sex, because of their dislike of their own bodies or their fear of a partner's evaluation. Many single adults are hyperanxious about their own genitals, so becoming sexual with another individual heightens their anxiety.

The important thing is to examine your motivations. For instance, even single adults who dislike oral sex, may "give" oral sex if they or their date see it as something of a "consolation prize." The question for a lot of single adults is "will you *settle* for oral sex?"

Why do single adults say yes to oral sex? Most single adults answer in one of two general rationales: (1) to "enhance the relationship" and/or (2) "to please the partner." Do any of these responses sound familiar?

- "I do it to strengthen my relationship with my partner."
- "I do it to make my partner happy."
- "I hope that doing it will make my partner know that I like him/her."
- "I do it to let my partner know he/she is special to me."
- "I hope that doing it will make my partner like me."
- "I hope that doing it will make me close to my partner."
- "I only do it because my partner wants to."
- "I do it only if coerced."
- "I do it because it would threaten the relationship if I said no."
- "I do it because I just couldn't say no to my partner."[6]

Like vaginal sex, oral sex can be exploitative. Oral sexual intimacy may be motivated by hidden agendas on the part of both parties: "Now *maybe* he will like me." Some single adults have come to accept oral sex as a negotiated compromise. However, if the man is pushing for as much sexual intensity as he can get (particularly pushing the woman's hand or head toward his crotch), it's abusive, unhealthy, and illegal!

Another questionable motivation is using oral sex as "sex *lite*" or as a way to preserve virginity. Certainly, the intense experience of orgasm through oral sex raises questions about the meaning of the intimacy. The prizing of virginity does not always stop couples from having oral sex. Since "going all the way" to some people means only full penetration of the vagina, oral sex is not "sex." If you find yourself saying, "Well, at least we didn't go all the way," you might ask yourselves if you are just playing word games with sexual issues.

Whatever your attitude, you must remember that sexually transmitted diseases can be transmitted through oral sex. The risk of getting an STD or HIV via receptive oral sex appears to be lower than through anal or vaginal sex—but it is not necessarily a zero chance of transmission.[7]

144. How common is anal sex?

Anal sex has long been practiced by heterosexuals, particularly as a means of birth control. Only since the appearance of AIDS have anal sex practices become a topic for serious discussion. According to several studies, around 25 percent of women and men have experienced or tried anal sex (10 percent in the last year; only 2 percent the last time they had sex). Many report using anal stimulation as part of foreplay.[1] Yet, it is difficult to get an accurate reading on how common anal sex is, since many are reluctant to admit to having had anal sex.

Some single adults do not consider anal sexual intimacy as "the real thing." Because it doesn't risk pregnancy, anal sex is therefore permissible in their thinking, and to engage in it is a way of maintaining their virginity. Whatever your attitudes, remember that receptive anal penetrative sex without a condom is considered the *most* risky sexual practice.[2] More medical experts recommend protection be used, suggesting both a condom and Nonoxynol 9, a spermicide, because condoms do break at a higher frequency in anal sex.[3]

CHAPTER 14

Single and Concerned about STDs, AIDS, and Other Realities in Singleland

145. What are sexually transmitted diseases?

Sexually transmitted diseases (STDs) are infectious diseases spread through sexual contact with an infected partner. They may also be transmitted from an infected mother to her child through passage in the birth canal. STDs include gonorrhea, syphilis, genital herpes, non-specific urethritis, hepatitis B, venereal warts, chancroid, chlamydia, and molluscum contagiosum (lesions on the genitals).

The term *sexually transmitted diseases* has replaced "venereal diseases" and "social diseases" because it includes some diseases, such as AIDS, that may be initially acquired through non- sexual means (such as a needle stick) but transmitted sexually.

The United States has the world's highest incidence of STDs— about 12,000,000 new cases every year.[1] The Center for Disease Control estimates that 44 million Americans have some sort of STD.[2] STDs are a "hidden" epidemic because many single adults are *asymptomatic*—infected but have no symptoms. Divorcing or divorced persons who suspect or know that their spouse was sexually unfaithful need to be examined for STDs. You may think it unnecessary: "Oh, it was an affair with only one person." But who has that one person slept with? No one wants an STD as something to "remember me by" or to complicate future relationships. An STD's impact can be devastating, physically and emotionally.

ESTIMATED ANNUAL NEW "WINNERS" IN THE STD LOTTERY[3]

STD	Annual Number of New Cases	Prognosis
Chlamydia	4,000,000	curable
Trichomoniasis	3,000,000	curable
Pelvic inflammatory disease	1,000,000	curable
Gonorrhea	800,000	curable
Genital warts (Human papillavirus)	500,000–1,000,000	treatable but not curable
Genital herpes	200,000–500,000	treatable but not curable
Syphilis	101,000	curable
HIV/AIDS	80,000	not curable

Many single adults—particularly young males—have a notion that an STD is merely a sexual "rite of passage" or part of "sowing one's wild oats," to be cured with a shot of penicillin. However, these days some STDs have treatment-resistant strains. Complications include infertility, ectopic pregnancy (outside the uterus), meningitis, and arthritis.[4] STDs may facilitate the transmission or acquisition of HIV.[5]

146. Why are STDs increasing?

Because nonmarital sex is so common; the two go hand in hand. Since the early 1970s health care professionals, counselors, and social scientists have been alarmed by the increase in STDs among adolescents and young adults (the next generation of single adult). Reasons cited for the increase include: (1) increased premarital/nonmarital sexual contact, (2) increased heterosexual experience with multiple partners (who have had multiple partners, too), (3) declining average age of first sexual experience, (4) unrealistic perception of risk ("not me!"), and (5) decline in the use of condoms prior to 1985.[1] Moreover, researchers are also alarmed by a "relapse" phenomenon, with again increasing rates of STDs, particularly among the young. Some people experience a temporary period of fright and practice "negotiated safety." Others may be less cautious in a relationship than if dating around. Some swear to "turn a new [sexual] leaf," but do not sustain it. "Behavior change and its maintenance cannot be assumed to be permanent."[2] To avoid STDs a single adult must have a *sustained* behavioral change.

147. How can I protect myself against STDs?

No sexually active individual is totally immune from an STD: rich/poor, male/female, heterosexual/homosexual, educated/uneducated, churchgoer/nonchurchgoer, first timer/many timer. Have sex (especially unprotected or risky sex) and you've bought a lottery ticket. STDs are not caused by a specific sexual practice. But chances of transmission of AIDS or rectal gonorrhea can be enhanced through unprotected anal sex, because of the delicate linings of the rectum. The risk of acquiring an STD also increases dramatically with multiple exposures to an infected partner and with multiple partners in one's sexual history. One study found that among women, of all ages, who reported "many" partners, 46 percent had "almost no" or "very little" knowledge of STDs.[1] Here are the best suggestions.

Be informed. Know what STDs are and how they are transmitted.

Abstain. Take a "sexual sabbatical."

Be sexually responsible as an adult. If you have sex, abstain from sexual behaviors that put your partner (and their future partners) at risk. If you choose not to abstain, use a condom responsibly (insuring against breakage or spillage).

Watch for physical warnings. Discharges, sores, and rashes may be signs of sexual infection. Be curious if a partner insists on total darkness for intimacy.

Seek medical attention. Ignoring symptoms will only complicate matters. Getting treatment can be a problem if your family doctor is a friend, or you are in a small town and worry about confidentiality. You may need to look for a public health clinic. But go! Remember, you will need to abstain from all sexual activity until medical treatment has been completed.

Seek spiritual or psychological assistance. Having or having had an STD can be emotionally threatening or damaging. Some single adults have felt like "lepers" or "unclean." Explore the spiritual implications of having this STD.

These days, don't assume anything. It is not enough to say, "You look like a nice person, so you must be safe." Admittedly, asking about your partner's medical history can douse the romance. However, many "nice" people have risky sex (especially when drinking) or have been married to or involved with people who have had unsafe sex.

148. Is AIDS a risk to single adults?

Acquired Immune Deficiency Syndrome (AIDS) is a threat to anyone who either has or has had multiple sexual partners or is sexually intimate with someone who has. AIDS is caused by a retrovirus commonly named HIV (human immunodeficiency virus). The virus attacks several types of human cells, including a key cell of the body's immune system, the body's first line against illness. Thus, an individual with an advanced HIV infection is vulnerable to "opportunistic" infections and malignancies associated with immune dysfunction. Generally, these diseases and other complications of HIV infection are terminal,[1] although HIV+ (positive) individuals are now living longer after diagnosis due to advances in treatment. In fact, some are now labeling AIDS a *chronic* disease rather than a terminal disease due to significant treatment with protease inhibitors.[2] Unfortunately, many single adults have mistaken this medical development for a cure. *Not!*

By January 1, 1996, 9.2 million people worldwide were estimated to have died with AIDS, including 358,000 Americans (302,000 men, 50,000 women, and 6,000 children).[3]

149. How is AIDS spread?

AIDS is spread primarily through four means:

1. sexual activity involving the exchange of body fluids: semen, blood, vaginal secretions;

2. the sharing of contaminated needles and syringes by users of intravenous drugs;

3. infected mothers transmitting the virus to their fetuses during pregnancy or during childbirth;

4. medical accidents, such as needle-pricks.

AIDS is *not* spread by casual contact such as kissing, hugging, or shaking hands. "Epidemiologic studies have *consistently* failed to reveal any increased risk in transmission from close, nonsexual contact with HIV-infected persons." [1]

150. Isn't AIDS a gay disease?

At first, AIDS was thought to be a disease of homosexual men and was initially labeled, *Gay Related Immune Deficiency Syndrome, GRIDS*. But it is now clear that the AIDS virus does not discriminate. Worldwide, over 70 percent of HIV infections result from heterosexual behavior.[1] *HIV is a reality for heterosexuals as well as homosexual single adults.* The percentage of homosexuals among Americans diagnosed with AIDS has declined to about 65 percent.[2] At the same time, there has been a startling increase of infection among heterosexuals, especially among women and people of color.[3]

Many single adults gained a false sense of comfort because of the persistent agendizing by political and religious conservatives: "When you violate moral, health, and hygiene laws, you reap the whirlwind. You cannot shake your fist in God's face and get away with it!" or "AIDS is God's judgment on homosexuals!" They think that AIDS is a gay disease and therefore, AIDS cannot touch them. Wrong!

151. So who is at risk for AIDS?

Everyone. AIDS is no respecter of persons: You play, you pay!

AIDS EXPOSURE CATEGORIES AND RATES OF INFECTION IN THE UNITED STATES[1]

Source of exposure	% of total infected
Male homosexual or bisexual contact history	54
Injection drug use history	24
Injection drug use history + homosexual/bisexual history	7
Heterosexual contact history	6
Receipt of blood transfusion	2
Hemophilia/coagulation disorder	1
Undetermined	6

Studies conducted by the American Medical Association, the Public Health Service, the Center for Disease Control, and the National Institutes of Health have identified the following groups as at increased—if not high—risk for AIDS.

• homosexual and bisexual men who are sexually active

• persons who share needles or syringes while injecting drugs or who have done so in the past

• male or female prostitutes, sex workers, and their sexual partners

• persons with hemophilia who have received clotting factor products

• infants of high-risk or infected mothers

• individuals who have a seropositive AIDS antibody blood test

And—and most critical to the readers of *Singles Ask*—*individuals who have had sexual relations with any of the above.*[2]

Here are "before bedtime" questions to ponder:

1. Is my romantic partner bisexual? Or homosexual? If you think the answer might be yes, would she/he admit it? (See question 171).

2. Did my romantic partner have a blood transfusion between 1975 and 1985 (before strict enhanced blood testing procedures)? This is an important question for older single adults who may have been married to a person who had a blood transfusion during this period.

3. Has my romantic partner ever experimented with IV drugs?

4. Has my romantic partner slept with any of the above?

5. Does my romantic partner know all the answers to questions 1–4 for all of his/her sexual partners?

6. Is my partner willing to be completely honest about his/her sexual past?

152. How threatening is AIDS to single adults?

There is no cure for AIDS, and no vaccine to prevent AIDS is expected in the foreseeable future. Any vaccine developed would be effective only in preventing or managing infection, not in curing existing cases.[1] An estimated 2,000,000 Americans are HIV+ and thus are capable of spreading the virus to others; a significant percentage are unaware of their status.[2] Remember, the fact that a person has the HIV virus does not mean he/she has AIDS *yet*. Eventually, all HIV+ persons will develop a medical condition that warrants a full-scale AIDS diagnosis. In the meantime, they might go on with their lives (romantic and sexual) perhaps for as long as a decade without knowing that they are infected or having symptoms. An individual could be "as healthy as a horse" but still be spreading the virus. The recent medical developments with protease inhibitors do significantly reduce the viral load (the amount of virus that can be detected in the blood). By taking these powerful drugs, some individuals "suddenly spring back, rebounding with energy" and a new lease on life.[3]

Theoretically, AIDS threatens any single adult who is sexually active. Former Surgeon General Dr. C. Everett Koop offered a threefold approach to AIDS prevention: monogamy, abstinence, and responsible use of condoms and spermicides, a concept described as *abstinence plus*.[4] Koop's warning ignited controversy among many pious people who prefer to stick their heads in the sand and quote slogans.

153. The person that I am dating says that he had the HIV test and was negative. Doesn't that mean he's safe?

Being negative means that *on the day* the blood sample was obtained, the HIV antibodies were not present. "Presuming that you are negative simply because you'd tested negative once before—or because you've never tested but believe you have not been unsafe—is not a wise presumption and can put your partner[s] at risk." [1]

154. What about safe sex?

The preferred term, these days, is *safer* sex. Nothing is "absolutely, positively, 100 percent, money-back guaranteed safe" except total abstinence! *Any* sex carries some risk, especially when it is spontaneous or is influenced by drinking or drugs. Without forethought pregnancies and infections happen.

Highest risk behavior: Practices that transmit HIV infection
[See Appendix 4 for detailed list]
- Anal intercourse without a condom
- Vaginal intercourse without a condom
- Oral sex with contact of sexual fluids (ejaculation or pre-ejaculation fluids)

Safer-sex: Practices that significantly reduce risk for HIV infection
- Intercourse (anal, oral, vaginal) protected with latex condom

Safest-sex: Practices unlikely to transmit HIV infection
- "Outercourse" (activities that do not involve intercourse or penetration), such as mutual masturbation with minimal contact with partner's sexual fluids.[1]

155. I am getting married, so should I be tested for HIV or STDs?

Definitely. *Both of you should.* It's better to know now and deal with it than not to know. If the tests come back positive, you will want solid medical and psychological assistance to "process" the information and make wise decisions concerning a shared future, especially if you want children. Remember, an AIDS test verifies the presence or absence of the virus only on that particular day. There is about a six-month window, for most, between the infection and the detection of the virus in the blood. So, if a person says, "Oh, not to worry—I've been tested already and I was negative," your follow-up questions should be: (1) When? and (2) Have you been sexually active since the test? Any negative result is only as safe as the last partner—including you. Some would suggest that you take the tests together and receive the results together.[1] This avoids any temptation to lie should the tests come back positive for AIDS or for an STD.

156. What about condoms?

Dr. Koop was right on target in saying that condoms are an essential protection. I wish that more people had been more compassionate toward Dr. Koop, who has been a friend to single adults. My understanding of sexual behavior is that we are always called, and empowered to be responsible sexually. You may well make the decision—as many single adults do—to be sexually intimate within certain parameters. I challenge you to be safe for yourself, your partner, and future partners. I agree with Dr. Jeffrey Kelly: "A person will be most fully protected from HIV if he or she never has sex outside a monogamous relationship with an assuredly faithful uninfected partner. This is a viable goal for some people, but not for most of those persons who are at greatest risk. The use of condoms during sex provides significant but not absolute protection from HIV infection (as well as STDs)."[1]

Maybe you're going to become a monk in an isolated desert monastery or join Mother Theresa's order. But, sooner or later, sexual opportunity or temptation will come and you will have to face the "c" question. For sexually-active single adults today, regardless of their age, condoms are a must—every time, no exceptions.

157. But won't I be able to tell if a person has AIDS, or is in a high risk group, or has an STD?

No. You will not. Only a fool would believe "I can tell." June Osborne, dean of the School of Public Health at the University of Michigan, reminds us, "It isn't group membership but behavior that puts [you] at risk. Not who you are but what you do." [1]

Seriously weigh a romantic involvement with someone who has had a drug dependency or usage in the past and has not been tested. They may have gone years without doing recreational drugs, may even sing in the church choir, but the virus can still be present. Getting tested is essential to good decision making.

Finally, "people may lie, not remember, or distort things about their past." [2] Few people want to own up to anything that shatters their carefully constructed and maintained self. The excuse "that was a long time ago" may have to be confronted so that a future has a chance for you.

CHAPTER 15

Single and Asking about Bisexuality and Homosexuality

158. What is bisexuality?

Bisexuality is another sexual reality in Singleland. Some single adults may sleep with partners of the opposite sex, as well as with partners of the same sex. AIDS specialist Anthony P. M. Coxon notes, "Whether they are truly bisexual or not, between 10 and 20 percent of gay-identifying men currently have sex with women."[1]

Bisexuals are attracted to and may have sexual contact with both sexes. Three types of bisexuality have been identified. Type A is transitional—predominately heterosexual but moving toward homosexual. Some who are married will initially self-identify as bisexual; then, after a death of a spouse, divorce, or "coming out" experience they will self-identify as homosexual.

Type B involves genuine attraction to both sexes.

Type C involves an erotic attraction to the same sex but an emotional attraction to the opposite sex. This accounts for the numbers of married males who have occasional or episodic sexual contact with other males, often called "trade."

Sexual orientation may be identified by three criteria: desire, behavior, and/or self-identity. The researchers for *Sex in America* reported that, "a substantial portion of [the] women (13 percent in their study) do not consider themselves lesbians even though they both desire other women and have had sex with women."[2] Similarly,

MSMs—men who have sex with men—may self-identify as homosexual, bisexual, or heterosexual.[3]

Some researchers identify *heterosexual homosexuals* who attempt to dispel their anxieties about their orientation through heterosexual behaviors. Some lesbians use pregnancy as a way to challenge rumors of homosexuality. They may marry, have children, and bake cookies for the PTA, but eventually they face a crossroads, perhaps after the children are grown: do they stay in the marriage? or do they divorce and live as lesbians, perhaps in a relationship?

Some religious conservatives experience homosexual feelings but believe homosexual behaviors to be wrong, evil, or unnatural. They may engage in heterosexual behavior in an attempt to change or hide their sexuality, in what one therapist labels "adaptive strategies." [4] They believe: "I am what I *do*; therefore, if I do enough heterosexual acts, I *am* heterosexual."

Many adults who are homosexual will not identify themselves as gay to avoid social, economic, and religious stigma[5] or rejection by family, friends, employers, or church communities. Individuals going through a divorce may be reluctant to disclose (let alone declare) that they are homosexual for fear that it would impact family and public response to the divorce, and perhaps complicate child custody or the ability to pay child support or alimony. Homosexuality is an ingredient in no few divorces, whether it is acknowledged publicly or not. Some people have decided to come out only after significant sexual sampling with partners of the same sex that may have put their spouses or sexual partners at risk for an STD or HIV. In some cases, a spouse being diagnosed with an STD has forced the issue into the open.

With the growth of "conversion" ministries and programs, many adults who have had same-sex partners renounce the gay "lifestyle," reidentify themselves as "ex-gay" and, as proof of their conversion, marry or recommit to making a heterosexual marriage work. The issue, however, is *sustained* conversion. Some zealous women who have had sex with homosexual men "to win them over" felt they were on something of a holy mission. On the other hand, there is the experience of the woman whose husband died of AIDS, who explained, "I took my vows 'for better or worse' seriously . . . now I feel like the world's biggest fool. I really thought I could change him. I ended up an HIV+ AIDS widow."

Wait just a minute, you might say. If a spouse is gay, how could he even get sexually aroused by a woman? Well, even eunuchs can get aroused.[6] In actuality, he is aroused *with* a woman, perhaps by fantasizing about a man while having sex with the woman.

Stanley Siegel, a psychotherapist with extensive experience with counseling homosexual and bisexual men, observes that some individuals identify "milestones" in their sexual histories that warrant an identification as a homosexual. Some never explored their homosexual feelings or interests until after marriage. Some so fear negative consequences that they avoid homosexual contacts by conscious will. Some erase memories so as not to contradict their determined world view.[7] "For the sake of the kids" or for the continuation of an economic lifestyle, some spouses are willing to work out an "accommodation" with gay or lesbian spouses allowing for occasional "safe sex" same-sex encounters while continuing the marriage (just as some have continued a marriage despite knowing that their spouse was involved with someone else).

Some therapists question the notion of bisexuality. Psychiatrist Richard Isay says, "True bisexuality in men is probably rare ... Most of the men I have seen who label themselves bisexual do so simply because they are in conflict about being homosexual."[8] The label "bisexual" is not nearly as stigmatized as homosexual.

159. I dated a man I came to realize was bisexual. How do I get over my feeling that I wasted the years involved with him?

Many single adults have come to the pained reality that the individual they love is bisexual or homosexual—sometimes, even before their partner accepts it. Sometimes, however, they are not free to disclose that reality to family or friends because it would "out" their partner. So comments like, "It's too bad that you and Ken couldn't make it; you made such a great couple" or "Such a nice young woman" stimulate a lingering pain. Richard Isay, having counseled many men, says that the bisexually-defined male eventually "has to make a realistic and reasonable assessment of the importance, on the one hand, of the gratification obtained from social respectability and a longstanding relationship with spouse and children and, on the other hand, of the desire to feel more authentic by expressing his inherent sexuality and establishing a personal and social identity as a gay man."[1] Simply put, he cannot long have it "both ways."

Some partners have decided that they cannot continue in such a relationship, for long-term considerations. While it *might* work out ("This is just a phase, you know, like a mid-life crisis"), reality says it won't! Some couples do create long-term friendships.

160. What percent of single adults are homosexual?

For a long time, the figure of 10 percent (based on Kinsey's research) was used. Now estimations are generally more conservative. The conservative Family Research Institute estimates 3 percent of the adult population; the Janus Report suggests 9 percent of males and 5 percent of females.[1] Based on her study of women, researcher Laurel Richardson estimated that 14 percent of *single* men and 4 percent of *single* women were homosexual.[2] Carefully reread that sentence: not the total population, but the *single adult* population. Keep in mind that because of prejudice and sampling bias, the question of how many persons are homosexual is ultimately unanswerable.[3] We also need reminding that adults who are homosexual or bisexual are not statistics but people who breathe, work, love, and bleed. Considering them as statistics dehumanizes them.

Are the number of homosexuals growing? The number of "out" homosexuals is growing but overall, no, say Hunt and other experts. "There is no growth in the actual numbers. What has happened is that more homosexuals than formerly have stopped keeping it a secret and come out into the open,"[4] particularly in the nineties.

New, more methodologically precise national studies indicate that 2 to 3 percent of adult men acknowledged sexual contact with another male in the previous year.[5] The most precise research by Binson, Gagnon and others reports 2.6 percent of men studied admit to having a male partner in the last year, and 5.3 percent of males since age 18.[6] However, activists and researchers question that number. How many males are going to admit to a total stranger, even in a research study, that they have engaged in anal sex or fellatio with another male?

However, the 10 percent number can be used accurately to identify the percentage of highly educated white males (10.8 percent) and never-married *urban* men (10.6 percent) who reported same-sex activity. The highest prevalence rates of reported homosexual behavior were found in the central cities of the twelve largest SMSAs[7] (Standard Metropolitan Statistical Areas, which in 1994 were New York City, Los Angeles, Chicago, Houston, Philadelphia, San Diego, Phoenix, Dallas, San Antonio, Detroit, San Jose, and Indianapolis).[8] Gagnon explains, "More than 9 percent of men in the nation's twelve largest cities identify themselves as gay. But just 3 to 4 percent of men living in the suburbs of these cities or in most of the larger cities of the nation say they are gay, and about 1 percent of men in rural areas identify themselves as gay."[9]

Clearly, the percent of males who self-define as homosexual or gay impacts the dating patterns and sexual behaviors of all single adults in that area. Despite the large numbers of single men in large cities, there are fewer men to date and potentially marry. However, one must remember that one-third of the men who had sex with men also reported having sex with women.[10] If you are a woman living in a major metropolitan area, you may well have dated a homosexual or bisexual man.

Lesbians also cluster in cities. Gagnon's study defines a lesbian as a woman who has had a female sexual partner in the years since turning eighteen, and identifies as lesbian 6.2 percent of women in largest cities and 2.8 percent of women in rural areas.[11]

161. Are there different types of homosexuality?

Instead of homosexuality it is more accurate to talk about homosexual*ities*. One definition does not fit all. Indeed, some researchers think it is wiser to talk about homosexual behaviors, since some who have same-sex intimacy will never self-identify as gay or lesbian. Three potential classifications seem possible: (1) those who are sexually attracted to persons of the same sex, (2) those who have had sex with persons of the same sex, and (3) those who identify themselves as gay or lesbian. *MSM* (men who have sex with men) may be a more precise term than *gay*. Significant numbers of men who have occasional passive sexual fellatio would not identify themselves as homosexual, although they participated in homosexual behavior. Many heterosexual single adults occasionally have or have had homosexual thoughts, feelings, or dreams and some have had fleeting behaviors which can be labeled *homoerotic.*[1]

Situational homosexuals are heterosexual individuals who engage in homosexual acts under certain circumstances. They may live in a culture that does not stigmatize bisexuality or in an environment deprived of sexual contact with members of the opposite sex, such as prisons. Some single adults (particularly women) become emotionally involved with prisoners, initially responding to personal ads, becoming pen pals, even marrying them. The large U.S. prison population (1995: 1,127,132) and the spiraling rates of HIV infection and full-blown AIDS among prisoners[2] should be a concern for those who become romantically involved with prisoners or ex-prisoners.

During adolescence, some single adults had same-sex experiences to orgasm which are described as sexual experimentation rather than expressions of sexual orientation. Judd Marmor, an authority on gender issues, offers a helpful working definition: "[A homosexual] is motivated in adult life by a definite preferential erotic attraction to members of the same sex and usually (but not necessarily) engages in overt sexual relations with them."[3]

162. Are there "stages" in homosexuality?

Psychologist Stanley Siegel suggests that defining oneself as gay unfolds in recognizable patterns or stages.

Stage 1: The individual acknowledges feelings in private (first to self, then to a "trusted" other or others). This is a time of experimentation and exploration during which the individual modifies public behavior and remarks selectively. This single (or married) adult might go to a gay bar on occasion (say, on a business trip out of town) but would not put a rainbow flag on the car or wear an AIDS ribbon into a Sunday school class or to work. This individual would laugh defensively at a joke ridiculing gays or lesbians.

Stage 2: The individual "debuts" into a small group of homosexuals. This "social identification" helps single adults shift their self-definition from *homosexual*—society's language for who they are—to *gay man* or lesbian woman.[1]

Stage 3: The individual moves from private world of being gay to the public world. The individual actively lobbies "for his full right to be who he is in all (or most) circumstances, openly confronting prejudice and bigotry." [2] Thus, the individual becomes part of the gay and lesbian "community" and solidifies his/her status as a gay or lesbian person. Not all people make a painless, easy linear transition. The individual must carefully consider what sacrifices may be involved in coming out or being "outed." Some find the closet a revolving door—a three steps forward, two steps backward progression.

The following model might be helpful in understanding the battle process individuals must delicately transverse to come to terms with their sexual identity, to own their sexual truth:

The wondering	"I wonder if . . ."
The fearing	"No. I can't possibly be . . . No way!"
The testing	"Could I be?"
The experimenting	"How does this particular behavior feel?"

This could lead to

The rejecting	"No, now I know that I am not."
The accepting	"I am a homosexual."
The deciding	"I will keep that part of my life under control." "I have got to be honest about who I am."
The disclosing within the family within the friend network within the support network: church, neighbors, work colleagues	"I have something I need to tell you . . ."
The embracing	"I am gay and not ashamed."
The refining	"This is who I am . . ."
The championing	"I am gay and proud!"

Can you understand why the process may take years? Admittedly, some face the decision only later in life. Others take the secret to their grave.

163. Is there a difference between being *lesbian* or *gay* and being *homosexual*?

Most heterosexuals use the words *homosexual* and *gay* interchangeably; however, that is imprecise. A man could be homosexual but not gay. While both are attracted to individuals of the same sex, *gay* is a philosophical or political term, specifically, a social and political statement of pride and acceptance of one's homosexual orientation. Hence we have gay or lesbian bookstores, restaurants, softball leagues, political associations, and churches. Referring to oneself as lesbian or gay indicates that one has accepted a homosexual orientation and interaction.

Anthony Coxon, an AIDS researcher, notes, "A significant portion of men who have sex with men do not identify themselves *in any way* with the gay community."[1] In fact, this individual may vehemenently reject the gay community, or even be homophobic. So, a person could be homosexual—have sex with or be attracted to people of the same sex—and not be gay or lesbian.

164. Sometimes I wonder if the guy I am dating is gay. He never makes any moves on me. Should I ask him? How can I be sure he's telling me the truth?

There are a lot of closeted gay men romantically involved with straight women; the same is true of lesbians. That he "hasn't made any moves" would be welcomed by a lot of women. Admittedly, it can be confusing and troubling to you, especially if you want this relationship to work or have invested a lot emotionally in it. One single professional said: "I didn't suspect John was gay. That thought never crossed my mind. So when he made no moves on me, I thought it was because something was wrong with *me*—too fat, too ugly, something. After a while, it was something of a relief to find out he was gay." Some women, particularly wives, have protested: "If only I were more of a woman, I could overcome his orientation." Some have difficulty ever romantically rebuilding after such a relationship.

Ask. Don't put it in a confrontational tone: "OK, buster, are you gay!?" Remember, he could be having sex with men and still not identify himself as gay; or he could answer no, truthfully. Tell him that there is something you want to talk about. Before you ask, spend some time thinking what you will do with his answer. If he admits, "Yes, I am," who are you going to tell—and who are those persons going to tell? Or will you erupt in a screaming rage, "Get out of my life! You _____!"

If he is homosexual, he may not be at a point where he is ready to make that admission to himself, let alone to you. So take your time. If you have any doubts, certainly ask before you sleep with him or before you marry him.

Many people discover that someone they care about is homosexual. The romance ends, but the relationship can unfold into a solid friendship. This requires two incredible people and time to make that new relationship evolve into a new reality. You will need at least one trusted person, probably a professional, or someone who has "walked this path," to help you process this reality. Linda, who discovered her "guy friend" was gay, explained: "I always felt that, even though Mike hurt me a lot, the pain that he was going through in 'coming out' about his homosexuality in a world that is predominately heterosexual must far exceed mine. So I suppressed my pain and anger to 'be there' for my friend."

165. What about homophobia?

Suzanne Pharr defines *homophobia* as "the irrational fear and hatred of those who love and sexually desire those of the same sex."[1] The debate heats up over the preciseness of the term (not the reality of homophobia) since *phobia* means simply, "a fear, usually irrational." Some believe *heterosexism* to be a broader term, defined as "both the belief that heterosexuality is or should be the only acceptable sexual orientation and the fear and hatred of those who love and sexually desire those of the same sex."[2] Every day in this country, homosexuals are beaten, fired, verbally abused, even killed simply because of their stated or assumed sexual orientation. Indeed, they are attacked not because they are "feared" but because they are hated. Some label this disdain *homohatred*.

Public rhetoric fuels the hatred, claiming "Gays are everywhere." Yet the most conservative studies say only 1 percent of the population is homosexual. How could they be a threat when they are outnumbered ninety-nine to one?[3] The dialogue is clouded by the recitation of myths: "Gays recruit . . . gays molest little boys." In reality the highest percentage of sex offenders who molest children are married, heterosexual males.[4]

166. What stand can I take on homophobia if I believe homosexuality is wrong?

Sociologist Tony Campolo has confronted the traditional "hate the sin/love the sinner" approach, accurately noting that some single adults hate the sin and the assumed sinner, too. "It seems to me that we as Evangelicals have to, in accord with Romans 1, take a stand against forms of behavior that violate what we believe Scripture is teaching. The gay and lesbian community fully understands this. What they can't understand is the hate and the vile things we say about them. They only see us as people who are reaching out with condemnation."[1]

Caring single adults must spend time thinking through this issue, and not just rehashing the party line or old stereotypes and myths. Indeed, many single adults have been stunned to discover a friend is gay but are surprised that their friend does not fit the stereotypes. It can be an eye-opening and soul-stirring experience. Too many single adults are willing to let others make up their minds for them rather than wrestle with the issues themselves.

The United Methodists have taken a strong stand on the issue as a denomination (although not all individual United Methodists agree) with the statement: "Homosexual persons no less than heterosexual persons are individuals of sacred worth. All persons need the ministry and guidance of the church in their struggles for human fulfillment, as well as the spiritual and emotional care of a fellowship that enables reconciling relationships with God, with others, and with self."[2]

While United Methodists "do not condone the practice of homosexuality" and consider homosexual behavior "incompatible with Christian teaching," the denomination has gone on record in their

Book of Discipline, declaring "that all persons, regardless of age, gender, marital status, or sexual orientation, are entitled to have their human and civil rights ensured." [3]

167. I am not homosexual. What has homophobia got to do with me as a single adult?

As a heterosexual, you can be a victim of homophobia as quickly as a homosexual can. Suppose in a job interview, the interviewer notes that you are thirty-five and never-married, and wonders: "Why *aren't* you married?" Even though he/she cannot legally ask that question, "*Could he/she be* . . . ?" darts through the mind. That wonderment could be enough to tip the job to another candidate. It is subtle and unprovable, but it is discrimination.

Homophobia fuels men's fear of other men and of independent strong-willed women, who may be dismissed as *ball-breakers* (*balls* being a euphemism for testicles). Warren Blumenfeld identifies numerous ways that the whole society pays for homophobia.[1]

Homophobia locks all people into rigid, gender-based roles that inhibit creativity and self expression. It demands traditional careers and traditional roles. It says, "Bring back TV's Mr. Cleaver and Dad Walton," that era when "men were men," which means "in charge."

A woman in a nontraditional job has to endure lots of suspicion about her sexuality, expressed as innocently as "Who are you dating these days?" Women in the military have to prove that they are real women—sadly, sometimes with sexual favors—lest they risk being turned in as lesbians and dishonorably discharged from the military.[2]

Homophobic conditioning compromises the integrity of heterosexual people by pressuring them to treat others badly, contrary to their human nature. It brings back the great Bunkerisms like "All those people" or "All you people," or "Nothing personal, you understand," which if applied to blacks or Hispanics, could complicate your life quickly. Yet they remain all too easy to say about gays and lesbians.

Homophobia inhibits one's ability to form close, intimate relationships with members of one's own sex, especially for men. That's why men have acquaintances rather than friends; that's why some men marry in order to have a best friend. They fear that if they spend too much time with same-sex friends, then someone will ask, "Wonder if . . . ?"

The list of homophobic "don'ts" for men is the size of the average metropolitan area phone book. Break or even bend one of them and you could be labeled weak or a "*sissy*" or worse: a "*fag*!!!" "Fag!" always is accompanied by exclamation marks. Ever wondered why, unlike women, men always go to the restroom alone or insist on having a empty seat between them and another man—even a friend—in a movie theater?

Phillip Culbertson argues that homophobia (which he defines as the fear of homosexuality and the fear of homosexuals, in general) not only sabotages men's relationships with peers, but also relationships with their sons, fathers, brothers, nephews, and cousins. It is why men stop touching their male children around age five.[3] Despite the beer commercials that tease viewers: "I love you, man," fathers fear having "sissy" sons.

Homophobia generally restricts communication with a significant portion of the population, and limits family relationships. It's homophobia rather than homosexuality that threatens the family. Family members say incredibly hateful things: "Get out!" or "You're no longer my son/daughter." Such stories are legion in the gay community. One man told his outed friend, "We can't be friends anymore because someone might think I'm gay if I have a gay friend."

Homophobia encourages premature sexual involvement. Young males are too easily pressured to be hyper heterosexually active and to do the macho-male madness to prove to themselves and others that they are "normal." This motivates the "stud" mentality among men struggling to define their masculinity. Many who act out hyper-masculinity are trying to prove they are not gay or to disguise their sexual orientation.

Homophobia can be used to stigmatize, silence, and, on occasion, target people who are perceived or defined by others as gay, lesbian, or bisexual but who are actually heterosexual. Being perceived as "pro-gay" itself can invoke rage and a response like: "it takes one to know one!" Try challenging a verbal gaybasher telling a crude joke by the copy machine at work and see what happens.

Sadly, single adults—particularly those who have never married—may so fear being thought of as homosexual that they internalize their fears to lash out at those who are homosexual, and laugh the loudest when gays are targeted by cruel jokes.

168. The office where I work is very homophobic. I am often asked, "And why aren't you married?" There are lots of anti-gay jokes and mimicking around here. How do I react to this unhealthy work environment without making them think that I am gay?

A homophobic work place impacts everyone who works there, whether you laugh at the anti-gay jokes or not. Gays are about the only group in this country that is still held up to ridicule in the workplace. However, that is changing as more corporations develop policies that discourage or prohibit harassment. Xerox, Apple Computer, Quaker Oats, Sony, US West, Wells Fargo Bank, BankAmerica Corporation, and Microsoft are among those that consider such anti-gay humor or discrimination grounds for dismissal.[1] Better think twice before you demonstrate your homophobia—it could cost you your job.

Be willing to "break ranks" and stand up to your colleagues, especially if it means stand up *for* a colleague. You could be ridiculed or teased. You could be dismissed for being "idealistic" or "out of touch" or the dreaded, "politically correct." If female, you could be challenged: "You're not one of those femiNazis, are you?"[2] In fact, challenging your colleagues could cloud your name, your future. But if you, as a person of faith, believe "in the worth and dignity of every human being," then you cannot just go along acting as if you don't hear the slur or innuendo.

You could respond, "Why do you say/think/feel that way?" or, "It makes me uncomfortable to hear you talking that way. I haven't found that stereotype to be true."[3] You may choose to approach the individual in private: "You know, as a professional and a person of faith, I had some problems with something you said." It's easy to sing or quote the prayer of St. Francis of Assisi, "Lord, make me an instrument of your peace." It is easy to translate, "Where there is hatred, let *someone* sow love." But remember, Francis prayed, "let *me* sow love."

CHAPTER 16

Single and Coping with Widowhood

169. Why do some widowers remarry so quickly?

"His wife's not even cold in the ground!" That cliché captures the tendency of widowers to remarry quickly, particularly those who are older or have young children. Generally, widowers marry younger women on the assumption that a younger wife will survive them and be in a position to provide care, particularly if the widower cared for a wife during a long illness. The question in many widowers' minds is simple: "Who will take care of me if I become ill? Who will care deeply and intentionally about my well-being?" Particularly if the widower has adult children who live halfway across the country, or if he has a strained relationship with them. Unfortunately, remarrying may even further strain the relationship.

For other widowers, dating seems insane. It's like being thrown into a deep relationship pool and ordered to "Swim!" Andrew Young, former Ambassador to the United Nations, was asked why he remarried "just eighteen months" after his wife died of liver cancer. "Was it difficult to start over again *so quickly*?" Young responded, "I was twenty-two when I first married; the only life I'd known was married life. I needed a relationship of trust and permanence. Dating wasn't for me."[1]

170. How do I know the widow/er I am dating is over the first spouse?

The goal is not to get over a previous mate(s) but to have *reconciled* with the loss. This culture encourages those who have lost a mate to fast-forward the grief work, just as we use microwaves to speed up food preparation. Sadly, many believe that a new marriage is proof that they are "over" their loss. Some cannot handle their deep emotional pain—a pain that even threatens their health and makes them more vulnerable to illness and heart disease.[1] Some thrust themselves into premature dating or new relationships as a way of avoiding their grief work. Healing is delayed, if not sabotaged; sooner or later it sneaks back. Bang!

Emotionally healthy people do not get over the loss of a spouse but incorporate that loss into their life story. They give themselves time to do thorough healing rather than expect a new marriage to be the agent of healing. But often it seems easier to focus on the future and forget the past. For example, Theodore Roosevelt, as a widower and remarried, never again mentioned his first wife, Alice, to their daughter *in her entire life*. Nor did he mention her in his autobiography. It was as if Alice Roosevelt had never existed for him.[2] He illustrates the "tough man" approach to grief.

The issue becomes clouded when children are involved. You must assure them that you have no intention of replacing or "deleting" the parent they lost. You can, however, offer them a special relationship, even as you are a unique second spouse to their parent. But some children will never want to blend you into the memories of their "real" parent.

171. How can I be sure that the widower I am dating isn't comparing me to his late spouse?

Assume that he is comparing—either consciously or unconsciously—and assume that his children, friends, neighbors are comparing as well. He may have initially asked, "Will I ever meet someone who can 'live up to' my late spouse?" Now the question is, "Can X (you) live up to my late spouse?" The quicker the relationship begins, the more critical (even vicious) the comparing can be, as President Woodrow Wilson discovered when he married Edith Galt, a widow, only eight months after his first wife's death.[1] You won't be able to stop the comparing, but you can handle it with grace. In her book, *Second Wife, Second Best*, Glynnis Walker captured the reality that you may experience, at least initially. "Much of the anguish of second marriages" revolves around the "stress of coping with a ghost that always seems to be lurking . . . the idealized version of a dead former spouse."[2] The rougher the times, the more the ghost intrudes: "Ah, she was a saint!"

Memories prevent some people from ever remarrying. Some widowed people do not feel single but feel still married to the deceased. They feel they would dishonor the departed by dating. There has to come a moment of redefining themselves as single, as happened for Estelle Shyres, a widow, who took off her wedding ring, handed it to her daughter and said, "I'm not married anymore."[3]

172. A widow and I have a wonderful relationship. How am I supposed to deal with her adult children who think that I am after her money?

The suspicion is common, especially when there are sizeable financial assets. All it really takes is one suspicious adult child to think you are after a parent's money, and the issue starts percolating. If that adult child verbalizes the concern to siblings, soon they are questioning your motives. If the widow has money while you have significant debt, and the children see it as a premature relationship (especially if they have not had time to mourn), the issue can become complicated, ugly, and ultimately unwinnable.

Your do have options. Dialogue with or confront the concerned adult children and try to reassure them about your intentions. Remember this phrase: *not so fast*. Give them time. If there is a more sympathetic family member, build a bridge through her or him to other family members. You may need a third party "ambassador."

Ask yourself these questions:

• Do any of my actions give the impression that I am in this relationship prematurely?

• Do I fully understand the underlying concerns of the adult children?

• Are we rushing into this remarriage? What could be gained by waiting?

• Is there an ex-spouse? Will this further complicate our relationship?

Be sure you execute a prenuptial agreement that spells out the financial details; make sure that family members know the provisions. While you are preparing a prenuptial, review your wills, as well.

173. I enjoyed a good active sex life with my late husband. But I hear about so many men who are impotent. How can I be certain to have a healthy sex life in the next relationship?

If you want me to encourage a little sexual "auditioning" before the big "I do," think again. A partner could pass the audition and still give a lousy performance. Impotence is a significant issue for many men in our aging and stress-focused culture. Try to replace your concern about an "active sex life" with a desire for healthy intimacy. Can you feel vulnerable and intimate with each other? Remember, health problems such as diabetes, prostate cancer, or other serious illness can invade a healthy sexual relationship at any time, changing it radically. You will have few certainties in a new marriage.

Impotence happens. But it only destroys relationships in which the couple puts all their "eggs" in the intercourse basket. With a little imagination and loving assurance, even impotent men can still have a healthy sex life.

174. What is the difference between a second marriage for a widower and a second marriage for a divorced person?

Depends upon the particular people. Dr. Steve Bearden, a counselor, says that a relationship is only as emotionally healthy as the two individuals involved. If both have an accurate assessment of the previous marriage(s) and have thoroughly done their grief work, their life experiences should make them wiser about making a commitment.

175. The man I am dating has been widowed *and* divorced. What should I consider before I get serious with him?

Increasingly, more single adults, are "1+1": once divorced *and* once widowed (or 2+1, 2+2 . . .). Whether they admit it or not, some people still assign a sympathetic, nonjudgmental value to the death of a mate but a wary, judgmental value to a divorce. Either way, before you consider another marriage you need to know that the past has passed and that is has been a good tutor!

Some individuals who had poor first marriages feel devastated when a second marriage ends in death or divorce. Some participants in my grief groups have boldly demanded, "Why did this happen? We had everything going for us! Why didn't my *first* spouse die?"

Ask yourself, "What has this person learned from the marriage and loss?" Is he bitter? Is she angry? Cynical? Wiser? Resentful? Less trusting? More caring? Here are the key areas for reflection:

• How are the relationships with in-laws, particularly if there are younger children? Remember that former in-laws are the children's grandparents, great-grandparents, etc.

• What is the financial situation? The economic differences between the death of a mate and a divorce may be dramatic. In either case, understand that the person you are dating may need a working spouse to afford the lifestyle of the previous marriage(s).You need to ask, "To what degree do finances motivate this relationship?"

• How will *all* the children involved respond to the new relationship, including your children?

• Has there been counseling? Would you both be willing to go for counseling in the future?

• Has your friend "owned up" to responsibilities for the divorce?

• Has the individual adequately grieved and paid attention to both marital losses?

• Are you both emotionally healthy?

• Are either of you rushing into something or running away from something?

• How have sexual needs been addressed in the "in-between periods"?

• Does your friend view you as "Messiah" or "The Rescuer"?

• Are legal, financial, and tax issues resolved or secure?

• Is this person angry at God for the death or divorce?

• How evident are the ghosts of the former spouse?

• How attached is this individual to the "symbols" of the previous marriages: rings, cars, vacation homes, jewelry, pictures, clothes, the bed?

• Does the individual believe she/he can be a whole person without marriage?

Some who are widowed or divorced say, "I *have* to be married to be somebody." One young widow was reminded, "You were a whole person before you met Greg, and you can be a whole person *after him*. It's time for you to remember that!"[1] It is difficult for some to perceive a future—a real future—on their own. One widow, three months after her husband's death, noted in a thank you note to house guests: "Something that you said in the country stunned me so—that you hoped I would marry again. You were close to us so many times. There is one thing you must know. I consider that my life is over and I will spend the rest of it waiting for it really to be over." Little did Jackie Kennedy know, when she wrote that note in 1964, of the brilliant future she would live.[2] You might conclude that you could have a more brilliant future by not remarrying or by not marrying a particular individual.

Also consider a significant legal ramification. What if you marry, and this previously divorced and/or widowed person dies before you? Some divorce settlements include a "will contract" that prohibits former spouses from altering the current will in any way that would disinherit (or economically disadvantage) the children—or heirs—from a previous marriage. Under such a provision, you, a new spouse (and any new children) could be left with nothing but legal fees, a financial mess, and an emotional nightmare. Glynnis Walker warns that, in settling estates, "There's No Such Thing as an Ex-Wife,"[3] particularly if all the legal details were not tidied-up before the remarriage and death. The former spouse and first marriage children could turn all their emotional baggage into legal actions against you.

CHAPTER 17

Single and Coping with Divorce

176. I am divorced. What can I do that will help me readjust to single life?

As a divorced single adult, I know some of the struggles of readjustment. Here are my suggestions for successfully readjusting:

Find a good counselor. It's too easy to play district attorney or martyr—to arrange the facts in such a way as to convince the jury (your peers, your family, your lawyer, work colleagues) of the wrongs and indignities your former spouse inflicted on you. A skilled counselor will help you reflect on the facts and deal with your feelings.

Accept your fair share of the responsibility for the divorce. Every divorce has two sides. That's one of the reasons our judicial process uses the adversarial system. Unfortunately, that same system often goads people into bitter, one-sided views of their marriages and poisons their views on future relationships. Meanwhile, the lawyers laugh all the way to the bank.

You may be 5 percent responsible or 55 percent. Whatever it is, own up to it. Your healing and your chances for a healthy recovery and possibly a good subsequent marriage will be enormously increased by fully owning your contributions to the failures of the marriage. But don't lay claim to more than your fair portion of the blame.

Resist being the martyr. It will be tempting to conclude that you have the world's messiest divorce. You don't! Someone, somewhere has it worse. If you take on the martyr's role, you will delay—if not sabotage—your recovery. If you take on the whiner's role—"Oh, poor me . . . "—you'll drive away people who could help you as well as someone who could love you.

Look for a healthy divorce recovery group. In your community find those support groups for people surviving divorce. These groups exist to help people grow through the experience. You will find affirmation for your courage and for your progress. You will find a place to trade readings of the divorce roadmap. You will discover caring people who have "been there/experienced that!" and who will be there to help you grow through this loss experience and thrive because of it.

Share your feelings. Many divorced persons, especially men, keep their feelings bottled up inside; as a result, some could be labeled "emotionally constipated." Some turn to socially accepted painkillers such as workaholism, alcohol, prescription drugs, gambling, credit-card binges, or easy sex. Find someone with whom you can talk out your feelings. Or write in a notebook or at a computer keyboard. Ignore sentence structure, grammar, punctuation, and spelling. Ignore self-censuring thoughts. Just write out those feelings.

Don't fast-forward your grief. Grief is a normal part of the divorce process, especially if you have been blindsided. I've seen people shrug off the pain, pour themselves into their work or children, and try to "Lone Ranger" their way through the whirlwind of divorce, humming "I did it *my* way!" A few made it. Others, unfortunately, didn't. It's OK to be angry! Mad! Depressed! Sexually frustrated! But it's not OK to ignore or camouflage your feelings. Grief can be a great tutor.

Keep a journal. When you were a child, your parents may have made marks on the wall to monitor your growth. A journal can do the same thing. It will also give you a safe place to record your thoughts and wonderings and a place to go back to to discover your growth.

Read. Browse the shelves of bookstores or the library to find some good reading on divorce. You may want to read my book, *I Wish Someone Understood My Divorce* (Augsburg, 1986) or Jim Smoke's classic, *Growing Through Divorce.*

Don't rush into another relationship. Give yourself enough time (*years*—not weeks or months) to heal and to reconcile with the loss. By waiting, you increase your chances for a healthy remarriage. Avoid looking for love in all the wrong places; a premature marriage is a wrong choice and will only give you the chance to walk into your lawyer's office and say, "I'm back."

Guard your heart. Beware of the one who volunteers: "I know just what you need: Me!"

Stand before the mirror at least once a day and say: "Nothing could be more threatening to you than a premature romantic relationship!" Invest in your future: give yourself time to heal.

177. How can I overcome the fear of being hurt again?

It's natural for divorced individuals to fear getting hurt again. Yet many actually volunteer for a return visit to Hurt City. Over time, a high percentage will diffuse the fear, but unfortunately, a few become life-long prisoners. How can you avoid falling into that trap?

Consider your best interests. If you live your life based on fear, you may spend the rest of your life alone. Do you really want to live solo? Do you really want to believe that "all men or all women are alike!"? [1]

Examine your choices. If you start dating, if you become a work-aholic, if you pour yourself into your hobbies, your children, or volunteer responsibilities, you may be running away from your problems rather than working to resolve them. Fright tends to stimulate flight.

Imagine your future. God wants you—you!—to have a great future. Look ahead five or ten years. Are you going to be as angry then as you are now? As cynical? If you embrace your fear and nourish it, you will lose many opportunities to experience love. Taking risks is a basic part of the single life. Honestly own your fears of being hurt again. Don't rivet any more thin layers of sheet metal over your fragile heart for protection. Move on with your life in spite of your fears. You may initially have to bluff your fears to move on. As I've said before, "Live your life *now!*" Or, as one divorced friend reminds me, "Living well is the best revenge!"

Suppose I were to offer you a chance to make $500 by driving me to my next speaking appointment. "Show me the money!" you scream, grabbing your car keys. But I have one small stipulation: You have to cover up the windshield. You can only use the rearview mirror to drive. Would we even leave the curb safely? Why is the windshield so wide and the rearview mirror so small? Because where you are going is more important than where you have been. Yet most divorced people have the proportions reversed. They have huge rearview mirrors that capture every painful experience in their lives. Then they peer into the future through the tiniest of windshields. The big temptation for divorced people is to get stuck in past-tense living!

Sometimes, the future is wrapped in thick San Francisco-style fog. But it's still there. Your task today is to actively imagine and cooperate with that future. Be patient and do not settle for a discount future.

Appraise your needs and expectations. Exaggerating your needs or trying to "make up romantically for lost time" is another way of avoiding being hurt again. While you have a right to expectations of a new relationship ("This person will never hurt me like my ex hurt me!"), be careful about putting the new could-be-the-one up on a pedestal. Be careful about nurturing unrealistic needs that will cause you to idealize some relationships and avoid others. These days, romantic relationships are hard, hard work.

Give yourself time. Give yourself *lots* of time. Take plenty of time to rebuild and to heal. You are not ready for the future until you have finished the business of the past. Time is one luxury that you can afford during this period. Be generous with yourself and this bud of a relationship.

Recognize that if you want satisfying relationships, you will have to work at them. Sometimes it's three steps forward and two steps backwards. Are you making choices that result in repeated hurt and rejection? Are you volunteering to be hurt? Do you always blame the other person for the failure of the relationship? Your relationships are not going to be any better than you are willing to make them.

Be aware of the statistical realities. An estimated 60 percent of remarriages fail. Where children are involved, the rate of dissolution rises to 75 percent![2] Choose to step beyond your fears before they strangle you or entangle you in unhealthy, going-nowhere relationships.

178. Why does a first relationship after divorce or the death of a spouse hurt as much or more than the divorce or death?

Possibly because we come to a new relationship so needy. We behave like huge emotional sponges. Our need is so great that we may allow fantasy and an appetite for romance to dominate our thinking. Some of us, like three-year-olds, want someone to kiss away our "owies." We reenter the world of dating (or *redate*) with unrealistic expectations. We may be unwilling to take the time to heal thoroughly—to get beyond the scabs. We want some "rescuer" to ride into our lives and "make it all better," so that we can have a Hollywood storybook ending and live "happily ever after."

A new relationship will require risk. Unfortunately, some redate with a set of scales: "I put in so much, and therefore expect you to put in enough to balance the scales. If you don't reciprocate (or do so as speedily as I wish), I feel rejected."

Others rush into a new relationship "heart first." It's tempting to ignore the little warning bells sounding all around us. Sadly, there are single adults who will take advantage of your vulnerability—emotionally, financially, and sexually. You may wake up some morning with a triple whammy! So go slow, keep both eyes open and both feet on the ground, and keep a close watch on your heart.

179. How will I know when I am ready to marry again?

Before you seriously contemplate remarriage, you need to vigorously grapple with these questions:

Have I forgiven my ex? It doesn't matter what your former spouse (or spouses) did or did not do—have you forgiven him or her? Do you still fume every time you hear their name or voice? Active forgiveness may still be necessary, even if your former spouse is deceased.

Have I forgiven myself? Have you accepted responsibility for your role (however large or small) in the demise of the marriage? Have you forgiven yourself? Maybe you took the tough, wounded victim's profile: "After all I've done for you! This is the way you treat me!!!" Did you douse any possibilities of reconciliation?

Has enough time elapsed for healing and reconciliation? Give yourself time. If you are still carting around a backpack stuffed with problems and tensions from your divorce—or from a less-than-perfect marriage that ended in death—you are not ready for another relationship, let alone another marriage. By *reconciliation* I do not mean going back to a mate. I mean significantly reducing the hostilities between you and your ex—especially if there are children.

Is there unfinished business from the previous marriage? Do you owe back alimony? Child support? Then pay up before you take on the responsibilities of a new marriage and before you start another family. If the person you are considering marriage with has unpaid alimony/child support, remember, you may end up helping to pay it.

Who should I tell about my decision to remarry? You may not be able to resolve all the conflicts to everyone's satisfaction. But a "Surprise! We got married!" could produce anger, resentment, and complications for you. You need to seriously consider informing your ex—especially if you have children under age eighteen. Talking to all the "players" on the field of your new romance could make you more aware of any potential sabotage to your new relationship (sabotage that might make the pain you have already experienced seem minor-league!).

Is marriage now the best choice? There are good choices for second marriages and there are poor choices. What are your motivations for marriage? Motivations have to be honestly confronted. In itself, a second marriage is no proof that you are over your previous mate(s). More time might turn a mediocre choice into the best choice. But a premature or rebound relationship will only give you another ex, sooner or later.

Invest in good remarital counseling. A woman asked, "I've been married five times. Do you think some counseling might be helpful?" "Couldn't hurt!" I answered. The best choices only come when you give them time to route themselves to you.

180. How do I tell single men that just because I am divorced and want to be held, I am not "hot to trot"?

Myths die hard. Many men cling to the notion that a recently divorced woman, as one man explained, "has physical needs" and therefore, needs "servicing." After all, he added, "She is sexually experienced." Many males, single and married, assume that a divorcee will be more likely to have sex.

Be aware of the signals you send to men. If you don't want a sexual come-on, say so. Communicate your wishes and desires clearly and unapologetically. One woman talked about her shock, when, after a meal and a movie, her date paused outside the theater and said, "Your place or mine?" Without hesitation, she replied, "Neither" and walked away. Never apologize for or question a choice your heart says is wise!

Be cautious about sending mixed signals that may confuse a man or encourage him to make his "big move" or that lead him to assume that now all he needs to do is "up the ante" persuasively. Some men hear your no and conclude: "Ah, she's playing hard to get. She doesn't want me to think she's easy or sleeps around."

You may have to ask point-blank: "Why do you think that I am sexually available?" Such a confrontation may discourage him from making future assumptions—about you or about other women. You could be doing him a big favor. But if he doesn't respect the boundaries that you establish and value, don't go out with him again.

Here are some approaches to use. You may have to use more than one, because some men seem to have trouble getting simple messages through their thick, hormone-clogged skulls.

The direct approach. "Do you think I am easy?" or "Let's get one thing straight!"

The indirect approach. Look at him, then smile and say, "You know, some men think all divorced women are easy to make. Why do you think they think that?" This at least puts the subject on the table for further discussion and possible insight.

Choose your words carefully. In the games of dating, it's easy to misinterpret cues and comments and body language. For example, if you tell (or laugh at) suggestive stories or jokes, he'll assume more than you might want him to assume.

Some men are as afraid of the protocol as you are and are just bungling their way through it—ad libbing rather than thinking first. If either of you stumble into off-limits territory, put your thinking cap back on and make it clear what you want and don't want.

Expect the big move. Be prepared to deal with it. But don't use a nuclear warhead on an ant colony.

Don't send mixed signals. Men can be annoyed or confused by sudden stops just short of their intended goal. Did you lead this person to an assumption of sexual availability? If so, apologize, but don't back down.

Know your dates. The world may have changed since you last dated. For many men today, sex is an expected payoff, the current version of yesteryear's goodnight kiss. Get to know a man before you say yes to a date or you may be saying no more times than you bargained for.

Consider paying for the date. Researchers are discovering links between "who pays for a date" and expectations of sex. In one major study, single adults "indicated that if the woman allows the man to pay all the dating expenses rather than splitting the expenses, some men think it is more justifiable for him to have sex with her even against her will." ("Look how much money I spent on you. Don't I get something *in return?*") Those men who "accept" forcible date rape are less likely to call it "rape," have more traditional attitudes toward women, are more "self-sexually permissive," and are more likely to blame the woman and society.[1] In another study, when confronted with rape scenarios, many male respondents explained, "Well, he did spend a lot of money on her" and were reluctant to condemn the rapist's behavior as "definitely unacceptable."[2] Date rape is a part of the relational repertoire of too many men who prey on divorced and divorcing women. Know your dates!

181. Why is dating so different when you've been divorced? Every one I've been out with seems to have only one or two things on their mind: sex or marriage.

Emotionally wounded and needy individuals make up a large part of the American divorced population of 17.6 million.[1] Some single adults are what I call *ICT*, Intensive Care Technicians: "Oh baby, I know what you need—a big dose of me!" Although it can be disguised as "tender loving care," it's loaded with hidden agendas and expectations.

Initially, sexual intimacy can alter moods. Sex is a great anesthetic to numb our pain. However, like any anesthetic, it wears off. Loneliness and emptiness sneak back—sometimes while you're still under the sheets in that awkward silence than can follow an orgasm. Sometimes you lie in the dark wondering, "How much do I *really* know about this person?" These days, that also means of this individual's previous sexual partners.

Healing from a divorce takes time—lots of time. You have to be willing to invest in your healing process by recognizing that some people are not safe for you.

182. The man I am seeing is still married to his wife. But he's going to get a divorce. How long should I wait around for him?

You've waited too long already! If he's not available now and all of the time, he's not available, period. Wake up and smell that cappuccino. Here's a great Availability Test for identifying unavailable men or women.[1] This one's not for you if

- He/she is with someone, but promises to leave soon.
- He/she is with someone, but doesn't really love that person.
- He/she is with someone, but says they are not intimate anymore (Sure!).
- He/she is with someone, but is just staying till the kids get older.
- He/she is with someone, but that someone knows about you and it's "cool."
- He/she is with someone and isn't leaving, but likes hanging out with you.
- He/she just left someone and *might* be reconciling.

If you put a mental check mark by any one of the listings, this one is unavailable, regardless of his promises. How do you know that in a decade he won't be using these same explanations with the next woman he is seeing "on the side"? If it worked once for him, he may well try it again.

I would add that he's unavailable if his heart is still recovering from the last ended or ending relationship. He needs time to heal and to process the last relationship before launching a healthy new relationship with you. (Unless, of course, you want to volunteer to be a temporary or transitional relationship until he gets back on his romantic "feet.")

CHAPTER 18

Single and Coping with an Ex

183. How can I learn to cope with an ex constantly calling and upsetting me?

Divorce alters relationships, but it does not necessarily terminate them. Unlike a guillotine, divorce does not always produce a clean amputation. Sometimes jagged, infected edges complicate our lives and the lives of our children. Most have a difficult ongoing relationship with an ex-spouse; a few evolve into a friendship, often "for the sake of the kids." If you are divorced and remarry, you become involved in a "triangle relationship": you, your new spouse, and your ex-spouse.

A new relationship cannot solve any unfinished business from a divorce. Don't pretend it's over if there are issues that need to be settled or when the original decision isn't working out and needs to be resettled. Clearly, peaceful coexistence becomes complicated when one party rushes into a premature new relationship or marriage. And the triangle becomes a quadrangle if you both jump into a new relationship.

An ex may "lay low" for months, even years, and then show up with a grin and an "I'm back!" So this may not be an issue for you today but it could be tomorrow. How can you deal creatively with an annoying and pesky ex? How can you be responsible and responsive?

Let your ex know what you find annoying. It might not be intentional—some ex-spouses are just habitually annoying.

Keep conversations brief and focused. Keep phone calls brief and to the point. Be assertive: "I am hanging up now. Good-bye." Since you pay your phone bill, you have control over the incoming as well as outgoing calls. Invest in caller identification (so you can tell when it's your ex that is calling) and a good answering machine to "screen" your ex's calls. Consider any phone call from an ex to be a "collect" call. Do you wish to accept the emotional charges?

Take the offensive. "I am so glad you called, because I have a few things I need to discuss with you" (this is especially effective if your ex owes alimony/child support).

Tell a joke. "You know, I heard the best joke the other day . . . " Humor diffuses tension.

Assume responsibility for your feelings. Rarely do we own our anger. We don't say, "I became so angry at you!" but rather, " You made me so mad!" Wait. Who's in charge here? You or your ex? Take responsibility for your reactions. If you keep responding in the old patterns your ex knows so well, you compound the issue. Rewire your circuits and surprise your ex. Don't let it get to you. One friend keeps her junk mail piled by the phone so she can sort while her ex rants and raves. She occasionally mumbles monosyllabic responses: "*Huh . . . well . . . oh . . . yeah.*"

Don't be baited. Don't be goaded into saying things you will regret later. Some exes are like skilled fishermen who invest lots of time preparing their lures. If your ex is playing the baiting game, your refusal to play diffuses the fun. Dorothy Nevill offers this wise tidbit: "The real art of conversation is not only to say the right thing in the right place but to leave unsaid the wrong thing at the tempting moment."[1] Ignore the temptation.

Set reasonable time limits for a conversation. Try "I just set the timer for six minutes. What's on your mind?" or "If you would like to talk about this, let me suggest you call between 5:30 and 6:30 p.m." Be specific. Late night calls only compound the irritation and leave you rehashing the conversation all night: "I should have said . . . " Avoid these unless you want to be sleepless in Buffalo, Louisville, or Dallas and no fun to be around the next day.

Pray. Use undesired phone calls as an opportunity to pray with your ex. "Now before we talk, let's just have a little prayer, OK?" This either changes the whole tone of the conversation or shortens it. Pray before you call your ex or before you answer his or her call. Just offer a quick, "Lord, help me in this conversation."

Never turn your children into delivery messengers. "You can tell your father that I said . . ." This is definitely a lose-lose strategy! In the divorce you received custody *of yourself*—take responsibility for *yourself!*

184. How do I handle jealousy over my ex's sex life?

I assume you mean their presumably active sex life. Would you be jealous if your ex was celibate? Curiosity not only "killed the cat" but has delayed or sabotaged a lot of healing after messy divorces. Your ex is responsible for his/her own sexual choices as well as for modeling wise relational choices to your children. And so are you. Don't be a sexual snoop.

Sure, you may feel like you are on a sexual "diet" while your ex is feasting! That's life. Get used to it. No useful purpose is served if you spend time brooding over tidbits of information (supplied by children and friends) and trying to "color in" the details with your imagination. The Psalmist counsels, "In your anger [or loneliness] do not sin. When you are on your bed [perhaps the bed you once shared with your ex] search your heart and be silent" (Psalm 4:4). Be silent is great advice.

Remember, some people lie or at least exaggerate about their sex lives. Your ex may still try to arouse your irritation by dropping little hints about what may or may not be true. Also, remember that divorced people often use sex as an anesthetic—something to dull the pain and sense of loss and rejection. So your ex may be acting out sexually but sowing the seeds for major league hurt down the road.

Don't dwell on what your ex is doing. Don't point out your ex's sexual sins to your children—whatever their age. If your ex has a sexual partner (or someone you assume is a sexual partner) be careful what you label them and remember that "little ears" overhear and pass on your tidbits and commentary. If you rehearse some label in your mind you may slip and your children will hear, and then your ex will hear and it's escalation of conflict time.

If your ex's sex life leads to an STD, will you still be jealous? Then why be jealous now? Your brain and soul cells have something much more important to concentrate on: your own great future!

Don't go tattling or whining to family, children, in-laws, neighbors, friends, or Ann Landers. What your ex-spouse does (or does not do) sexually is none of your business—*unless you can show that it directly harms your children.* Never use your children as detectives to help you gather dirt, er, information that might help you reopen child custody issues or negotiate with your ex. ("Oh, he has a girlfriend, does he? . . . Oh, you heard her in the bathroom at 3 a.m?") You may, of course, have legitimate questions or concerns about what goes on when your children are with your ex. Direct your questions to your ex.

185. Can my ex and I have sex?

Many divorced couples have sex at some point. In one research study, 8 percent of second wives reported that their husbands "saw their first wives for sexual reasons." [1] The percentage is no doubt higher among those who have not remarried. Some participants in my seminars declare that even the *notion* of "ex-sex" is obnoxious. Yuk! Perhaps absence and abstinence do make the heart grow fonder (and do tend to sentimentalize memories). However, a little trip down sexual memory lane seldom eliminates the problems and attitudes that led to a divorce. Ask yourself, again, "What am I pretending not to know here?"

"Can we have sex?" is not the right question. "*Should* we?" is more appropriate. What's the motivation? Is there a hidden agenda? Are you using sex to "butter up" the ex, say, for some more money this month?

One woman described occasional sex with her ex as "our way of saying goodbye gradually." [2] Maybe so, but remember, sexual intercourse and permanent commitment go hand in hand—even for ex-spouses. If you do have sex, you still always wonder who your ex has slept with and who that individual has slept with. You may end up with something to remember an ex by that you don't want. My best advice is: Nip it in the bud.

186. Should I try for reconciliation or should I consider my divorce a decisive ending point?

Reconciliation with *reality* is the goal of the healing after divorce. We reconcile to the loss, to the divorce, to the changed circumstances—financial, emotional, and spiritual—and we move on. Sometimes we have to schedule a heart-to-heart with ourselves to have a reality check. So by *reconciliation*, I do not mean remarrying your ex but settling disputes between you, deliberately and significantly reducing the tension, especially if there are children who are affected by your continued hostilities.

Your divorce severed a legal relationship. It will take time for your emotions to match the legal reality. Many divorced people cling so strongly to a hope for reconciliation or for a "coming to the senses" that they are devastated when the ex marries again.

Divorce gives you permission to focus your energies on the future rather than on the past. The tap of the judge's gavel is like a starter's gun for you—to begin a process of healing, nurturing yourself, organizing your agenda for a good life, and moving on. As a divorced person, I have found great encouragement in words about Abraham's choice after the death of Sarah: "Then Abraham *rose up*" (Genesis 23:3). That is the goal for every divorced person: (1) thoroughly do your grief work, (2) rise up, and (3) move on.

187. I didn't want this divorce. Now my ex wants to be my friend. How can I be a friend to him? Should I try to create a friendship with my ex?

Divorce doesn't end problems or relationships; it changes them. You're no longer husband and wife, but you can choose from a variety of models for your new relationship, or you can create your own relational path. Some couples manage to stay "buddies." As one woman said, "Well, we have been together all our lives." You still have common turf, particularly children and perhaps grandchildren. You share friends and memories. Lots of your history is mingled or overlaps. You may still interact socially. This is especially true in small towns or communities.

Some couples put aside differences and spend holidays (or portions of holidays) together "for the benefit of the children."

Most aren't so fortunate. Put many ex-couples in the same space and you'll soon dial 911. Here are some post-divorce prototypes to avoid:

• *Grudge-Matchers* have a lot of unresolved issues, perhaps below the surface. It doesn't take much to push their buttons. They keep track of who is "ahead" and match each other, grudge for grudge.

• *Time-Bombers* are just waiting to explode. You feel like you are walking through a mine field when you are around them or communicate with them. Any step could be explosive.

• *Guerillas* launch an attack and then run for cover.

• *Revengers* snarl, "My ex will pay for this!" Little wonder about the popularity of the movie, *The First Wives Club*. Revenge is seductive. But plotting revenge wastes energy that could have been invested in building your own future. It's not unusual for revengers to end up in court again (and again), with meters running for two lawyers. Sadly, some revengers and their revenge objects end up dead!

Some couples work hard for a friendly divorce, but that's not always possible to achieve or maintain. Over time, new experiences and new relationships will change the mix. Particularly if in a later marriage there are financial pressures that make honoring alimony or child support commitments difficult. Generally, the new spouse resents money going to the previous family, and eventually resentment gets nasty. Some couples keep up an appearance of friendship to minimize conflict, pain, and feelings of guilt. Some individuals act friendly so that they can more easily circumvent or challenge the guidelines for visitation, alimony, and child support.

You may not be able to be friends just yet. But in time you may—if enough seeds of friendship and kindness are planted. The apostle Paul said, "If it is possible [and in some circumstances it is not], as far as it depends on you, live at peace with everyone" (Romans 12:18). Surely ex-spouses are included in Paul's category, *everyone*. The key phrase is "*if it is possible*." After some divorces, there isn't a lot of possibility.

188. I can't talk to my ex. But there are some things I'd like to get off my chest. Help!

I'm not sure what is included in "get off my chest." Some of us have stored so much inside that we're ready to detonate! We keep stuffing hurts, slights, and emotional outrages into plastic bags, to insure their freshness. We have huge stockpiles of wounds.

First, do not turn your children into couriers to relay anger-dripping messages to your ex. "Tell your mother for me . . . " Anger-based communication only intensifies barriers, so the stuff you "get off your chest" will be replaced by new stuff.

Consider composing a "Letter to My Ex." Even if you do not send it, the exercise will be healthy for you.

Sit down and put into letter format all that is on your mind and heart. Forget grammar and spelling. Just let the words flow. This draft could end up in the trash can, so get free.

Let the draft sit for a while. There's no rush.

Slowly reread the letter. Silently. Now aloud. Left out something? Overstated anything? Is this something you would want your children to see? Assume they will see it at some point.

Remember the three phrases, the ten words that could make a difference to your healing. They could offer the olive branch to your ex—and, like a boomerang, to yourself:

I was wrong. (Don't add, "but, of course, not as wrong
   as you!")

I am sorry.

Will you forgive me?

Ask yourself, "What is my motivation, now that I have this down on paper?" Are you trying to wound your ex? Revenge in an "in-your-face" style merely ups the ante in the hostilities.

Circle or highlight the key words or phrases. Using those key words, compose a free-verse poem about what you have felt writing this letter. Some single adults have found free-form poetry to be a better, more flowing venue for expressing their feelings.

Ask yourself: "Is this going to help or hurt?" Think not only of your ex but also your children, who may well see this letter, as well as your ex-in-laws (the grandparents of your children), your ex's new spouse or spouse-to-be, friends, neighbors, etc.

Ask a trusted friend to read the letter. Talk with your friend about the letter and consider their editorial suggestions.

Let the letter sit, again. For a day, a week, a month.

Reread it. No great writing is a first draft. Besides, you may have forgotten some key point.

Do another draft.

When you have a draft you feel comfortable with, consider the options. Ask God for the wisdom to know what to do with your "Declaration."

Do another draft.

Decide what to do with it:

> *Do nothing with it.*
>
> *Mail it to yourself.* The process of dropping this letter in a mailbox can be healing.
>
> *Make a copy and mail the original.* Ask God to pave the way for the receipt of the letter, that it might be favorable to dialogue.

Destroy the letter, either by burning it or by tearing it in pieces and flushing it down the toilet. After all, by writing this letter, you have "flushed" some pain out of your life.

Move on with life. Life is too precious to be wasted.

In my experience as a divorced person, I have found that the more time I invested in finding the right words, the better the dialogue and the less likely my words would be to wound or to be misunderstood. The Psalmist was right, "A gentle answer turns away wrath, but a harsh word stirs up anger" (Proverbs 15:1).

Remember, coping with an ex is like breaking a horse: Take it slow and take it easy.

CHAPTER 19

Single and
Coping with
Single Parenting

189. I am a single parent with three children. How do I deal with their curiosity about my singleness?

Without knowing your age or your children's age, I will offer two responses. First, assuming your children are still at home and that you are an "active" single parent, I would hope that you do not douse your children's curiosity. Certainly you can establish some parameters for their curiosity. However, singleness is a reality in their world and the world of their friends and in television and movies, so they already have a head start in wondering. Most children want a clear sense of security that you are going to be there for them.

Barbara Schiller, head of Single Parent Family Resources, identifies one crucial issue. "Address their stated or unexpressed fears: I am going to be here for you. Listen carefully to what your children are saying and are not saying." [1]

Your children need to know that you value them and that you do not see them as a hindrance to your own future. Younger children may entertain a fantasy for your eventual reconciliation with the co-parent, for things to be "like they were." You may have to delicately but deliberately burst that entrenched fantasy.

The single life, especially dating, may threaten your children, especially when they detect or even suspect that a relationship is getting serious. They may fear that if you meet the right one and remarry, that person could walk out on you and them, too. It is essential that you remind them that your marital status does not threaten them. Reassure them—repeatedly—that they have a place in your heart and in your priorities for the long term. Keep that commitment.

If you are a single parent with adult children, they may be concerned about your remarriage, particularly if you have significant assets. I remember my surprise when my seventy-four-year-old mother announced, "I don't think I'll remarry." I didn't know she was thinking about it. Remarriage can bring a real sense of relief in some cases; tension in others. In some families, however, there may be one son or daughter who wants to act as "protector" of the surviving parent or the family inheritance (sometimes with less than pure motives), and this can create great conflict. This can intensify distress between you and your child/ren and between your friend and your child/ren. It can create a wedge between the you and the object of your romantic interests. Earl, a seventy-five-year-old widower, wanted to remarry. His son, a physician, fumed, "Daddy, you're making a fool of yourself! You're too old to have these kinds of urges!" Earl pleaded with me, "What should I do?" I asked about the reaction of his three daughters; they supported him with "Daddy, we just want you to be happy." Earl married a wonderful woman and the three daughters danced at his wedding. His son ended up making a fool of himself by not attending.

190. How can a single parent explain the dating process to children when it obviously confuses them?

Children today understand the dating process somewhat better than previous generations because they have friends whose parents are divorced, dating, and/or remarried. Television has also exposed most children to the issues involved. But don't assume anything. Before your first date, you will still want to lay some groundwork.

Some parents make the mistake of going out on a date without telling the children where they are going and when they will be back. The children need to know that dating will not reduce the quality time you have with them. Even though it does add one more commitment to your already busy schedule as a single parent, you need to make certain that your children understand they have not been relegated to second place among your priorities.

Don't be surprised if your child is hostile to a person you are seeing, or becomes hostile upon realizing that this could result in marriage and a step-relationship. Expect some sulking or acting out—or in older children, the silent treatment or slammed doors. Realize that it will take time for your children to get used to the idea that you and their other parent are not going to get back together.

Be aware that children will be sensitive about being sent to their rooms so that you can have privacy with your friend. They will be sensitive to body language and any suggestion that they are "in the way" of romance. They may harbor feelings of rejection and suffer because of it. Good communication between your children and your friend is very important in the early relational foundation-building. These encounters may be anxiety-producing for the never-married single adult dating a single parent. It's tempting to think (even say) "If that were my child, I'd . . ."

With older children, at some point you will need to confront the issue of sexuality—yours! Your children will have questions about your sexual choices. What you say, what you do not say, and what you do will plant seeds that you may have to live with later, particularly as you offer them guidance in dealing with their own sexual choices.

Reassure your children that no one is going to take the place of their other parent. Ask them to give your new relationship a fair chance. Ask them to try hard to get to know—and possibly eventually like—the person you are seeing. Help them understand that liking your friend is not a betrayal of their love for their other parent.

Anticipate the questions. Always tell the truth, because the truth will eventually come out.

191. I am a single parent who has high standards—quite different than my ex. Do I simply ignore his past and present or should I tell my children?

I am not certain what composes your ex's "past and present" but I do know that the public rationale for a divorce and the private reasons may be quite different. For example, it's one thing if your ex does drugs, is an alcohol or substance abuser, or has a criminal record. But what is *your* motivation? The single parent needs to make certain that disclosure is not a "settling of a score" or revenge.

Children have a way of figuring out what's going on, on their own, or with a little prodding from an older brother or sister. They have a subtle suspicion when the truth or the entire truth is being withheld or parceled out to them. The key questions for you are: (1) What does each child need to know? and (2) How will this knowledge affect their relationship with the co-parent and with each other? How will a child emotionally process the data? Will it seem that you are simply settling the score or badmouthing your ex? Even if the data is factually true, you could lose, as well.

Wise single parents have decided never to say anything negative about an ex and never to return the volley when the ex is negative about them. As one single parent said so accurately, "Faults and all—he is *still* my child's father."

192. As a single parent, how do I explain my sexual choices to my children?

These days children are going to assume some level of sexual involvement. Your honesty needs to be appropriate; how old are they and are they able to understand? Just don't try to hide the relationship from them. This can become an issue if you have teens and are giving them the "Just Say No!" lectures yet your behavior contradicts you, so what they hear from you is, "Do as I say and not as I do." It would be unwise for you to allow your children to find you and a friend in a compromising position. And don't pump your children for information on the dating or sexual realities of your ex: "Is your father still seeing . . . ?"

193. I was married to a homosexual man. I had no idea about his orientation until long after we were married and had children. Most people think that I initiated the divorce for "irreconcilable differences." So I have taken lots of heat—even from my family—for being the initiator. Do I need to reveal his sexual orientation to the children?

In many divorces, homosexuality is a factor to some degree (one in five homosexuals in one research study identified themselves as having been heterosexually married). One single mother explained that she could not disclose her husband's sexual orientation because in their conservative community the disclosure would destroy him professionally and socially, and, more importantly, would have a negative financial impact on the children.

Lots of spouses learned to accommodate homosexuality as an ingredient in the marriage, at least for the sake of the children or appearance or lifestyle. As long as extramarital sexual activity is avoided or confined to certain agreed-to boundaries, the marriage continues. However, the onset of AIDS has threatened this balanced silence. In some cases, vindictive spouses or ex-spouses can use or threaten to use the knowledge for financial or child custody advantage.

In few cases does homosexuality interfere with fathering or mothering. You have a right to request that the co-parent not sleep with a lover or significant other when the children are there. You do not have a right to keep your children from seeing their co-parent because of your attitudes about homosexuality.

The issue can become troublesome if the entire family takes on "the secret," especially as teens attempt to cope with their own emerging sexuality and with the pronounced homoprejudice in our society. If the co-parent's orientation becomes known or is suspected, children may face taunts and teasing: "Your dad's a fag!" Things becomes far more complicated when the co-parent has a lover and they decide to live together; there is considerable latitude in how courts view such an arrangement. In some cases vengeful parents can make it difficult for the co-parent to have meaningful visitation privileges. One word of caution if you're considering this strategy: You can win this battle initially but lose the war over the long haul.

Many parents simply accept that this is reality and work to determine what is best for the children. Admittedly, in the age of AIDS, you may have to address some of your children's concerns about the threat of a co-parent or their lover contracting AIDS. Moreover, early in the divorce process, the partner may not be "out" and you will have to keep the information to yourself. You have to be careful not to disclose this to friends who are the parents of your children's friends, since the word may very well get back to your children, and you may have to answer, "Why didn't you tell me/us? What *else* have you kept from us?" [1]

194. What are the difficulties a never-married man faces in dating or marrying a woman with children?

This is a big reality. The older you are and the longer you are unmarried, the more likely you are to date or marry someone with children. Here are some factors you should be aware of:

Somewhere (even if only in memory) there is a father—an ex or a deceased husband. Surviving spouses tend to accentuate the positive in their deceased mates or to practice "selective memory." Divorced persons tend to focus on the negative characteristics and histories of their exes. Either way, comparisons will be made. The father may not be active in the children's lives, but he does have some influence on their fantasies, expectations, and trust, even if deceased or only present on special occasions, such as birthdays or holidays.

Some children nourish a fantasy about their parents getting back together and the whole family living "happily ever after." Clearly you threaten the fantasy. Other children may have clearly defined ideas of what their new stepparent should be like; they may want you to "make up" for the deficiencies of the other parent.

Some children, particularly sons, have become ad hoc "men of the house." While their perception of reality may be skewed or exaggerated, it is important that you proceed slowly building a relationship with them as well as with their mother. You are constructing an "in addition to" rather than "in place of" relationship.

Some children cling to a new male—any new male. They may have wanted each man their mother has dated to be their stepfather. Do you make the cut? Many will be hungry for a male relationship. Your relationship with their mother may not develop into marriage, but you may hate to pull the plug on the emotional bond with the child/ren fearing that you will hurt them. Other children have seen a long succession of men come in and out of their lives—"here today, gone tomorrow." They might refuse to open up to you, since they see you as merely "the latest" romantic interest of their mom.

The children may be a constant reminder to you (or to your family) that their mother has been previously married. Some men (and their mothers) think of stepchildren as "emotional baggage" that they could do without. This becomes especially apparent when trying to schedule your life during holidays or school vacations when custody must be shared.

The children and their mother have a "shared" history—a past that you are not part of. So there may be inside jokes, or conversations that begin with, "Remember the time we . . . ?" (and you are not part of that *we*). Ex-in-laws may be less than thrilled with you, particularly if they suspect you were a factor in the divorce.

The children may be discipline-challenged. They may not be on their best behavior, and they may test you to check out the boundaries of your love or tolerance. Remember, you may be a friend of their mother or may even be her fiancé, but you are not a sheriff with a "We're going to have some law and order around here!" agenda. "What those kids of yours need" will only douse the romantic flame. Your indictment of the child's misbehavior translates as an indictment of the single parent's parenting skills.

If you are dating a single parent with young or small children, you may feel you are dating a crowd or are in a fishbowl. Little eyes and little ears seem to be everywhere. There may be problems with finding (or paying for) frequent babysitters. Get used to dating *with* the kids.

Children get sick. A single parent's schedule generally revolves around the children. So you have a big romantic evening planned but it has to be mothballed because Dr. Mom is needed at home or Dr. Mom is calling home every ten minutes.

These factors need to be considered seriously. However, lest the portrait be too negative, remember that children can be wonderful. I had dinner with a friend and his new family—a widow and her two young sons. I noticed small gold bands on the children's ring fingers, so I asked about them. The boys answered, "Our Dad [my friend] gave them to us when he married our mom. *He wanted to marry us, too.*"

Being involved with another adult's children is an awesome responsibility. You can have considerable positive influence if you go into it with your eyes and your heart "wide open" and if you work to keep your communication lines open.

You do need to ask some questions. What are the motives of this single parent? Does she want a husband? A father figure for the children? A second income? A combination of the above? Those are tough, even menacing questions, but they should be asked before you become involved in the relationship. Never overlook this troublesome fact: approximately 75 percent of remarriages with children fail.[1]

195. What are the difficulties a never-married woman faces in dating or marrying a man with children?

The previous question may be applicable to anyone, a man or woman, who is dating someone with children. However, there are certain issues that apply most often to women dating men with children.

In a large study of second wives, in which 61 percent had never been married before, Glynnis Walker discovered that a majority felt that they worked "to help their husbands meet support payments for their first family." One in three said that they could not afford to have their own children because they were supporting children from the husband's previous marriage. (Of course, that could be a frustration, not only for you, but for your parents, especially those who want their *own* grandchildren, not "built-in" or "prepackaged" stepgrandchildren.)

Two-thirds of the participants reported that they were inadequately prepared for marriage to someone who had been previously married. One in four participants indicated that at times they felt "their husbands were still married to the first wife."[1] Moreover, some ex-spouses become vindictive if the first spouse remarries, including restricting (or complicating) the father's participation in the children's lives "as a punishment for remarrying,"[2] or if the children become "too close" to the stepmother.

Simply put, you will need lots of diplomatic skills for the inevitable tough times when your relationship with your spouse becomes complicated. Ask the wicked stepmother from the fairy tales.

196. Do children have a veto power over the future of their parents?

It's easy to suggest that the reference point be "What's best for the children involved?" The reality is that many children do exercise some degree of veto power. The threat, "I'll go live with Dad/Mom" can be persuasive. The threat does not have to be verbal; your otherwise friendly son or daughter may make your date feel as welcome as a child molester at a PTA meeting. Or they might "live and let live" as long as it is only a dating situation, but once marriage is on the horizon, all bets are off. The "child from hell" stuns everyone in his/her path. Sadly, siblings can turn against each other on the issue. An ex may be a sideline coach, encouraging the sabotaging behaviors. You need to decide whether your ex learns of your wedding plans through you, your children, or the grapevine.

The reality is that no small number of relationships and remarriages are deliberately sabotaged and even destroyed by children: "If it hadn't been for the kids . . . " In fact, some couples have chosen to live under separate roofs because of the stresses with the children.

This merits The Conversation. Dr. Bobbie Reed has wisely suggested that the single parent first carefully audit the situation, considering how each person involved will be affected or impacted by the marriage, especially when it involves "blending" two families and redefining living space or economic priorities.[1] Diane Swaim has counseled hundreds of single parents and works to empower them in their role *as parents*. "I am the parent as long as the children are under age. I will consider what is best for them. It is irresponsible not to consider their opinions. But I still believe in being 'The Parent.'"[2]

Single parents have an incredible responsibility to their children. For many it's twenty-four hours a day for 365 days a year. Yet you agreed to this responsibility when you had the sex that conceived them. You agreed to at least see them to young adulthood. The best way to do that, given the high divorce rate in second marriages, is often to remain single until the children are young adults.

Counseling offices are crowded with children, teens, and young adults who feel that no one cares about them or that they are second priorities in the lives of one or both parents. "Why didn't someone ask *me* what I think? What I feel? What I want?" So, veto power? No! Input? Definitely.

197. Why do men want to date women without children?

Frankly, because in the minds of many, other people's children translate as "problems." Big problems. Every day, in blended families and dating families, the lines are drawn and skirmishes fought. Almost no issue is too small to become a battleground, particularly with the charge of favoritism. "*His* kids get away with murder."

Scanning the personals, readers repeatedly find, "No children." Even the phrase, "*Children OK*" can be deceptive. "OK" does not mean enthusiastic acceptance. Moreover, given the number of women without children in the available pool of single adults, men do not *have* to date women with children. For many—particularly men who are older and have already raised a family—the presence of children means an ex or a ghost of the perfect mate ("God rest his soul"), and that spells T R O U B L E!!! Most men have heard the stories: "I love her . . . but not those children."

Single parents have to beware of the "law-and-order" date or prospective mate, who resembles the hired gun or the sheriff in the B-Western, riding into town to restore law and order. Or the woman who wants to bring "civilization" to your humble abode. The date who is motivated to "make it up to the kids" or becomes "the kids' pal" may expect your children to "rise up and call me blessed." Be warned: that could be the *last* name they come up with.

Some single parents are so emotionally involved with their own children from a previous marriage that they cannot enthusiastically take on another's. If you are considering marriage, it's especially important that you and your future spouse agree about having additional children together. A new baby could be a unifying factor or a disunifying factor, particularly if unplanned.

Many men fear marrying a woman with a child. Rather than getting involved and having to wrestle with that decision, they simply do not date women with children. Admittedly, children do limit freedom, especially in these days of entitlement, what with swimming, ballet, skating lessons, Brownies, soccer, etc. Even scheduling a babysitter can cramp your single style.

198. I love this woman but I cannot stand her ex. The children spend part of their time with him. I am positive that he is poisoning their minds against me. How do I get along with him?

For some, the issue is about control. Obviously, the woman could not live with this man, but he still has some ability or desire to reach into her life and influence her relationships. To deal with this you will need The Conversation. "My friend, *this* is reality. I am marrying your ex. Get used to it!" Perhaps her ex fears that you will launch a campaign to delete him from an active role in the lives of his children. You need to reassure him that you do not intend to do that. Meet him, on his turf or neutral turf, and say, "How can we get along for the sake of the children?"

You may choose a third party (hopefully someone with some experience in this arena) as a referee for the meeting or to make it into a "trialogue." Or you may choose to do this by mail, e-mail, fax . . . Or be creative and rent a billboard: "Hey, Bill. I am marrying your ex. Let's be friends."

199. The woman I am dating has four impossible children under age sixteen. I love her but how can I deal with those out-of-control children?

Love is not going to be enough in this situation. If you know the children are impossible, you need to assume that they will continue to be impossible for the foreseeable future, at least long enough to zap the energy out of your relationship with their mom. Some children are skilled strategists; they can launch insurgency campaigns against you as the new person in their parent's life. They may never get a chance to know you, but it will be their loss. Don't volunteer for grief patrol by ignoring the intentions of these children. They will create ways to pit you against their parent unless you both anticipate and recognize this tendency.

Sometimes you can establish a beachhead by getting to know one child and asking, "Just give me a chance." Always reaffirm that you do not intend to replace or obliterate their other parent.

This problem is common when a newly divorced or widowed parent begins premature dating, or when the children have not yet accepted the divorce or the death. Ask yourselves, "What is the big rush?" Decide to give the relationship and the children time. *Lots of time.* But keep alert to the small issues that can mushroom into significant ones, and never underestimate the power of an ambush.

Finally, you can make it as a single parent, and you can make it as an influence on the children of someone you love and marry. But you have to go into these relationships with your eyes and heart wide open.

CHAPTER 20

Single and Seeking a Good Counselor

200. Why do I need to talk to a counselor? Can't I just work this out on my own?

All of us have questions, wonderings, puzzlements, doubts, frustrations, confusions, and predicaments about this incredible capacity called sexuality. But it's finding courage to talk "about sex in a way that can actually help us become more satisfied with our experiences that is so important and badly needed," reminds sexuality specialist, Patrick Carnes.[1]

Single adults cannot make sense of sexuality in a vacuum or "on their own." Even those who seek out an assumed safe monastic life soon discover that sexuality catches up with them. Some, who have been less than kind in regard to the sexual failures or foibles of others or who have self-righteously commented, "I certainly *don't* need a counselor!" have found the tables turned on them. We have to integrate our sexuality with our spirituality—and that is no small task. If we cannot, sooner or later we will "turn to relationships with *objects*—the false gods, in the biblical sense, of alcohol, money, sex, food—whatever seems to fill the void inside."[2] Sexuality can easily become idolatry for a single adult.

In order to put the puzzling or troublesome pieces of my sexual life together and make sense of my stories, and my black-and-blue sexual bruises, I need someone to whom I can disclose my great secrets and small shames, as well as my shadow. I am grateful to the gifted counselors and spiritual directors who have helped me sort through my questions and make sense of them.

What Victoria Alexander contends is necessary for the healing of grief, is also necessary for mental, spiritual, and sexual health:

I need to be able to put my feelings and my fears and stories into words.

I need to be able to say the words aloud.

I need to know that those words—and the pauses—and the tears—and the laughter (at times) have been heard.[3]

From my own puzzlements with my sexuality, I would add:

• I need to have someone who will listen all the way to the end of my sentences.

• I need someone to take seriously the black-and-blue realities of trying to make sense of sexuality as a single adult. I don't want to be patted on the head or to hear, "There, there."

• I need someone who can hear my failures. I don't want or need someone who thinks their spiritual gift is "kicking my rear end!" (such counselors are numerous).

• I need a trained, credentialed, licensed counselor—whether psychologist, social worker, or pastor.

201. **What is crucial for counseling to be successful?**

Two elements are critical: the choice of a counselor and your willingness to be trustingly vulnerable, to bring *all* of yourself into the counseling. If counseling is to be effective, I need to be able to relate comfortably and unapologetically to the counselor, especially when discussing my sexuality and sexual choices, things that I may never have admitted to anyone, including myself. My friend, Susannah Fitzgerald, a social worker, insists, "Without feeling psychologically safe with a counselor," a counselee will not be "able to share that which is most personal" and which demands attention.[1]

The counselor must be comfortable with her own sexuality in order to encourage me to explore my sexual issues. Frankly, some counselors—despite all their training—have blind spots on certain sexual issues and choices.

202. How can I find a competent counselor?

Ask your minister or physician for a referral. Ask friends. Ask through employee assistance at work. You may be referred to any one of several different types of counselors, either in private practice or in a community mental health service. Mental health helpers include the following:

Psychiatrist: a physician with advanced training in psychiatry who treats mental disorders (and is able to prescribe drugs for treatment)

Psychologist: a nonphysician with graduate training (preferably a Ph.D.) in human behavior

Clinical social worker: an individual trained in providing social and human services

Counselor: a person trained in counseling, who works in the mental health field or in a church setting

Marriage and family therapist: a clinician who specializes in working with relationship and family problems

Therapist: a person trained in a variety of therapeutic techniques for dealing with human behavior

Minister: a person either ordained or authorized to do lay counseling, particularly on the spiritual dimensions of an issue. Not all ministers, however, are gifted as counselors. Some ministers believe their role as minister means to bring "law-and-order."

Make an initial appointment.
Ask about their credentials, training, and memberships in professional organizations.
After your first appointment with a counselor, reflect on these questions:
Was it easy to talk to this person?
Did the counselor show genuine respect for me?
Did the counselor ask good questions about all the aspects of my life or only about my sexual or romantic issues?

Did the counselor offer "instant" solutions?

Did the counselor project the attitude of "having all the answers"?

Did the counselor take me seriously?

Can I trust this counselor with my stories and my secrets?

Dr. John Larsen, with incredible experience both in counseling and in training counselors, cautions, "Your counseling experience will likely be more productive if you select a counselor whose values are generally in line with yours. It is perfectly acceptable to inquire about the counselor's values before you begin or continue a counseling relationship." [1] It is also valuable to inquire about the counselor's attitudes on singleness.

Think of a counselor as a guide or "stretcher" (rather than a "shrink"). Is this a skilled helper who can help you stretch to understand and embrace your sexuality and your realities? Or is this a "shrink"—a common euphemism. Good counselors are not Ms. Fix-It of the emotions: three sessions and "There now, you're all fixed."

Give your counselor time, and give of yourself and your stories. You only waste their time and delay your healing and growth if you play games or withhold essential information.

If you are uncomfortable with an individual after an initial visit move on to another referral. These days, almost anyone can hang out the shingle and call themselves a "counselor," particularly in the religious community. The "fit" between you and a counselor is essential for a successful counseling experience. Keep asking for recommendations.

Consider counseling an investment, not an expense. You may find psychological services that are covered by your insurance plan or a counselor who charges in proportion to your income. Check out your employee assistance program. You may want to seek out services through community mental health services. I have never regretted the money I have spent "renting" ears and perspectives. It is a wise time and money investment.

203. I have a friend who goes to a spiritual director. What is that?

You may want to take advantage of what is called *spiritual direction.* Spiritual directors (sometimes called *spiritual friends*) are trained in the spiritual disciplines, and their counseling focuses on the spiritual aspects of an issue. They help us sort out what God is doing in our lives. Often spiritual directors are priests, nuns, or pastors of mainline churches who consider spiritual guidance one of the privileges of their calling and offer it to people who are not members of their congregations or even their denominations. Spiritual directors often have the power to hear confessions and generally include prayer as part of their approach. Many do not charge for their guidance.

What is seemingly a sexual issue may be a spiritual issue. In fact, the issue may have developed because we have built rigid boundaries between the spiritual and the sexual. Any sexual issue is touched by our understanding of God and grace. Most psychologists, however, focus primarily on the sexual or relational dimensions and, only lightly if at all, on the spiritual aspects. The spiritual director reverses those priorities. The spiritual director's question may often be, "What is God saying to you in *this*?" Little wonder that, in our most intense sexual moments, we say or scream, "O God!" Patrick Carnes concludes that it makes sense that "so many people chase after sex with such desperate abandon. Whether or not they know it, they are searching for God." [1] I agree. Our wrestling with sexual questions is really a wrestling with the question of what it means to be a human being, a child of God, a one-of-a-kind miracle. For those single adults who perceive God as the original author of "Thou-shall-not!," especially eager to clobber us for our sexual sins, discovering God's grace and mercy through the guidance of a spiritual director can be life-changing and soul-renewing.

204. Isn't going to a counselor admitting that something is wrong with me?

No. Never be ashamed to see a counselor. If people challenge you, it's generally a good indication that they need the services of a psychologist. Mental health care and theological professionals are "one of the ways God has designed so that we do not remain estranged from him" (2 Samuel 14:14). The following sentence has brought hope to thousands of single adults seeking recovery: "I trust in God who is continually moving me toward healing—physically, mentally, emotionally, and spiritually—if I want it, and sometimes even beyond my acceptance and awareness." [1]

APPENDIX 1

The "I Can" Affirmations

(Read aloud, inserting your name after I and before can.)

I *can* define myself by measures other than my mean dating frequency

I *can* date well
> I *can* date healthy individuals
> I *can* know what I want in a relationship
> I *can* invest in healthy relationships
> I *can* reconcile with previous romantic losses
> I *can* respect the dignity and worth of every single adult I date

I *can* lower the defensive barricades into my life
> I *can* be open to romantic surprises
> I *can* invest in a romantic future

I *can* make intelligent romantic choices

I *can* say no to any level of intimacy that challenges my decision making

I *can* make responsible sexual choices and decisions

I *can* abstain from irresponsible intimacy

I *can* always act like a responsible adult

I *can* be celibate

I *can* encourage my friends to have healthier romantic lives

"I *can* do all things through Christ who strengthens me!" (Phil. 4:13)

APPENDIX 2

The
Conversation

Reflect: Carefully reflect on the key areas (attitudes, actions or inactions, behaviors, habits) that concern or distress you.

Prioritize: Decide which issues merit deliberate confrontive dialogue.

Edit: Write out what you are thinking and feeling.

Choose: Find kind but firm words with which you can frame and voice your concerns.

Anticipate: Recognize that the initial reaction may be negative.

Dress Rehearsal: Rehearse your words in front of a mirror or with a friend.

Ground Rules: Find an appropriate opportunity and a setting so that you won't be interrupted.

Request a Fair Hearing: Ask the individual(s) to hear you out— all the way to the end of each sentence.

Think It Through: Ask the individual(s) to consider what you have shared before responding. Agree to do likewise.

Time Out: Remember that initial responses may be less than what you expected and may demonstrate that the individual(s) did not really "hear" you OR is unwilling to accept responsibility for some of his/her choices.

Invite Further Conversation: Keep talking together to clarify the issues.

APPENDIX 3

A **Confession** for **Single Adults**

We confess that at times we have not been honest with you, with ourselves, with those we have dated, with those we have loved, and with those who have loved us.

We confess that we have not honored the sexuality that you so deliberately created for us.

We confess that we have not remembered how fearfully and wonderfully you made us.

We confess that we have allowed the culture to intimidate us with its biases, sexual norms, polls, and stereotypes.

We confess that we have allowed the culture to define what is esteemed, coveted, normalized, and valued.

We confess that we have been obsessed with and have overvalued anatomy and physique and have devalued the individual.

We confess that we have coveted the sexual capacities and choices of others.

We confess that we have not respected ourselves and those with whom we have shared intimacy.

We confess that we have used, abused, and confused this marvelous capacity called sex.

We confess that we have pushed the boundaries—to see how far we could go and to get what we wanted—and thus have disrespected those with whom we have shared intimacy.

We confess that we have focused on the sexual now, on immediate expression and pleasure.

We confess that we have not been mindful of the sexual struggles, the sexual histories, and the sexual pain of others.

We confess that we have too easily dismissed the sexual longings, questions, and struggles of others.

We confess that we have too readily judged others for their sexual choices, mistakes, and realities.

We confess that we have not recognized and appreciated the sacred worth of those with whom we have been intimate.

We confess that we have willingly participated in the sexual devaluing of others, either with our silence or by teasing, ridiculing, pressuring, mocking, and depreciating them.

We confess that we have not acted or loved with clean hearts and clear intentions; we have thought more of ourselves than of others.

We confess that we have not asked you to bless or redeem our sexuality, that we have not asked you to remind us continually that the incredible capacity for sexual expression is your gift.

We confess that we have not thanked you or expressed gratitude for so wondrous a gift as human sexuality.

Help us, O Lord, to appreciate the wonder, power, and mystery of your good gift of sexuality.

Remind us, O Lord, that we have been redeemed with a great price.

Empower us, O Lord, to take seriously this incredible gift of sexuality.

Guide us, O Lord, to be responsible stewards of these sexual capabilities that you have given us.

Rekindle our resolve, O Lord, in all ways to honor you, ourselves, and our neighbors sexually—through body, mind, and spirit.

Amen.

Appendix 4

Sex Intimacy Guidelines

The scientific and medical communities have developed guidelines to help distinguish sexual practices that carry a high risk of sexually transmitted diseases, especially the HIV infection, from those that do not. Single adults, whether sexually active or not, need to be aware of these guidelines before engaging in sexual behaviors. Remember a behavior could be sexually safe or "safer" but not be emotionally safe. A "just this once" decision could have profound long-term medical, psychological, and spiritual consequences.

Totally safe sex—no risk
    Abstinence from all sexual behaviors
    Solo masturbation

"Safer sex"—extremely low or no risk
    Touching, hugging, massaging, caressing
    Social (dry) kissing

Probably safe—very low risk practices (small theoretic risk)
    French (wet) kissing
    Mutual masturbation (if no cuts on hands, no ulcers or lesions
        on the genitals of either partner)
    Vaginal sex with a male or female condom (condom must be
        put on before *any* penetration)
    Fellatio with condom

Cunnilingus with dam (place latex dam over partner's
vaginal area before oral contact)

Anilingus with dam (place latex dam over anus before
oral contact)

Using one's own sex toys (vibrators, etc) that have not been
in contact with body fluids

Anal sex with condom (condom put on prior to penetration)

Mutually monogamous sex between two persons who have no
HIV risk factors and who have been tested and are negative

**Possibly unsafe: no strong proof but some evidence that
transmission can occur**

Fellatio without a latex dam (oral sex to ejaculation;
swallowing semen)

Cunnilingus without a latex dam (oral contact with partner's
genital area and vaginal secretions)

Anilingus without a latex dam

Unsafe sex: high risk of transmitting HIV

Anal intercourse without a latex condom (highest risk is to
receptive partner)

Anal penetration by finger or vibrator followed by intercourse
without condom

Vaginal intercourse without a male or female condom

Sex with numerous individuals

It must also be noted that the HIV virus and other STDs may be
present in the male's pre-ejaculation sperm droplets; for example in oral
sex or vaginal sex before full ejaculation. Thus, pregnancy or infection
is possible without ejaculation.

Source: Herminia Palacio, "Safer Sex" in *The AIDS Knowledge Base: A Textbook on HIV
Disease from the University of California, San Francisco, and the San Francisco General
Hospital*, ed. by P. T. Cohen, M.D., Merle A. Sande, M.D., and Paul A. Volberding, M.D.
Boston: Little Brown and Company, 1994, 10.6-7,8.

NOTES

I:1.   Kathleen Norris, *Cloister Walk* (New York City: Riverhead Books, 1996), 98.

1:1.   "Valentine Late or Never," *USA Today*, 14 February 1997, 1.

1:2.   Alice Peppler, personal correspondence to author, 19 February 1997.

2:1.   Sam Jones Papers, box number 312, Woodruff Center, Emory University, Atlanta, Georgia.

2:2.   Albert Bushnell Hart and Herbert R. Ferleger, eds., *Theodore Roosevelt Encyclopedia* (New York: Roosevelt Memorial Association, 1941), 329.

4:1.   H. Norman Wright and Marvin Inmon, *Preparing Youth for Dating, Courtship, and Marriage* (Eugene, Oreg.: Harvest House, 1978), 47.

5:1.   "How to Bury a Millionaire," *People*, 21 August 1995, 40–41.

8:1.   Liz Curtis Higgs, *One Size Fits All and Other Fables* (Nashville: Thomas Nelson, 1993), 150.

13:1.   Greg Flood, *I'm Looking for Mr. Right But I'll Settle for Mr. Right Away* (Atlanta: Brob House, 1986), 50.

21:1.   Warren Farrell, *The Liberated Man: Beyond Masculinity* (New York: Random House, 1974); Lillian Rubin, *Intimate Strangers: Men and Women Together* (New York: Harper and Row), 1983.

27:1.   Linda A. Jackson and Olivia D. McGill, "Body Type Preference and Body Characteristics Associated with Attractive and Unattractive Bodies by African Americans and Anglo Americans," *Sex Roles* 35:5/6 (1966), 295–305.

29:1.   Arthur A. Rouner, Jr., *Struggling with Sex: A Serious Call to Marriage-Centered Sexual Life* (Minneapolis: Augsburg, 1987), 62.

29:2.   Constance L. Shehan, "Consequences of Dating a Married Man," *Medical Aspects of Human Sexuality* 21 (January 1987): 99.

30:1.   Ray E. Short, *Sex, Love or Infatuation: How Can I Really Know?* (Minneapolis: Augsburg, 1978), 15–16.

30:2.   Ibid., 16.

31:1.   Ellen Fein and Sherrie Schneider, *The Rules: Time-Tested Secrets for Capturing the Heart of Mr. Right* (New York: Warner, 1995), 78.

32:1.   Katie Roiphe, *Last Night in Paradise: Sex and Morals at Century's End* (Boston: Little, Brown & Co., 1997), 138–139.

35:1.   William Worden, *Grief Counseling and Grief Therapy: A Handbook for the Mental Health Practitioner*, 2d ed. (New York: Springer, 1991), 16.

35:2.   Ibid., 18.

36:1.   Roy W. Fairchild, *Finding Hope Again: A Guide to Counseling the Depressed.* San Francisco: Harper&Row, 1980, 34-35.

39:1.   Short, *Sex, Love, or Infatuation*, 150.

40:1.   Evelyn M. Duvall and Reuben Hill, *Being Married* (Boston: D.C. Heath, 1960), 122.

41:1.   U.S. Bureau of the Census, *Statistical Abstract of the United States: 1996*, 116th ed. (Washington, D.C., 1996), Table 64, page 57; model suggested by Marshall Kirk and Hunter Madsen, *After the Ball* (New York: Bantam, 1989), 300.

42:1.   Barbara De Angelis, *The Real Rules: How to Find the Right Man for the Real You.* New York: Dell, 1997, 141–151.

43:1.   *Statistical Abstract of the United States: 1996*, 96–97.

43:2.   Laurel Richardson, *The New Other Woman: Contemporary Women in Affairs With Married Men* (New York: Free Press, 1985), 5.

43:3.   "Too Late for Prince Charming," *Newsweek*, 2 June 1986, 54–57; "For 30-Year-Old Educated Woman, Marriage Picture is Slim," *Kansas City Star*, 16 February 1986, 1.

43:4.   U.S. Bureau of Census, *Statistical Abstract of the United States: 1996*, 96-97.

44:1.   Eric Fruge, *Single Parent Family Skills Workshop* (Lexington: University of Kentucky, 1997).

47:1.   Connell Cowan and Melyvn Kinder, *Women Men Love, Women Men Leave* (New York: Clarkson N. Potter, 1987), 143.

52:1.   Barbara De Angelis, *The Real Rules*, 97.

53:1.   Sidney B. Simon, *Getting Unstuck: Breaking Through Your Barriers to Change* (New York: Warner Books, 1988), 28–30.

59:1.   Lisa Tuten, as told to Ellen Sherman, "Trail of Terror: I Was Stalked," *McCall's*, 1 August 1995, 57, 59.

60:1.   Henry Kissinger, quoted in *The New York Times*, 19 January 1971.

65:1.   Leo Rosten, *Leo Rosten's Treasury of Jewish Quotations*, New York: Bantam, 1980, 315.

66:1.   Abraham Lincoln, cited in *Respectfully Quoted: A Dictionary of Quotations Requested from the Congressional Research Service*, ed. Suzy Platt (Washington, D. C.: Library of Congress, 1989) 233.

67:1.   Lenore Weitzman, cited in "Socioeconomic Class and Family Change," in *The Encyclopedia of Marriage, Divorce and the Family*, Margaret DiCanio, ed. (New York: Facts on File, 1989), 450. See also p. 178.

68:1.   Eric Schlosser, "The Business of Pornography," *U.S. News and World Report*, 10 February 1997, 42–52.

68:2.   William Knoke, *Bold New World: The Essential Road Map to the Twenty-First Century* (New York: Kodansha, 1996), 35.

69:1.   Schlosser, "The Business of Pornography," 49.

69:2.   Ibid.

70:1.   Susan Sprecher and Pamela C. Regan, "College Virgins: How Men and Women Perceive Their Sexual Status." *The Journal of Sex Research* 33:10 (1996), 8.

70:2.   David J. McKirnan, Joseph P. Stokes, Lynda Doll, and Rebecca G. Burzette, "Bisexually Active Men: Social Characteristics and Sexual Behavior," *The Journal of Sex Research* 32:1 (1995), 65–66; Diane Binson, Stuart Michael, Ron Stall, Thomas J. Coates, John H. Gagnon, and Joseph A. Catania, "Prevalence and Social Distribution of Men Who Have Sex with Men: United States and Its Urban Centers," *The Journal of Sex Research* 32:3 (1995), 245–46, 249.

71:1.   Shari Roan, "Woman, 63, Gives Birth, Could Set Record," *Kansas City Star*, 24 April 1997, A-1.

71:2.   Amanda Spake, "The Choices That Brought Me Here," *Ms.*, November 1984, 50.

71:3.   William H. Masters, Virginia E. Masters, and Robert C. Kolodny, *Masters and Johnson on Sex and Loving Behavior* (Boston: Little, Brown & Co., 1986), 532–33; "Chlamydia—The Silent Danger." *Medical Aspects of Human Sexuality* (July 1991), 19.

72:1.   Michael Precker, "Is Bigger Better?" *Dallas Morning News*, 8 February 1994, C-1.

72:2.   Glen Wilson and David Nias, *The Mystery of Love: How the Science of Sexual Attraction Can Work for You* (New York: Quadrangle, 1976), 25.

72:3.   Elizabeth Sneed, "Briefs That Let Men Pad Their Assets," *USA Today*, 16 February 1995, 20.

72:4.   Richard Martin, cited in Sneed, "Briefs," 20.

73:1.   Richard Stengel, "Men As Sex Objects," *M*, July 1992, 72.

73:2.   Naomi Wolf quoted in Stengel, 75.

73:3.   Ibid., 76–77.

73:4.   Leland Elliott and Cynthia Brantley, *Sex on Campus: The Naked Truth about the Real Lives of College Students* (New York: Random House, 1997), 11.

73:5.   Betty Van Wagner, "The Man in the Mirror," August 1989.

73:6.   Elliott and Brantley, *Sex on Campus*, 8.

75:1.   Paul Millman and "The Guys," *Buy Book, Get Guy* (New York: Perigee/Berkeley, 1997), 84.

77:1.   "How to Claim Your Share of the 1800 Book-a-Year Genre," *Writer's Digest*, February 1997, 20–24.

79:1.   Higgs, *One Size Fits All*, 150.

79:2.   Plato, *The Symposium*, trans. B. Jowett, in *The Dialogues of Plato*, vol. 3 (New York: Bigelow, Brown and Co., 1914), 317–19.

80:1.   Maurice Lamm, *The Power of Hope* (New York: Rawson, 1995), 160.

81:1.   Nadine Marks, "Flying Solo at Midlife: Gender, Marital Status, and Psychological Well-Being." *Journal of Marriage and the Family* 58 (November 1996): 918.

83:1.   Sprecher and Regan, "College Virgins," 8.

83:2.   Art Ulene, *Safe Sex in a Dangerous World* (New York: Random House, 1987), 32.

83:3.   Harvey Cox, *The Secular City: Secularization and Urbanization in Theological Perspective*, rev. ed. (New York: Macmillan, 1966), 183.

83:4.   Ira L. Reiss, *Premarital Sexual Standards in America* (Glencoe, Ill.: Free Press, 1960), 202.

83:5.   Evelyn Eaton Whitehead and James D. Whitehead, *A Sense of Sexuality; Christian Love and Intimacy* (New York: Doubleday/Image, 1989).

84:1.   Michele Ingrassia, "Lifestyle: Virgin Cool," *Newsweek*, 17 October, 1994, 64.

85:1.   Sean D. Sammon, *An Undivided Heart: Making Sense of Celibate Chastity* (Staten Island: Alba House, 1993), 103.

86:1.   Matthew Kelly, *A Call to Joy: Living in the Presence of God* (San Francisco: HarperSan Francisco, 1997), 103–4.

89:1.   See Leo Steinberg, *The Sexuality of Christ in Renaissance Art and in Modern Oblivion* (New York: Pantheon, 1983); see also James B. Nelson, *Between Two Gardens: Refections on Sexuality and Religious Experience* (New York: Pilgrim, 1983), 105; William E. Phipps, *The Sexuality of Jesus* (New York: Harper and Row, 1973), 97.

90:1.   "St. Matthew," *The Interpreter's Bible*, vol. 7, George A. Buttrick, ed. (Nashville: Abingdon, 1951), 297.

90:2.   Tim Stafford, "Intimacy: Our Latest Sexual Fantasy," *Christianity Today*, 16 January 1987, 26.

92:1.   Archibald Hart, *The Sexual Man* (Dallas: Word, 1994), 111.

92:2.   Elliott and Brantley, *Sex on Campus*, 18, 171–173.

92:3.   Bob Berkowitz, *His Secret Life: Male Sexual Fantasies* (New York: Simon and Schuster, 1997), 13.

93:1.   Whitehead and Whitehead, *A Sense of Sexuality*, 104.

94:1.   Stuart Miller, *Men and Friendship* (Los Angeles: Jeremy P. Tarcher, 1983).

95:1.   National Geographic Society, *The Incredible Machine* (Washington, D.C.: National Geographic Book Service, 1986), 162; Philip Whitfield, *The Human Body Explained* (New York: Henry Holt , 1995), 142.

97:1.   Robert J. Sternberg, cited in Robert J. Trotter, "The Three Faces of Love," *Psychology Today* September, 1986, 46–54.

97:2.   Karen Lebacqz, "Appropriate Vulnerability: A Sexual Ethic for Singles," in *Christian Perspectives on Sexuality and Gender*, Elizabeth Stuart and Adrian

Thatcher, eds. (Herefordshire, England: Gracewing/Fowler Wright Books, 1996), 426–27.

99:1.   Adrian W. Zorgniotti and Eli F. Lizza, "Taking the History of a Patient With Impotence," *Medical Aspects of Human Sexuality* (August 1991), 55–58. This is often described as "blunt perineal trauma." See also Irwin Goldstein and Larry Rothstein, *The Potent Male: Facts, Fictions, Future* (Los Angeles: Body Press, 1990), 75.

99:2.   L. R. Schover, "The Multiaxial Problem-Oriented System for Sexual Dysfunction: An Alternative to DSM-III," *Archives of General Psychiatry* 39 (1982), 614–19.

99:3.   Masters, Masters, and Kolodny, *Masters and Johnson on Sex and Loving Behavior*, 483–84.

99:4.   Guy Kettelhack, *Dancing Around the Volcano* (New York: Crown, 1996), 111.

99:5.   Katie Roiphe, "Is AIDS Hysteria Being Used to Keep You Virginal?," *Cosmopolitan*, April 1997, 68.

99:6.   Ibid.

100:1. Patrick Carnes, *Sexual Anorexia: Overcoming Sexual Self-Hatred* (Center City, MN: Hazelden Books, 1997), 2–3.

100:2. Ibid., 21.

101:1. Ibid., 60.

102:1. Naomi Wolf, "Bring Back Petting, The Time-Tested Answer to Teen Sex," *USA Today*, 24 June 1997, 13A.

102:2. Beverly Miller and John Marshall, "Coercive Sex on the University Campus," *Journal of College Student Personnel*, 28:1 (1987), 38–47.

102:3. Tim Stafford, *A Love Story: Questions and Answers on Sex* (Wheaton: Campus Life Books, 1986), 56–57.

103:1. Peter J. Gomes, *The Good Book: Reading the Bible With Mind and Heart* (New York: William Morrow, 1995), 25.

103:2. Ibid., 20.

104:1. Duane Swierczynski, "Kiss and Tell," *Men's Health*, April 1998, 83.

104:2. Valerie Frankel, "Almost Sex," *Mademoiselle*, October 1996, 153.

104:3. Robert Francocur, cited in Frankel, "Almost Sex," 152.

105:1. Carnes, *Sexual Anorexia*, 15.

105:2. Patrick Carnes, *Out of the Shadows: Understanding Sexual Addiction*, 2d. ed., (Minneapolis: ComCare, 1992), 110–12.

105:3. Sex and Love Addicts Anonymous, "Addiction and Recovery." (W. Newton, Mass.: The Augustine Fellowship, 1990), 2–3.

106:1. Elliott and Brantley, *Sex on Campus*, 32.

106:2. Ellen Sweet, "Date Rape: The Story of an Epidemic and Those Who Deny It," *MS*, October 1985, 56.

106:3.   "Date/Acquaintance Rape," University of Missouri at Rolla, 2, Internet document.

106:4.   Elliott and Brantley, *Sex on Campus*, 224.

107:1.   "Date/Acquaintance Rape," 2.

107:2.   Isla L. Lottes and Martin S. Weinberg, "Sexual Coercion Among University Students: A Comparison of the United States and Sweden," *The Journal of Sex Research* 34:1 (1996), 71.

107:3.   Charlene L. Muehlenhard and Melany A. Linton, "Date Rape and Sexual Aggression in Dating Situations: Incidence and Risk Factors," *Journal of Counseling Psychology* 34:2 (1987), 186, 190.

108:1.   "Date Rape," World Wide Legal Information Association, 1 March 1997, 2, Internet document.

108:2.   Jeffrey A. Kelly, *Changing HIV Risk Behavior: Practical Strategies* (New York: Guilford Press, 1995), 119.

109:1.   Jean O'Gorman Hughes and Bernice T. Sadler, Project on the Status and Education of Women, 4, Association of American Colleges, internet document.

110:1.   David Scott, *Bachelor's Little Book of Wisdom* (Merrillville, Ind.: ICS Books, 1996), 25.

111:1.   Craig A. Hill and Leslie K. Preston, "Individual Differences in the Experience of Sexual Motivation: Theory and Measurement of Dispositional Sexual Motives," *The Journal of Sex Research* 33:1 (1966), 31–32.

114:1.   Matthew Kelly, *A Call to Joy*, 103–4.

115:1.   Arieh Bergman, "HPV Infection in Men: Severing the Link to Cervical Cancer," *Medical Aspects of Human Sexuality* (December 1991), 20.

115:2.   Mantak Chia and Douglas Abrams Arava, *The Multi-Orgasmic Man* (San Francisco:HarperSan Francisco, 1996), 207.

117:1.   Dietrich Bonhoeffer, *The Cost of Discipleship*, rev. ed. (New York: Macmillian, 1963), 47.

119:1.   Armstead Maupin, *Maybe the Moon* (San Francisco: HarperCollins, 1992), 57.

120:1.   Alan D. Wolfelt, "Grief" (Presentation given in Olathe, Kans. to clients of Frye Funeral Home and area clergy, 13 February 1991).

121:1.   Elizabeth Kuster, *Exorcising Your Ex* (New York: Fireside, 1996), 11.

122:1.   Rosten, *Leo Rosten's Treasury of Jewish Quotations*, 389.

123:1.   Diane Swaim, personal conversation with author, 20 February 1997.

123:2.   C. Everett Koop, *Surgeon General's Report on Acquired Immune Deficiency Syndrome* (Washington, D.C.: U.S. Department of Health and Human Services, 1986), n.p.

123:3. Bergman, 20.

124:1. Elliot Zaret, "Sexual Abuse of Children Remains a Hidden Crime," *Kansas City Star*, 27 March 1996, E-4.

124:2. Mary P. Rowe, cited by Jean O'Gorman Hughes and Bernice T. Sadler, Project on the Status and Education of Women, Association of American Colleges, April 1987, 6, internet document.

126:1. Harvey Cox, *The Secular City: Secularization and Urbanization in Theological Perspective*, rev. ed. (New York: Macmillian, 1966), 180.

126:2. Reiss, *Premarital Sexual Standards in America*, 83–84.

127:1. Sprecher and Regan, "College Virgins," 14.

130:1. *Webster's Ninth New Collegiate Dictionary* (Springfield, Mass.: Merriam-Webster, 1983), 630.

130:2. Lisa Schiffren, quoted in David Whitman, "Was It Good for Us?," *U.S. News and World Report*, 19 May 1997, 60.

130:3. Jennifer Grossman, cited in Whitman, "Was It Good For Us?," 64.

131:1. Hill and Preston, "Individual Differences in the Expression of Sexual Motivation," 30.

131:2. Ellen Dissannayake, *Homo Aestheticus* (Seattle: University of Washington Press, 1992), 223.

132:1. Anne Brener, *Mourning and Mitzvah* (Woodstock, Vt.: Jewish Lights Publishing, 1993), 15.

134.1. *Information Please Almanac: 1997*, 50th ed. (Boston: Houghton Mifflin, 1997), 434.

134:2. Whitman, "Was It Good for Us?," 60.

135:1. Dissanayake, *Homo Aestheticus*, 223.

135:2. Fein and Schneider, *The Rules*, 108, 110–111.

136:1. De Angelis, *Ask Barbara*, 104–5.

137:1. Jack Morin, *The Erotic Mind: Unlocking the Inner Sources of Sexual Passion and Fulfillment* (New York: HarperCollins, 1995), 28.

137:2. Herant A. Katchadourian and Donald T. Lunde, *Fundamentals of Human Sexuality*, 2d ed. (New York: Holt, Rinehart, and Winston, 1975), 274.

137:3. Robert T. Michael, John H. Gagnon, Edward O. Laumann, and Gina Kolata, *Sex in America: A Definitive Survey* (New York: Little, Brown & Co., 1994), 166.

137:4. Ibid.

137:5. Janus Report, quoted in Hart, *The Sexual Man*, 119.

137:6. Ibid., 136.

137:7. Michael et al., *Sex in America*, 158.

137:8. Ibid., 163.

137:9. Ibid.

138:1. Irma Kurtz, "Agony," *Cosmopolitan*, April 1997, 60.

138:2. Michael et al., *Sex in America*, 164.

138:3. J. Kenneth Davidson, Carol Anderson Darling, and Laura Norton, "Religiosity and Sexuality of Women: Sexual Behavior and Sexual Satisfaction Revisited," *The Journal of Sex Research*, 32:3 (1995).

138:4. Michael et al., *Sex in America*, 164–65.

139:1. Jonathan Kirsch, *The Harlot by the Side of the Road: Forbidden Tales of the Bible* (New York: Ballentine, 1997), 137–44.

139:2. Hart, *The Sexual Man*, 141.

140:1. Morin, *The Erotic Mind*, 27; Berkowitz, *His Secret Life*, 13–33, 133–36.

140:2. Michael et al., *Sex in America*, 166.

140:3. Ibid.

140:4. Barry McCarthy, *What You Still Don't Know About Male Sexuality* (New York: Thomas Crowell, 1977), 210.

140:5. Ibid.

141:1. Morton Hunt, "Sexual Behavior in the 1970's," *Playboy*, October 1973, 84.

141:2. Richard Foster, *Money, Sex and Power* (San Francisco: Harper and Row, 1985), 124. See also Morton Kelsey and Barbara Kelsey, *Sacrament of Sexuality: The Spirituality and Psychology of Sex* (Warwick, N.Y.: Amity House, 1986), 223.

141:3. Michael et al., *Sex in America*, 166.

141:4. Lewis Smedes, *Sex for Christians* (Grand Rapids: Zondervan, 1976), 244, 160.

141:5   Hart, *The Sexual Man*, 118.

142:1. Masters, Masters, and Kolodny, *Masters and Johnson on Sex and Human Loving*, 45.

142:2. William A. Fisher, Nyla R. Branscombe, and Charles R. Lemery, "The Bigger the Better: Arousal and Attributional Responses to Erotic Stimuli that Depict Different Size Penises," *The Journal of Sex Research* 19:4 (1984), 380.

142:3. Wolf, *The Beauty Myth*, 153.

142:4. Judith Couchman, "The Big Deal About Breasts," *Clarity*, March/April 1994, 34.

142:5. Abraham Morgentaler, cited in Michael Precker, "Is Bigger Better?," *The Dallas Morning News*, 8 February 1994, 3C. See also Mary Remy, "Filing for An Extension," *Men's Health*, June 1997, 146–47.

142:6. Michaengelo Signorile, *The Signorile Report on Gay Men: Sex, Drugs, Muscles, and the Passages of Life* (New York: Harper Collins, 1997), 6–8, 133–144.

143:1. Anne A. Ehrhardt, "Sexual Behavior Among Homosexuals," in *AIDS in the World II: Global Dimensions, Social Roots, and Response*, edited by

Jonathan M. Mann and Daniel J. M. Tarantola (New York: Oxford University Press, 1996), 259.

143:2.   Jack Thomas, "Janus Study Shows America Is Still in Love with Sex," *Detroit Free Press*, 25 February 1993, 4D.

143:3.   Ruth Westheimer, *Dr. Ruth's Encyclopedia of Sex* (New York: Continuum, 1994), 192.

143:4.   Tara McCarthy, "Why I'm Saving Myself for True Love—But Getting Some Kicks in the Meantime," *Glamour*, June 1997, 193.

143:5.   Rhonda K. Reinholtz and Charlene L. Muehenhard, "Genital Perceptions and Sexual Activity in a College Population," *The Journal of Sex Research* 32:2 (1995), 155

143:6.   Ibid., 159.

143:7.   Anthony P. M. Coxon, "Behavior Changes Among Homosexual Men," in Chapter 22, "Male Homosexuality and HIV" of Mann and Tarantola, *AIDS in the World II*, 252; Ehrhardt, "Sexual Behavior in Homosexuals," 259.

144:1.   Michael et al., *Sex in America*, 144, 146–47; Elliot and Brantley, *Sex on Campus*, 138–39.

144:2.   Eliot and Brantley, *Sex on Campus*, 82-83.

144:3.   Jeffrey A. Kelly, *Changing HIV Risk Behavior: Practical Strategies* (New York: The Guilford Press, 1995) 72, 76. See also: David Wyatt Seal, "Interpartner Concordance in Self-Reported Sexual Behavior among College Dating Couples," *The Journal of Sex Research*, 34:1 (1997), 45, 51.

145:1.   Jacqueline Shannon, "Warning: STD Epidemic," *Cosmopolitan*, April 1997, 100.

145:2.   "Sexually Transmitted Diseases Account for Half of Most Common Infectious Diseases," *Single Adult Ministry Journal*, 119 (November/December, 1996), 1.

145:3.   Shannon, "Warning: STD Epidemic," 100.

145:4.   Masters, Masters, and Kolodony, *Masters and Johnson on Sex and Loving Behavior*, 532–33.

145:5.   Susan Y. Chu and James W. Curran, "Epidemiology of Human Immunodeficiency Virus Infection in the United States," in *AIDS: Etiology, Diagnosis, Treatment and Prevention*, 4th ed. (Philadelphia: Lippincott, 1997), 141.

146:1.   Ibid.

146:2.   Coxon, "Behavior Changes Among Homosexual Men," 254.

147:1.   "Sexually Transmitted Diseases," *Single Adult Ministry Journal*, 1.

148:1.   Jeffrey A. Kelly, "Changing HIV Risk Behavior," 2–7.

148:2.   Sandra Jacoby Klein, *Heavenly Hurts: Surviving AIDS-Related Deaths and Losses* (Amityville, N.Y.: Baywood Publishing, 1993), 13, 60.

148:3.   "Global Overview: A Powerful HIV/AIDS Epidemic," in *AIDS in the World II*, 17.

149:1.   Herminia Palacio, "Safer Sex," in *The AIDS Knowledge Base: A Textbook for HIV Disease*, edited by P. T. Cohen, Merle S. Sande, and Paul A. Volberding (Boston: Little, Brown & Co., 1994), 10.6–3.

150:1.   Bruce G. Weniger and Seth Berkley, "The Evolving HIV/AIDS Epidemic," in *AIDS in the World II*, 57.

150:2.   Palacio, "Safer Sex," 10.6–1.

150:3.   John W. Ward, Lyle R. Petersen, and Harold W. Jaffe, "Current Trends in the Epidemiology of HIV/AIDS," in *The Medical Management of AIDS*, 5th ed., edited by Merle A. Sande and Paul A. Volberding (Philadelphia: W. B. Saunders, 1997), 7.

151:1.   Jeffrey A. Kelly, *Changing HIV Risk Behavior*, 4.

151:2.   Ibid., 7–15. See also Institute of Medicine, National Academy of Sciences, *Confronting AIDS: Directions for Public Health, Health Care and Research* (Washington, D.C.: National Academy Press, 1986), 2.

152:1.   Institute of Medicine, National Academy of Sciences, *Confronting AIDS: Directions for Public Health, Health Care, and Research: Summary and Recommendations* (Washington, D.C.: National Academy Press, 1986), 2, 26.

152:2.   Marianne LeVert, *AIDS: A Handbook for the Future*, (Brookfield, CT: The Millbrook Press, 1996) 18.

152:3.   Signorile, *The Signorile Report*, 70.

152:4.   Koop, *Surgeon General's Report*, n.p.

153:1.   Signorile, *The Signorile Report* (citing report from Australia's Victorian Council/Gay Men's Health Centre), 313.

154:1.   Jeffrey A. Kelly, *Changing HIV Risk Behavior*, 72.

155:1.   C. Everett Koop, "Women Urged to Get Tested for AIDS Before Pregnancy," *Kansas City Star*, 25 March 1987; Signorile, *The Signorile Report*, 314.

156:1.   Jeffrey A. Kelly, *Changing HIV Risk Behavior*, 71.

157:1.   June Osborn, address to the American Medical Association meeting on AIDS and Public Policy, Chicago, 21 April 1987.

157:2.   Jeffrey A. Kelly, *Changing HIV Risk Behavior*, 76.

158:1.   Chu and Curran, "Epidemiology of Human Immunodeficiency Virus Infection in the United States," 137.

158:2.   Michael, et al., *Sex in America*, 177.

158:3.   Chu and Curran, 137.

158:4.   Vivienne Cass, cited in Stanley Siegel and Ed Lowe, Jr., *Uncharted Lives: Understanding the Life Passages of Gay Men* (New York: Dutton, 1994), 33. See also "The Dilemma of Heterosexually Married Homosexual Men," in Richard A. Isay, *Becoming Gay: The Journey to Self-Acceptance* (New York: Pantheon, 1996), 87–118; "More Anger After Divorce if Ex-Husband Is Gay," *Medical Aspects of Human Sexuality* (May 1991), 9.

158:5. David J. McKirnan, Joseph P. Stokes, Lynda Doll, and Rebecca G. Burzette, "Bisexually Active Men," *Journal of Sex Research*, 32:1 (1995), 66.

158:6. Sheila Anne Feeney, "Yes, I'd Like to Be Castrated, Please," *Kansas City Star*, 14 April 1997, D-2.

158:7. Siegel and Lowe, *Uncharted Lives*, 107.

158:8. Isay, *Becoming Gay*, 114.

159:1. Ibid., 117.

160:1. "How Many Gays Are There?" *Newsweek*, 15 February 1993, 46; Thomas, *Janus Report*, 4. See also, "Sex n' Condoms in the USA," *New Scientist*, 24 April 1993, 3; John Gallagher, "10% Reality or Myth," *Advocate*, 15 November 1994, 23–25.

160:2. Richardson, *The New Other Woman*, 3.

160:3. Alfred C. Kinsey, Walter B. Pomeroy and Clyde B. Martin, *Sexual Behavior in the Human Male* (Philadelphia: W.B. Saunders, 1948), 650.

160:4. Morton Hunt, *Gay: What Teenagers Should Know About Homosexuality and the AIDS Crisis* (New York: Farrar, Straus, and Giroux, 1987), 12–13. See also Bruce Voeller, "Society and the Gay Movement," in *Homosexual Behavior: A Modern Reappraisal*, edited by Judd Marmor (New York: Basic Books, 1980), 233.

160:5. Binson, et al., "Prevalence and Social Distribution," 246.

160:6. Ibid., 251.

160:7. Ibid., 252.

160:8. *World Almanac and Book of Facts, 1997* (Mahwah, N.J.: World Almanac Books, 1997), 386.

160:9. Michael, et al., *Sex in America*, 177.

160:10. Binson, et al., "Prevalence and Social Distribution," 252.

160:11. John H. Gagnon, *Human Sexualities* (Boston: Addison Wesley, 1977), 179.

161:1. Katchadourian and Lunde, *Fundamentals of Human Sexuality*, 328.

161:2. *World Almanac: 1997*, 960.

161:3. Marmor, *Homosexual Behavior, A Modern Reappraisal*, 5.

162:1. Siegel and Lowe, *Uncharted Lives*, 113–14.

162:2. Ibid., 114.

163:1. Coxon, "Behavior Changes Among Homosexual Men," 252.

165:1. Suzanne Pharr, *Homophobia: A Weapon of Sexism* (Little Rock, Ark.: Chardon Press, 1988), xi.

165:2. Warren J. Blumenfeld, *Homophobia: How We All Pay the Price* (Boston: Beacon Press, 1992), 15.

165:3. Joan Steinau Lester, *The Future of White Men and Other Diversity Dilemmas* (Berkeley, Calif.: Conari Press, 1994), 164.

165:4. John Malone, *Straight Women/Gay Men* (New York: Dial, 1980), 53.

166:1. Doug Newton, "Tony Campolo—In Your Face," *Light and Life*, May 1997, 7.

166:2. The United Methodist Church, *The Book of Discipline of the United*

Methodist Church 1996 (Nashville: The United Methodist Publishing House, 1996), 89.

166:3.   Ibid.

167:1.   Blumenfeld, *Homophobia*, 8–13.

167:2.   Michelle M. Benecke and Kirsten S. Dodge, "Lesbian Baiting as Sexual Harassment: Women in the Military," in Blumenfeld, *Homophobia*, 167–69. See also Pharr, *Homophobia: A Weapon of Sexism*, 26.

167:3.   Phillip Culbertson, *New Adam: The Future of Male Spirituality* (Minneapolis: Fortress Press, 1992). See also Carlton Elliott Smith, "Men, Sex, and Spirituality: An Interview," *The Other Side*, November/December 1993, 10.

168:1.   Rita Risser, "The New Diversity," *Professional Speaker* (December 1996), 6–7.

168:2.   Lester, *The Future of White Men*, 102.

168:3.   Ibid., 104.

169:1.   Claudia Dreifus, "Andrew Young: On Life, Sin, and the Murder of His Friends," *Modern Maturity* (March–April, 1997), 57.

170:1.   Georgia Dullea, "Men Often Devastated When the Wife Dies," *The Louisville Courier Journal*, 20 September 1983, C6.

170:2.   Elting E. Morison, "Roosevelt, Alice Hathaway Lee," in *Notable American Women 1607–1950: A Biographical Dictionary*, vol. III, Edward T. James, ed. (Cambridge, Mass.: Belknap Press, 1971), 191–192.

171:1.   Ruth Birnkrant, *Fascinating Facts About Love, Sex and Marriage* (New York: Crown, 1982), 156.

171:2.   Glynnis Walker cited in "Remarriage," *The Encyclopedia of Marriage, Divorce, and the Family*, Margaret DiCanio, ed. (New York: Facts on File, 1989), 395.

171:3.   Theresa Tighe, "Overcoming Loneliness With Living," *Saint Louis Post Dispatch*, 12 April 1994, 2D.

175:1.   Elizabeth Harper Neeld, *Seven Choices: Taking the Steps to New Life After Losing Someone You Love* (New York: Dell/Delta, 1990), 66.

175:2.   Ben Bradlee, *A Good Life: Newspapering and Other Adventures* (New York: Simon and Schuster, 1995), 262.

175:3.   Glynnis Walker, cited in *Encyclopedia of Marriage, Divorce, and the Family*, 395.

177:1.   Cowan and Kinder, *Women Men Love, Women Men Leave*, 21–26.

177:2.   DiCiano, *The Encyclopedia of Marriage, Divorce, and the Family*, 394.

180:1.   Muehlenhard and Linton, "Date Rape," 187.

180:2.   G. J. Fischer, "College Student Attitudes Toward Forcible Date Rape," *Archives of Sexual Behavior* 15:6 (1986), 457–66 (reported on Medline).

181:1.   *Statistical Abstract of the United States: 1996*, 54.

182:1.   De Angelis, *The Real Rules*, 68.

183:1.   Dorothy Nevill, cited in *Treasury of Women's Quotations*, Carolyn Warner, ed. (Englewood Cliffs, N. J.: Prentice-Hall, 1992), 70.

185:1.   DiCiano, *The Encyclopedia of Marriage, Divorce, and the Family*, 395.

185:2.   Ann Landers, "Couple's Divorce Didn't End the Sex," *Kansas City Star*, 30 March 1997, G-2.

189:1.   Barbara Schiller, personal conversation with author, 8 March 1997.

193:1.   DiCanio, *The Encyclopedia of Marriage, Divorce, and the Family*, 268.

194:1.   Ibid., 394.

195:1.   Glynnis Walker, cited in *The Encyclopedia of Marriage, Divorce, and the Family*, 395.

195:2.   Ibid.

196:1.   Concept developed in: Bobbie Reed, *Stepfamilies Living Together in Christian Harmony* (St. Louis: Concordia, 1980).

196:2.   Diane Swaim, personal conversation with author, 20 February 1997.

200:1.   Carnes, *Sexual Anorexia*, 203.

201:2.   Ibid., 337.

200:3.   Victoria Alexander, *Words I Never Thought to Speak: Stories of Life in the Wake of Suicide* (New York: Lexington Books, 1991), xv.

201:1.   Susannah Fitzgerald, personal correspondance to Harold Ivan Smith.

202:1.   John Larsen, personal correspondence to Harold Ivan Smith.

203:1.   Carnes, *Sexual Anorexia*, 336.

204:1.   William V. Pietsch, *The Serenity Prayer Book* (San Francisco: HarperSan Francisco, 1990), 66.

Printed in the United States
121585LV00006B/29/A